PERSPECTIVES ON WRITING
Series Editor, Susan H. McLeod

D1466441

PERSPECTIVES ON WRITING

Series Editor, Susan H. McLeod

The Perspectives on Writing series addresses writing studies in a broad sense. Consistent with the wide ranging approaches characteristic of teaching and scholarship in writing across the curriculum, the series presents works that take divergent perspectives on working as a writer, teaching writing, administering writing programs, and studying writing in its various forms.

The WAC Clearinghouse and Parlor Press are collaborating so that these books will be widely available through free digital distribution and low-cost print editions. The publishers and the Series editor are teachers and researchers of writing, committed to the principle that knowledge should freely circulate. We see the opportunities that new technologies have for further democratizing knowledge. And we see that to share the power of writing is to share the means for all to articulate their needs, interest, and learning into the great experiment of literacy.

Other Books in the Series

Charles Bazerman and David R. Russell (Eds.), *Writing Selves/Writing Societies* (2003)

Gerald P. Delahunty and James Garvey, *The English Language: From Sound to Sense* (2009)

Charles Bazerman, Adair Bonini, and Débora Figueiredo (Eds.), *Genre in a Changing World* (2009)

David Franke, Alex Reid, and Anthony Di Renzo (Eds.), *Design Discourse: Composing and Revising Programs in Professional and Technical Writing* (2010)

Martine Courant Rife, Shaun Slattery, and Dànielle Nicole DeVoss (Eds.), *Copy(write): Intellectual Property in the Writing Classroom* (2011)

Doreen Starke-Meyerring, Anthony Paré, Natasha Artemeva, Miriam Horne, and Larissa Yousoubova, *Writing in Knowledge Societies* (2011)

Andy Kirkpatrick and Zhichang Xu, *Chinese Rhetoric and Writing: An Introduction for Language Teachers* (2012)

Charles Bazerman et al. (Eds.), International Advances in Writing Research: Cultures, Places, Measures (2012)

Chris Thaiss et al. (Eds.), *Writing Programs Worldwide: Profiles of Academic Writing in Many Places* (2012)

Mike Duncan and Star Medzerian Vanguri, *The Centrality of Style* (2013)

EPORTFOLIO PERFORMANCE SUPPORT SYSTEMS: CONSTRUCTING, PRESENTING, AND ASSESSING PORTFOLIOS

Edited by Katherine V. Wills and Rich Rice

The WAC Clearinghouse
wac.colostate.edu
Fort Collins, Colorado

Parlor Press
www.parlorpress.com
Anderson, South Carolina

The WAC Clearinghouse, Fort Collins, Colorado 80523-1052

Parlor Press, 3015 Brackenberry Drive, Anderson, South Carolina 29621

Printed in the United States of America

Library of Congress Cataloging-in-Publication Data

Eportfolio performance support systems : constructing, presenting, and assessing portfolios / edited by Katherine V. Wills and Rich Rice.
    pages cm. -- (Perspectives on writing)
  Includes bibliographical references and index.
   ISBN 978-1-60235-441-8 (pbk. : alk. paper) -- ISBN 978-1-60235-442-5 (hardcover : alk. paper) -- ISBN 978-1-60235-443-2 (adobe ebook : alk. paper) -- ISBN 978-1-60235-444-9 (epub : alk. paper)
  1. Electronic portfolios in education. 2. Academic achievement--Evaluation. 3. English language--Rhetoric--Study and teaching (Higher) I. Wills, Katherine V., 1957- II. Rice, Richard Aaron.
  LB1029.P67E69 2013
  378.166--dc23
                                      2013019920

                                      1 2 3 4 5

Copyeditor: Don Donahue
Designer: Mike Palmquist
Series Editor: Susan H. McLeod

This book is printed on acid-free paper.

The WAC Clearinghouse supports teachers of writing across the disciplines. Hosted by Colorado State University, it brings together scholarly journals and book series as well as resources for teachers who use writing in their courses. This book is available in digital format for free download at http://wac.colostate.edu.

Parlor Press, LLC is an independent publisher of scholarly and trade titles in print and multimedia formats. This book is available in paperback, cloth, and Adobe eBook formats from Parlor Press at http://www.parlorpress.com. For submission information or to find out about Parlor Press publications, write to Parlor Press, 3015 Brackenberry Drive, Anderson, South Carolina 29621, or e-mail editor@parlorpress.com.

CONTENTS

ACKNOWLEDGMENTS

ePortfolios are considered "authentic assessment" learning tools. Reflecting over the process and the product built for end task, capstone, or assessment purposes can be enormously instructive. Working with contributors to edit this collection of essays; gathering advice from colleagues at both Texas Tech University and Indiana University Purdue University Columbus; bouncing ideas off members of our professional communities such as those in the fields of Computers and Writing, Writing Program Administration, Technical Communication, Rhetoric, First-Year Experience, Secondary English Education, and Assessment; discussing new directions and new emerging technologies with researchers in assessment, website design, interaction design, social media, mobile media, communication, and assessment areas; as well as working with the fabulously innovative people at The WAC Clearinghouse and Parlor Press, has been incredibly valuable to us. We want to thank Susan H. McLeod especially, the series editor, whose tireless work with our project is a model for all editors. Publishers Mike Palmquist with The WAC Clearinghouse and David Blakesley with Parlor Press have both been very generous with their feedback and time and direction. Thank you, Kathy Yancey and Barbara Cambridge and Darren Cambridge, for the amazing work you've done on portfolios over the years. Your work is a model for anyone and everyone working in this area. Thank you, Kanika Batra, for your editing work and support with the project. Further, we thank our anonymous peer reviewers, and we thank the many graduate students in training who reviewed and helped offer style and editing advice as part of their own coursework and development as scholars, including, specifically, Jessica Badger (Texas Tech University), Christopher Andrews (Texas Tech University), Melanie Doulton (Texas Tech University), Deborah Fontaine (Northwest Florida State College), Dan Lovejoy (Texas Tech University), Jon Ostrowski (Texas Tech University), Richard Rabil (Texas Tech University), Rhonda Stanton (Texas Tech University), and Xiling Wang (Texas Tech University). Finally, as with every project of this scope, the many students who have shared their thinking and ideas through our courses, through the courses of our contributors, through the courses cited in the scholarship of this text, and through the continuation of ideas from this collection, we are indebted and thank you. Just as the construction, presentation, and assessment of any ePortfolio is an authentic learning opportunity, the creation of this text and its continuation through Creative Commons licensing has been a wonderful learning experience. This live text will continue to grow. Please review additional examples and the ongoing programs discussed in this collection online through The WAC Clearinghouse's Open-Access Books page (http://wac.colostate.edu/books).

EPORTFOLIO PERFORMANCE SUPPORT SYSTEMS: CONSTRUCTING, PRESENTING, AND ASSESSING PORTFOLIOS

INTRODUCTION

Katherine V. Wills
Indiana University Purdue University Columbus

Rich Rice
Texas Tech University

Institutions of higher learning have dedicated much energy and many resources to assessment measurements and standards through individual tools, through high-stakes testing, and through ePortfolio management systems. An ePortfolio is a selected collection of work presented electronically. An electronic performance support system, specifically, is an integrated electronic environment designed to reduce complexity in order to make sense of things, to provide employee performance information in order to foster improvement, and to provide workers with a decision support system in order to maximize productivity. As higher education continues to learn from efficiencies and new technologies in the workplace that refine performance measurement, study knowledge transfer and Web 2.0 tools (Gerben, 2009), and develop viable and sustainable products through interaction theory and website design principles, this collection of essays from knowledgeable scholars and practitioners of ePortfolios helps foster increased understanding of intersections between ePortfolio composing, presentation, and assessment in the academy and workplace, including ideas for embracing electronic performance support systems. Ideas and the discussion related in this collection published by the WAC Clearinghouse are extended online through Creative Commons licensing, as well. Please consider purchasing the print version, but also freely link to and share materials in the online version.

Essays in this collection ask readers to consider ways in which ePortfolios, as distinguished from non-electronic portfolios, facilitate sustainable and measureable writing-related student development, assessment and accountability, learning and knowledge transfer, principles related to universal design for learning, just-in-time support, interaction design, and usability testing. The collection contributes to recent scholarship on ePortfolios and provides new dimensions to the field of portfolio development in the academic and in workplaces. Traditionally, portfolios have been considered valuable tools because in addition to embracing principles of validity and reliability as assessment measurements, they enable students to continue to learn as they construct their portfolios. Portfolios have specific audiences—most traditionally a program or a teacher in an institution. But institutions work to prepare students for the workplace (including academic workplaces), and the workplace demands much different forms of performance and support measurements. ePortfolios should be designed with scalability and potential workplace applications in mind.

The collection is categorized into four sections each with three essays (chapters) that conduct an intertexual discussion and point to possibilities and gaps for ePortfolios future discussion.

1. SYSTEMATIC PERFORMANCE SUPPORT SYSTEMS

We open the discussion with Kathy Yancey's seminal article, "Postmodernism, Palimpsest, and Portfolios: Theoretical Issues in the Representation of Student Work," which is reprinted with permission from the National Council of Teachers of English. Originally published in *College Composition and Communication* in 2004, Yancey's piece situates portfolios as reflective "exercises in remediation" in a public space. Classrooms, too, are public spaces.

Throughout the collection, contributors Rice, Ramsay Johnson and Kahn, Cambridge, Corbett et al., and others expand on Yancey's concept of how ePortfolios can iteratively resituate and reconstitute ePortfolio artifacts into new interpretive understanding. This ability of ePortfolios to not only reproduce, but also to reformulate meanings across time and space lends ePortfolios their additive possibilities. Adding one plus one artifact does not equal two, but more than two because of the variety of possible interpretations. The intentional gathering and remixing of artifacts lends to the viability of ePortfolios across workplaces and lives, as Yancey alluded to in her 2004 *CCC* article. We felt we would be remiss if we did not launch this collection with Yancey's piece because we knew her work would be foundational to the ePortfolio conversations of this collection. And, as Yancey predicted in her article and as this collection shows, digital portfolios are evolving nationally and internationally and attention should be paid to the intentionality of the development.

Yancey is Kellogg W. Hunt Professor of English and Distinguished Research Professor at Florida State University, where she directs the Graduate Program in Rhetoric and Composition (http://ncte2008.ning.com/profile/kathleen-yancey). She has served in several national leadership roles, including President of the National Council of Teachers of English; Chair of the Conference on College Composition and Communication; and President of the Council of Writing Program Administrators. In January 2013, she assumed the Presidency of the South Atlantic Modern Language Association. She also co-founded and co-directs the Inter/National Coalition for Electronic Portfolio Research, which has brought together over 60 institutions from around the world to document the learning represented in electronic portfolios. Editor of the flagship journal of writing studies *College Composition and Communication*, Yancey has authored or co-authored over 70 articles and book chapters and authored, edited, or co-edited eleven scholarly books, including *Portfolios in the Writing Classroom* (1992), *Reflection in the Writing Classroom* (1998), *Situating Portfolios* (1997b), *Delivering College Composition: The Fifth Canon* (2006), *Electronic Portfolios 2.0: Emergent Research on Implementation and Impact* (2009), and the forthcoming co-authored *Contexts of Writing: Transfer, Composition, and Sites of Writing*, which is a study of the transfer of writing knowledge and practice in college.

Rich Rice follows Yancey's principles and core values of representation in "The Hypermediated Teaching Philosophy ePortfolio Performance Support System." Rice directs the Multiliteracy Lab in the Texas Tech University Department of English, and he teaches using ePortfolios both online and face-to-face in the TTU Technical Communication and Rhetoric program. See http://richrice.com. He is a member of the Conference on College Composition and Communication's Committee on Best Practices for Online Writing Instruction. His recent articles are in the areas of new media knowledge creation, mobile medicine, basic writing and photo essays, remediated film, nontraditional graduate support systems, ePortfolios, and media labs. With Nedra Reynolds (2006a, 2006b) he has co-written the second editions of *Portfolio Keeping* and *Portfolio Teaching*. Reynolds is soon to release third editions. In this essay, Rice draws on research in electronic performance support systems in order to point out ways in which the traditional teaching philosophy essays fall short as a genre of invoking its intended audience and multiple purposes because of hypertextual and reflective exegeses similar to those in ePortfolios. He suggests that in order to become an effective ePortfolio support system, the teaching philosophy should be taught and received as a networked performance space. In this second essay, Rice opens by expanding on Yancey's belief that ePortfolios, like a palimpsest, can be "retooled." Rice then hints at upcoming ideas in Lauren Klein's essay that discusses how blurring the boundaries of social media and ePortfolios can enhance classroom and workplace experiences. Furthermore, Rice elaborates on Carl Whithaus' discussion later in the collection of teaching philosophies as a "thirdspace" from Grego and Thompson (2008). ePortfolios multiply opportunities for presenting the self in diverse *kairotic* performances such as hypermediated teaching philosophies.

Next, Lauren F. Klein details another systematic approach to academic portfolios using social media. Klein directs the portfolio program in the City University of New York's Macaulay Honors College (http://macaulay.cuny.edu/eportfolios/lklein). She is an Assistant Professor in the School of Literature, Media, and Communication at the Georgia Institute of Technology, where she also directs the Digital Humanities Lab. Her essay, "The Social ePortfolio: Integrating Social Media and Models of Learning in Academic ePortfolios," examines recent research in social networking. She points out how many users can apply ePortfolio systems and social network sites in order to bridge the academy and other workplaces. What can an ePortfolio be? An ePortfolio can shapeshift into almost anything, according to Klein. Her essay closes Section 1 by moving readers among Yancey's foundations, Rice's teaching philosophy constructions, and then Klein's worlds of social networking: practical and creative, personal and social, textual and digital. This builds a foundation for the essays in Section 2, Constructing the Bridge, which explores ePortfolio transitioning into nonacademic workplaces as sustainable academy-to-workplace programs, capstone courses, and feedback loops that improve the ePortfolio experience and product.

2. CONSTRUCTING THE BRIDGE

The first essay in this section is by Barbara D'Angelo and Barry Maid. "ePorts: Making the Passage from Academics to Workplace" builds on the idea that ePortfolios can be useful for both individuals and systems by talking about ePortfolios as passageway from demonstrating proficiencies and meeting programmatic outcomes to demonstrating entry-level skills in various workplaces. The essay situates perceived dichotomies of academic versus practical, and theoretical versus applied. A key finding in D'Angelo and Maid's ePortfolio evaluation is that "direct instruction in tools or software" is a common shortcoming. How can teaching institutions serve many stakeholders? Ultimately, the authors conclude teachers using ePortfolios must serve in their role as technical communication educators. Any institution rebuilding its use of ePortfolios would benefit from this analysis of Arizona State University's program. It serves as a technical communication bridge between the academy and the workplace. D'Angelo's publications include several book chapters and articles on the use of outcomes for curriculum development and assessment and on information literacy. Maid founded the Technical Communication program at Arizona State University in 2000 and headed it for more than 10 years. His recent publications are in the area of information literacy, writing assessment, online education, and independent writing programs. Most recently, with Duane Roen and Greg Glau, he is co-author of *The McGraw-Hill Guide: Writing for College, Writing for Life*, currently in its 3rd edition (2012). Learn more about these researchers' ongoing work at http://www.public.asu.edu/~bdangelo and http://www.public.asu.edu/~bmmaid.

Next, Karen Ramsay Johnson and Susan Kahn at Indiana University Purdue University at Indianapolis (IUPUI) highlight their perspectives on challenges embedded in capstone projects. The essay connects the dots with English majors and professional programs transitioning to careers or further study. Similar to the previous essay regarding ASU, the authors relate work being done at IUPUI, including integration of ePortfolios with other adopters across campus. Johnson and Kahn show the evolution of their work in relation to work from Barrett (2004), to matrices and webfolio work of Hamilton and Kahn (2009), to Zubizarreta (2009), and to Cambridge, Cambridge, and Yancey in *Electronic Portfolios 2.0* (2009). This chapter continues a thread on reflective process in ePortfolios that runs through the work of Darren Cambridge. Whether in the classroom or community, reflective process weaves through the collection. More than a case study of ePortfolios within the collection, Johnson and Kahn's piece shares the reflective experiences of four English Capstone students using ePortfolios. The feedback loop between students and authors/researchers shows that the technology of ePortfolios may not resolve inherent pedagogical and social problems. Readers are reminded that ePortfolios are always already "works-in-progress." Johnson has given numerous presentations on ePortfolios and their use in both Liberal Arts programs and in assessment. Kahn has published, presented, and consulted widely on faculty development, assessment, and electronic portfolios, including co-editing *Electronic Portfolios: Emerging Practices in Student, Faculty, and Institutional Learning* (2001). She currently chairs the Board of Directors of the Association for Authentic, Experiential, and Evidence-Based Learning (AAEEBL), the international association for ePortfolio practitioners.See http://academicaffairs.iupui.edu/plans/ePort for more discussion on IUPUI's approachs.

Karen Bonsignore in "Career ePortfolios: Recognizing and Promoting Employable Skills," writes about "City Tech," an organization that helps students prepare career ePortfolios. Bonsignore is Director of the New York City College of Technology ePortfolio Project (http://eportfolio.citytech.cuny.edu). She has offered numerous presentations on various ePortfolio, assessment, and technology related topics including, most recently, "Comprehensive Support for a Successful ePortfolio Project," "Designing an Effective Online eTutor Writing Assistance Program to Support Career ePortfolios at City Tech," and "Career ePortfolios: A Showcase of Student Work." This essay relies on student perspectives, but with the career ePortfolio and its multiple and diverse audiences in mind. Bonsignore's text brings into sharp relief the public life of the ePortfolio as an artifact for the marketplace. These portfolios offer significant advantages over traditional dossiers, including offering numerous versions. The program prepares students with competitive job market and graduate school admissions advice. Thus, the three discussions in Section 2 about constructing bridges examine the nuanced interplay of outcomes, reflection, and audience in variety of ePortfolio capstone courses and community projects.

3. PRESENTING INTERACTIVE DESIGNS

Geoffrey Middlebrook from the University of Southern California and Jerry Chih-Yuan Sun from National Chiao Tung University begin "Showcase Hybridity: A Role for Blogfolios" with a powerful volley to the ePortfolio field about the limitations of static approaches to ePortfolios. They encourage database-driven and more dynamic approaches to the ePortfolio imagination. Specifically, this chapter discusses a project at USC to implement a portfolio-based system. Hybrid "blogfolios" can result in flexible research processes for personal, intellectual, and vocational benefits. Middlebrook and Chih-Yuan Sun evoke Ali Jafari's (2004) positioning of students as stakeholders at the "cyber-table." Students and web bloggers do not only reproduce digital identity through content; their identity is developed through aesthetic, software, and media choices (Farmer, 2006). Chih-Yuan Sun has published journal and conference papers in the areas of online teaching and learning, student motivation, electronic feedback devices, OpenCourseWare, and ePortfolios. Middlebrook is the recipient of numerous grants and awards, among them the University of Southern California Provost's Prize for Teaching with Technology. For more information about current work, see Middlebrook at http://dornsife.usc.edu/cf/faculty-and-staff/faculty.cfm?pid=1003534, and Chih-Yuan Sun through http://blog.jerry-sun.net and http://elearning-lab.nctu.edu.tw.

Similarly, in "Accessible ePortfolios for Visually-Impaired Users: Interfaces Designs, and Infrastructures," author Sushil K. Oswal focuses on questions of interface and content design in ePortfolios for blind users. The chapter is relevant for those with other disabilities as well. Oswal's research is anchored in digital technology and the questions of accessibility for the disabled. Oswal established the First-Year Writing Portfolio Project at Middle Tennessee State University and the university's newly-minted Ph.D. program has to date resulted in three doctorate degrees on the topic of portfolios. Oswal received the C. R. Anderson Award for the work on his doctoral study of an Environmental Taskforce in a Japanese-owned corporation. He is currently a Technical Communication faculty of an Interdisciplinary Program at the University of Washington, Tacoma, with additional appointments in the Environmental Studies unit of his department and the Disability Studies unit of the University of Washington, Seattle. His discussion guides readers to Zaldivar, Summers, and Watson's chapter regarding what constitutes effective ePortfolio production and accessibility. For more information on Sushil K. Oswal's current work, see http://depts.washington.edu/disstud/faculty/sushil_oswal.

And the third chapter in this section comes from Darren Cambridge: "From Metaphor to Analogy: How the National Museum of the American Indian can inform the Augusta Community Portfolio." Cambridge's latest books on ePortfolios are well-cited throughout this collection. Cambridge works for the American Institutes for Research, and spends much time analyzing ePortfolio work being done around the world. Cambridge explores the use of a specific metaphor to suggest that the individual and the system must be better integrated. The metaphor he uses is that of a museum. Here, Cambridge studies the Augusta Community Portfolio project and uses details from the National Museum of the American Indian to suggest ePortfolio design must be highly interactive in order maximize effectiveness. Cambridge asks for a "balanced relationship between community ePortfolio authors and readers, developing design and content that both provides audiences with immediate value." The demands of public, academic, professional, and personal spaces should not override authentic literacy. This third section at once heralds, praises, and critically questions the value of interactivity of digital literacies. He co-leads the Inter/National Coalition for Electronic Portfolio Research; is third country coordinator for the Europortfolio project funded by the European Union's Lifelong Learning program; and serves on the board of the Association for Authentic, Experiential, and Evidence-Based Learning. He has developed technical specifications for IMS Global Learning Consortium and open source ePortfolio software through the Sakai Foundation. For more of Cambridge's recent work, see *Electronic Portfolios 2.0: Emergent Research on Implementation and Impact* (2009), and *Eportfolios for Lifelong Learning and Assessment* (2010). Links can be found at http://ncepr.org/darren.

4. AUTHENTIC ASSESSMENT TOOLS AND KNOWLEDGE TRANSFER

In the first essay of the last section, co-written by Steven J. Corbett, Michelle LaFrance, Cara Giacomini, and Janice Fournier, "Mapping, Re-Mediating, and Reflecting on Writing Process Realities: Transitioning from Print to Electronic Portfolios in First-Year Composition," the authors describe conditions critical to understanding how best practices are implemented. Specifically, they look at ePortfolios in first-year composition at the University of Washington through shifting attitudes, practices, and technological affordances. Academia, too, is a workplace. What results are enhanced by critical reflection, better understanding of learning processes, and a more specific understanding of audience? Corbett et al.s' student data models authentic and evidence-based learning in much the same way as Johnson and Kahn's. All authors draw attention to incremental changes in instructional practices, cultures of assessment, and institutional support that will have to go hand in hand with ePortfolio application at the programmatic level. Corbett is Southern Connecticut State University Co-Director of Composition (http://writing.colostate.edu/portfolios/portfolio. cfm?portfolioid=2870), LaFrance is at the University of Massachusetts, Dartmouth (http://michellelafrancephd.com), Giacomini is University of Washington Research Manager of Academic and Collaborative Applications (http:// sites.google.com/a/uw.edu/cara-giacomini), and Fournier is University of Washington Research Scientist of the Program for Educational Transformation Through Technology (http://depts.washington.edu/pettt/team). See their Web pages to learn more about their current work.

Next, Carl Whithaus' chapter, "ePortfolios as Tools for Facilitating and Assessing Knowledge Transfer from Lower Division, General Education Courses to Upper Division, Discipline-specific Courses," investigates relationships between ePortfolios and knowledge transfer at a divisional level general education program. Whithaus' work is of particular used to administrators, program directors, and internal and external assessment bodies. Whithaus uses Grego and Thompson's (2008) notion of "thirdspace" (previously discussed) to suggest ePortfolios can be used as valuable tools for outcome-based assessments of lower-divisions. How can knowledge transfer be tracked from lower-level courses though upper division, graduate, and beyond? Whithaus shares convincing cases for the use of ePortfolios from around the world. He has published two books that focus on writing instruction and information technologies: *Writing Across Distances and Disciplines: Research and Pedagogy in Distributed Learning* (2008) and *Teaching and Evaluating Writing in the Age of Computers and High-Stakes Testing* (Erlbaum, 2005). The three chapters of this last section, in some part, deal with measuring and improving writing skills through ePortfolios. The data gathering, reflecting and, and archiving functions of ePortfolios lend greater depth and validity than the traditional culminating student surveys. The archiving function (through use of databases) mentioned in Whithaus' text paves the way to Zaldivar, Summer, and Watson's final discussion that seeks to capture useful assessment data, student voices, and authentic learning. For more information on Whithaus' current work, see http://writing.ucdavis.edu/ faculty-staff/directory/whithaus.

Finally, Marc Zaldivar, Teggin Summers, and C. Edward Watson of Virginia Tech University ask us to consider once again strategies to use authentic and evidence-based portfolios to both teach and assess in "Balancing Learning and

Assessment: A Study of Virginia Tech's Use of ePortfolios." Specifically, the essay which closes our collection opens new questions for us, such as how do we encourage administrators and faculty and staff to see value in ePortfolio learning? What are the greatest challenges confronting us with ePortfolio performance support systems? Zaldivar is Virginia Tech University Director of the ePortfolio Initiatives and works with EDUCAUSE (see http://www.educause.edu/members/virginia-tech), Summers is Assistant Director of Virginia Tech's ePortfolio Initiatives (see http://eportfolio.vt.edu), and Watson is Virginia Tech University Director of Professional Development and Strategic Initiatives (see http://www.uopd.vt.edu/IT_Leadership/Scholar_Bios/Edward_Watson.html). This final chapter in the collection asks readers to reflect on useful assessment data with attention to student voices and authentic learning.

Ultimately, this gathering of thought-provoking essays asks how ePortfolios can be used not only to document past experience, but also to change the climate of learning and assessment on college campuses while preparing college graduates for successful job applications and careers. How do ePortfolios evolve into and out of workplace environments, public spaces, and across academic curricula? What are the benefits and drawbacks of authentic, evidence-based ePortfolios that link students' voices and their learning to ePortfolios and databases? ePorfolios are mediation of performance, participation, and (re)invention. Contributors present findings and recommendations based on their experiences and research using ePortfolios in a variety of institutional and workplace settings for a variety of purposes. Through additive uses of interactive media, databases, feedback loops, and global networking, ePortfolios are positioned to make continued and significant contributions to learning and knowledge creation. Please review additional examples and the on-going programs discussed in this collection online through The WAC Clearinghouse's Open-Access Books page (http://wac.colostate.edu/books).

REFERENCES

Cambridge, B., Cambridge, D., & Yancey, K. B. (Eds.). (2009). *Electronic portfolios 2.0: Emergent research on implementation and impact.* Sterling, VA: Stylus.

Cambridge, D. (2010). *ePortfolios for lifelong learning and deliberative assessment.* San Francisco: Jossey-Bass.

Farmer, J. (2006). Blogging to basics: How blogs are bringing online education back from the brink. In A. Bruns, & J. Jacobs (Eds.), *Uses of blogs* (pp. 91-103). New York: Peter Lang.

Gerben, C. (2009). Putting 2.0 and two together: What web 2.0 can teach composition about collaborative learning. *Computers and composition online,* (Fall 2009). Retrieved from http://candcblog.org/Gerben

Grego, R., & Thompson, N. S. (2007). *Teaching/writing in thirdspaces: The Studio Approach.* Carbondale, IL: Southern Illinois University Press.

Hamilton, S., & Kahn, S. (2004). Enhancing learning, improvement, and accountability through electronic portfolios. *Metropolitan Universities Journal, 14*(4), 90-101.

Jafari, A. (2004). The "Sticky" ePortfolio system: Tackling challenges and identifying attributes. *EDUCAUSE Review, 39*(4), 38-49.

Reynolds, N., & Rice, R. (2006a). *Portfolio keeping: A guide for students* (2nd ed.). Boston: Bedford/St. Martin's.

Reynolds, N., & Rice, R. (2006b). *Portfolio teaching: A guide for teachers* (2nd ed.). Boston: Bedford/St. Martin's.

Roen, D., Glau, G., & Maid, B. (2012). *The McGraw-Hill guide: Writing for college, writing for life.* New York: McGraw-Hill.

Whithaus, C. (2005). *Teaching and evaluating writing in the age of computers and high-stakes testing.* Mahwah, NJ: Lawrence Erlbaum.

Whithaus, C., & Lakin, M.B. (2005). Working (on) electronic portfolios: Connections between work and study. *Kairos: A Journal of Rhetoric, Technology, and Pedagogy, 9*(2). Retrieved from http://english.ttu.edu/kairos/9.2/binder2.html?coverweb/whithaus/cover.htm

Yancey, K. B. (Ed.). (1992). *Portfolios in the writing classroom: An introduction.* Urbana, IL: NCTE.

Yancey, K. B. (1998). *Reflection in the writing classroom.* Logan, UT: Utah State University Press.

Yancey, K. B. (2004a). Postmodernism, palimpsest, and portfolios: Theoretical issues in the representation of student work. *College Composition and Communication, 55*(4), 738-762.

Yancey, K. B. (2004b). *Teaching literature as reflective practice.* Urbana, IL: NCTE.

Yancey, K. B., & Weiser, I. (1997a). Situating portfolios: An introduction. In K. B. Yancey, & I. Weiser (Eds.). *Situating portfolios: Four perspectives* (pp. 1-20). Logan, UT: Utah State University Press.

Yancey, K. B., & Weiser, I. (1997b). *Situating portfolios.* Logan, UT: Utah State University Press.

Zubizarreta, J. (1997). Improving teaching through portfolio revisions. In P. Seldon, *The teaching portfolio* (2nd ed.), pp. 37-45. Bolton, MA: Anker.

Zubizarreta, J. (2004). *The learning portfolio: Reflective practice for improving student learning.* San Francisco: Jossey-Bass.

Zubizaretta, J. (2009). *The learning portfolio: Reflective practice for improving student learning* (2nd ed.). San Francisco: Jossey-Bass.

SECTION 1: SYSTEMATIC PERFORMANCE SUPPORT SYSTEMS

What our age needs is communicative intellect. For intellect to be communicative, it must be active, practical, engaged. In a culture of the simulacrum, the site of communicative engagement is electronic media.

—Taylor & Saarinen,
Imagologies: Media Philosophy (2004), p. 2

AFSMI-NJ, "Market to the Younger Generation Using Social Media,"
http://afsmi-nj.org/market_to_the_younger_generation_using_social_media

CHAPTER 1.

POSTMODERNISM, PALIMPSEST, AND PORTFOLIOS: THEORETICAL ISSUES IN THE REPRESENTATION OF STUDENT WORK

Kathleen Blake Yancey
Florida State University

What we ask students to do is who we ask them to be. With this as a defining proposition, I make three claims: (1) print portfolios offer fundamentally different intellectual and affective opportunities than electronic portfolios do; (2) looking at some student portfolios in both media begins to tell us something about what intellectual work is possible within a portfolio; and (3) assuming that each portfolio is itself a composition, we need to consider which kind of portfolio-as-composition we want to invite from students, and why.

> I was of three minds,
> Like a tree
> In which there are three blackbirds
>
> —Wallace Stevens

To begin at the beginning ...

One beginning for thinking about the representation of student work is located in the context of our own research. When someone talks about representation of student work, what's often being discussed is a mediated representation, that is, *our representation of that work*—typically presented as part. A number of issues locate this meaning of representation, many scholars and organizations—among them the CCCC—addressing them.

Backing up, we might consider an earlier beginning: *the representations of students that we as teachers invite or permit.* These representations, regardless of the form that they take (essay test, PowerPoint project, or portfolio), simultaneously invite certain constructions and (yet) provide the texts that we assess. Put differently, what we ask students to do is who we ask them to be. As important, these representations constitute a rhetorical situation, precisely (1) because they are immediate, direct, and substantive—composing, as they do, the material of our teaching lives and those of our students'—and (2) because they perform a double function—providing grist for the twin mills of identity and assessment.

(Yet) Another beginning is both professional and personal, the practices we've developed with and through the portfolios that began populating writing classrooms and programs over two decades ago. For many, portfolios played a major role in the quest for a better way of representing student achievement— qua grades—than summing their grades on individual essays. As a selected body of plural performances narrated by the writer in a reflective text and located at a particular point in time, portfolios seemed (and still seem) a representation preferable to incremental measures that seem, by contrast, to represent our successes as teachers at least as much as a student's successes as a writer.[1]

In other words, any representation is situated in multiple contexts. And: a single representation, regardless of how innocent it may seem, can also serve multiple intents and can also work to unintended effects. So here a small postmodern beginning—in the sense that I have abandoned a master narrative about representation of student work, calling instead upon what Richard Freed describes as a "proliferation of little narratives" or, in Clifford Geertz's terms, a "dialogue of local interpretations." Each interpretation presented above—

1. representation of student work *by* faculty;
2. representation by students of their own work *in response* to faculty;
3. representation of students by faculty *in the currency of* grades

—is located within its own context, its own narrative. Making sense of an issue—in this case, representation of student work—requires multiple contexts, fluidity, plurality. Or: in a postmodern world, what in earlier times might have regarded as fragmentation, indeterminacy, and heterogeneity are understood today as necessary virtues.

How we organize and represent the world: that too is the palimpsest of my title. In *The Practice of Everyday Life*, Michel de Certeau presents palimpsest as another kind of representation, focusing in his illustration on the map as type. Mapmaking itself, he says, is exemplar par excellence of representation: typically, maps seek through various representational devices to stabilize a fluid and dynamic space, which (admittedly) is a useful practice for those needing the direction maps provide. At the same time, of course, what goes unnoticed is that such a stable representation achieves this stability precisely through *mis*representation: a map fundamentally misrepresents the thing represented. Moreover, such representations, as the example of the Mercator map attests, are ubiquitous, and we are impervious. Seeking a radical design practice that would permit representation of multiplicity in maps of various kinds—located in perspectives oriented to territory, socioeconomic distribution, political conflicts, identifying symbolism, and the like—de Certeau found in *palimpsest* a new semiotic, a new means of showing the "imbricated strata" inherent in any space a map might mark. The space itself, according to de Certeau, *is* a palimpsest, which only becomes obvious if and when the means of representation are likewise multiple.

Taking a cue from de Certeau, Ben Barton and Marthalee Barton have discussed layering as one "palimpsest" method for accomplishing a fuller representation. As they suggest, we might think in terms of multiply layered maps of the world through which we achieve a representation.[2] As important, *whenever* we seek to "map" materially or metaphorically, we might go "multiple," as in the case of using x-rays—taken from various vantage points—to represent and thus assist in constructing a more accurate diagnosis.[3] And of course, we might use such multiple mapping to represent student development and achievement. Recently, literary theorist Michael Davidson has talked about a related concept, what he calls the role of *palimtext*—a specifically verbal application of palimpsest—in understanding any given work of an artist. He claims:

> The palimtext is neither a genre nor an object, but a writing-in-process that may make use of any number of textual sources. As its name implies the palimtext retains vestiges of prior writings out of which it emerges. Or more accurately, it is the still-visible record of its responses to those earlier writings. (Davidson, 1995, p. 78)

According to Davidson, reading a text *in its own developmental context*—that is, reading it as a palimtext, much as we read the final draft of a student text in the context of earlier drafts of that essay or a portfolio of finished texts in the light of earlier work, including notes and peer reviews and teacher commentary—is a best way of reading precisely because of the contextual framework it privileges. As important, both of these—palimpsest and palimtext—speak to the shifting relationships between context and text: to make meaning, they both include context as a central element of text.

Context is what allows us to understand, to interpret, to make meaning. It allows us to answer the question, "Relative to what?" "Relative to the multiple contexts from which the writing emerged, to the contexts made visible and made an explicit part of the reading," we reply. Related to teaching and learning, the idea of context allows us to interpret, to represent, in many ways, simultaneously. As teachers we do this as part of daily practice, often tacitly: interpret what we intend in the context of past experiences, relative to what we hope. Students likewise:

In a first instance (perhaps a default instance), a student represents learning within the *context of time past and present*: her past, for instance, explaining what knowledge she has brought with her from previous experiences to current time as she explores what she seeks to know now.

Concurrently, in a second instance, she represents what she is learning within the *context of space*: learning in multiple contexts concurrently, she notes what she learns in one setting, a class or service learning setting, for example, at the same time that she includes what she is learning in another class.

And in a third instance, she can do both in the *context of the subordinate* (the context of what might be), while she "translates" what she is learning into the context of the future, one where she may explore questions she cannot answer now or, alternatively, in a context more focused, that of her professional aspirations.

The inclusion of these contexts in our teaching and learning as a kind of palimpsest makes meaning more complex, more sophisticated (if not always more immediately coherent) as it makes it more specific, less anonymous.

Never more so than when we ask students to represent their work and, thus of course, their selves when we ask them to compose portfolios.

These claims—among them that an assessment (like a portfolio) constructs that which it purports to measure—aren't new. What is new, at least in terms of portfolios, is the medium in which they are created. Print portfolios, in classrooms and programs, have enriched writing programs for nearly two decades (Belanoff & Dickson, 1991; Yancey & Weiser, 1997); electronic portfolios, as the recent _American Association for Higher Education_ publication *Electronic Portfolios* (Cambridge) suggests, aim for analogous changes both in what and in how we learn and teach.

The student represented in each portfolio—print and digital—is not co-identical, however, principally because these spaces that students are invited to make their own offer fundamentally different intellectual and affective opportunities: that's my first claim.

Reprinted with permission from the NCTE. Originally published in *College Composition and Communication*, Vol. 55, No. 4 (Jun., 2004), pp. 738-761.

Looking at some student portfolios in both media begins to tell us something about what intellectual work is possible within a portfolio: that's my second claim.

And if it's so that the intellectual work made possible differs according to medium, then a question we need to consider when we design our courses isn't so much, portfolios or not, but which kind of portfolio, which kind of composition, and why? That's my third claim.

There are several ways to think about the resemblances between and differences characterizing print portfolios and digital portfolios; as a focus, I want to consider briefly the arrangement permitted within each and as context for that, the rhetoric of ancient Greece. As we know, when preparing a speech, ancient rhetors were advised to think in terms of the five canons of rhetoric: invention, arrangement, style, memory, and delivery. When speech was the primary text for rhetoric, delivery received the attention we might expect: a rhetor's intonation, physical gestures, and general demeanor were understood to influence both construction and reception of text. When medium became pluralized to the *media* of speech and writing, however, delivery changed, maintaining viability in oral contexts, largely disappearing from those of print. For those interested in writing, delivery became (as did memory) an invisible canon.[4] As Richard Lanham points out, however, with the addition of the digital to the set of media, delivery takes on a critical role.[5] More specifically, it brings invention and arrangement into a new relationship with each other: *what you arrange*—which becomes a function of the medium you choose—*is who you invent*. And: who you invent is who you represent. Or:

> If arrangement constrains and shapes what we invent, and
> if what we invent leads to what it is that we represent, then
> what arrangements do we require, request, or recommend?

And how do we invite and review these arrangements?

Within this rhetorical context, I want to begin (again) by thinking about how we arrange materials in print portfolios. Typically, we have three options: (1) in a genre-based way, according to the documents of the course (essay one,

> As in a file cabinet, information is organized into categories (file drawers), subcategories (file folders), and elements (pieces of information in the file folders) …. the information resides in the owner's portfolio, providing easy access to all the data needed to support a lifetime of formative and summative evaluations (my italics).
>
> —Truer and Jensen (2003, p. 27)

argument two, and so forth); (2) in an outcomes-based way, according to what a student knows and can do (showing evidence of conceptual understanding and applications of concepts); and (3) in an intellectual framework, according to major questions or key terms of the course (using work samples to answer questions like "what is rhetoric?"). A fourth option is possible, as well: some hybrid combination of the earlier possibilities. Most often, students are asked to use a document- or genre-based approach that mirrors the sequence of assignments; the tendency is for students in their portfolio arrangement to replicate the (linear) curriculum and their always-forward processes of development almost hand-in-hand. In addition, the notebook often encasing the portfolio underscores this sense of development in *its* linear representation of materials. And while it *is* possible to read such a portfolio hypertextually (Allen, Frick, Sommers, & Yancey, 1997), the medium makes such a hypertextual reading process more difficult, not less, and as important, the design of the notebook itself acts to frame what appears as a linear development of the student. (And it's worth noting that this forward-progress development is precisely what we teachers hope for, so it too matches neatly with our desires.)

Likewise, digital portfolios can take one of three principal arrangements, and in this case, since the three offer very different rhetorical opportunities, it's worth pausing a moment to define them. The first, what we might call an *online assessment system*, is a portfolio-qua-collection housed in a digital environment where students store preselected pieces of work in a commercially or institutionally designed template. Florida State University's Career Center, for instance, offers such a portfolio template that is keyed to nine attributes, such as creativity and communication, organized into a matrix allowing students both to analyze their development as they progress through school and to represent their accomplishments. Each portfolio in the Florida State career model opens with the same interface and offers basically the same navigational path.

More ambitious (and disconcerting) in its own way is the OpenSource University of Minnesota "cradle-to-grave" model of

CHAPTER ONE I AM BORN
Whether I shall turn out to be the hero of my own life, or whether that station will be held by anybody else, these pages must show.

CHAPTER LXIII A VISITOR
[The Penultimate Chapter]
What I have purposed to record is nearly finished; but there is yet an incident conspicuous in my memory, on which it often rests with delight, and without which one thread in the web I have spun would have a raveled end.

—*David Copperfield*
Charles Dickens

electronic portfolio, created for employees and students at all UM campuses. This portfolio model offers the user the ability to "store and selectively share information in that portfolio with anyone, anywhere, at any time," a feature the designers call a "virtual identity" (Truer & Jensen, 2003, p. 34). To add "self-reported information" into the portfolio, much as in the Florida State model, the "UM Electronic Portfolio owner fills out text fields in a template that corresponds to a portfolio element" (Truer & Jensen, 2003, p. 35). There are (as of this printing) sixty-five such elements, each one of which (name of institution attended, degrees earned, and so on) permits the user to attach a file or link to a URL. Portfolio owners can also "create new elements to meet specific needs" (Truer & Jensen, 2003, p. 35). As the careful reader will note, however, not all information in this portfolio model is "self-reported." The UM "administrative system," through the software PeopleSoft, automatically displays system information in each owner's portfolio. This includes the user's name, university ID photo, contact information, demographic information, and education records. An essential part of the UM Electronic Portfolio design is that system information is displayed dynamically. This means, first, that an owner cannot modify system-entered information, and, second, the portfolio always displays the most up-to-date information (Truer & Jensen, 2003, p. 36).

The opportunities for assessment in such a model are numerous, including advisors using it to help students in "placement and course selection"; instructors assessing "learning achievement"; and even the parents of students, with permission, checking to see how their student-children are progressing. (Interestingly, the parents are apparently checking their children's performance in the *single* course requirement represented in the prototypic model: *composition*.) The online assessment electronic portfolio, then, is portfolio-like in its capacity to collect exhibits and in its inclusion of opportunities for reflection. An online assessment system, however, is very un-portfolio-like, as we in composition studies have understood portfolios, in several ways, most notably in that each portfolio has *two* composers, (1) a student and (2) the system, with the system's override capability exerting greater authority.

A second model of digital portfolio, what we might call "print uploaded," is a version of portfolio that is identical in form to the print but that is distributed electronically. In this model, the reviewer typically links from an item on the opening page to a second item—and back, much as one does in the online version of university phone books. This model is particularly useful for students morphing into the digital from the print. Lizette Piccello, a teacher at Virginia Beach City Schools, uses this approach to help students move from one medium (print) to the next (digital), advising students, first, to create a Table of Contents, and, second, to link each entry in the table to the appropriate exhibit—and back (L. Piccello, personal communication, July 22, 2003). While such a model doesn't fully exploit what digital environments make possible (the inclusion of images and pictures, links to other sites, and audio, color and photographs), such a portfolio is very like the print model in its collection, selection, and reflection and, at the same time, like the digital in its use of technology to create connections. To use another metaphor, it's a bit like the interlanguage that a speaker of a new language creates between the home language (print) and the target language (digital), including elements of each in a hybrid design.

A third digital portfolio, the one I'll focus on here, is what we might call "Web sensible," one that through text boxes, hyperlinking, visuals, audio texts, and design elements not only inhabits the digital space and is distributed electronically but also exploits the medium. In other words, this model may include print texts, but it will include as well images and visuals, internal links from one text to another, external links that provide multiple contexts, and commentary and connections to the world outside the immediate portfolio. For example, in a portfolio composed inside a course, a student might include links to process pieces as well as to completed drafts; links to a streaming video that welcomes the portfolio reader and narrates the opening; links to the class blog as well as to a group PowerPoint presentation. An audio file may narrate the PowerPoint presentation, and the PowerPoint may also link to several Web pages that provide context for the concepts presented in the PowerPoint as well as links to an explanation of the kinds of links that are being used. The portfolio may also link to texts composed in other classes, some of which have separate reflections. The medium, then, is *media*; the links numerous and varied, connecting to multiple kinds of exhibits. Typically, as I have argued elsewhere (Yancey, 2004), the "Web-sensible" model offers at least two navigational paths, and it's not uncommon for a portfolio composer to suggest explicitly to readers ways to chart those paths. In this sense, the portfolio composer sounds much like the "Dear Reader" narrator of the Victorian, novel, each instructing the reader both how to *read* and how to *understand* the new genre:

Once you do get into this site, here are a few tips to help you with browsing. This site is divided into three parts: computers I work with, the hobbies I enjoy ... and my reputation. There are three ways to navigate this site. This homepage has all the links, with a short description of each neatly planned out. If you get lost, or want to jump to something, use the side frames. But first you should go to the reflective essay. It describes all the works in this portfolio and has links to them inside of it. If you want to see something else, simply come back to the homepage.

* * *

The most important part of this website is for you to leave it. You don't have to leave now, but there are some <u>really cool sites</u> out there.

—Matthew Yancey

The Web-sensible digital portfolio, then, offers a new kind of space for student work.

All of which allows me to suggest that these portfolios—the familiar model of print and the Web-sensible digital—are different in kind rather than degree and that their differences speak to the possibilities for student invention and representation.

As Jay Bolter and Richard Grusin explain in *Remediation*, and as Marshall McLuhan suggested before that, nearly every medium is re/mediated on another medium. In other words, consciously or otherwise, we create the new in the context of the old and based on the model of the old. Television is commonly understood to be remediated on film, for example, and the Web is commonly understood to be remediated on magazines. Remediation can be back-ended as well, as we see in the most recent CNN interface on TV, which is quite explicitly remediated on the Web. In early September 2003, *The Miami Herald* announced its remediated iteration, also intentionally based on the Web (S. Apostle, e-mail, September 15, 2003). As Bolter and Grusin observe, "Whenever one medium seems to have convinced viewers of its immediacy, other media try to appropriate that convention" (Bolter & Grusin, 2000, p. 9). The new, then, repeats what came before, while at the same time remaking that which it models.[6]

Portfolios are exercises in remediation. Like new media themselves, portfolios "emerge from within cultural contexts, and they re-fashion other media, which are embedded in the same or similar contexts" (Bolter & Grusin, p. 19). From this perspective, a print portfolio seems remediated on a book. Typically, it opens with a letter or table of contents, then proceeds in a linear fashion from beginning to end. It privileges a single story, typically an argument, or a narrative that argues; it highlights the story of development told by the writer; it culminates in a narrative of accomplishment. Like chapters in a book, the entries in the portfolio testify to this story line. Although the reader may move through the portfolio hypertextually, the linear arrangement of the book argues for a beginning-to-end reading. The reader of the portfolio is, more often than not, singular: the teacher. The portfolio is typically read in isolation, silently.[7] The portfolio, in other words, is public in the small sense: within the classroom. Because of the print medium, which outside of a school culture culminates in a publication that is only revised if the number of copies sold is sufficient, the argument is frozen in a particular spot of time: a print portfolio is, typically, published only once. And once published, the story opens, progresses, and most importantly, concludes. In sum, the arrangement of the portfolio, modeled on a book, provides for the invention of a particular kind of student: one who can state a claim, synthesize material, lead a reader through a tale of progress and achievement, and conclude.

Still, a print portfolio *is* a re-mediation: as such, it offers more and other than a book. A book itself, for instance, is the product of many processes, most of which are invisible: what we tend to see in the finished product is the trace of the processes that produced it. In contrast, a print portfolio, particularly a classroom print portfolio, can intend to show process, proposes to show the pulleys and galleys that went into the final publication as well as the final publication itself. Much like Coosje Van Bruggen's *Frank O. Gehry's Guggenheim Museum Bilbao*, which records in reiterative detail the museum's "conception through design and construction" (1997), a print portfolio often shows us the *how* of development as well as the achievements of it. In the terms of literary theorist Davidson, what a print portfolio offers, in this way of process and product, is a palimtext, the *still-visible record of its responses to earlier writings* (1992, p. 78).

As students compose the print portfolio, showing both the making and the made, they engage in activities that the authors of *The Myth of the Paperless Office* identify as knowledge making. The product of research into the activities of "knowledge workers," *The Myth of the Paperless Office* outlines the myriad processes of gathering, storing, and sorting of documents that writers use to "construct and organize thoughts" (Sellen & Harper, 2001, p. 61), processes that, the authors claim, rely quite explicitly on the presences and arrangement of print documents. Writers, for example, keep information available as "contextual cues to remind them of where they were in *the space of ideas*" (Sellen & Harper, 2001, p. 61, emphasis added). The "laying out of the paper reports," and the "time bringing together and organizing reports for themselves or other people" are two critical activities for making knowledge. Another is the following: "… act of flicking through these documents, bringing to mind what was important to them and why they were important. The main implication of all this is that paper is important because it makes information accessible and tangible and gives it a persistent presence." (Sellen & Harper, 2001, p. 63) The collection of the documents and the arrangement of them, as with portfolios, permit the cre-

> Whatever else learning may be, it is clearly a *disposition to form structures.*
>
> —Berthoff qtd. in Tinberg, 2002, p. 5

ation of knowledge needed in an information age. And the pattern, Abigail Sellen and Richard Harper claim, is consistent across a diversity of workplaces:

> Since the time of our study, we have noticed that when we look at most workplaces, it is easy to see who is engaged in intensive knowledge work: it is the person whose desk is strewn with paper. Find a desk littered with stacks of reports, written notes, and every inch of space used up, and you will find someone creating a document, planning work, or doing some other sort of deeply reflective activity. (Sellen & Harper, 2001, p. 72)

[In designing my digital portfolio] I do realize that it seems strange for me to include a section entitled "Visual Communication" ....
I decided ... for the following reasons. First, I eventually want to add more work from my Visual Communication course to the website. Much of the work I'd like to include is being finished up toward the end of the semester. I hope to eventually include it in the site. Second, I avoided the title of "Rhetoric" and used "Other" instead because I would like to leave space in that section available to include coursework I complete down the road in other classes.

—Cate Heatly

Portfolios, of course, are exercises in *deeply reflective activity*. More generally, print portfolios, by virtue of the medium, ask students to engage in processes leading to knowledge and processes associated with reflective thinking.

Not least, the coherence achieved in the print portfolio is a verbal coherence, as is the means of representation. Put in terms of Howard Gardner's multiple intelligences, print portfolios are more singular than plural (1993).[8] Digital portfolios, like their print cousins, are exercises in re-mediation; they can re-mediate in one of two ways. As we saw earlier, some electronic portfolios, even though they are created in a digital environment, remediate a print model. This portfolio is the academic analogue to the print catalogue, a genre that is written for the page, not the screen, and whose digitality serves two purposes: easier storage, quicker dissemination. As noted elsewhere, it is one version of print uploaded (Wickliffe & Yancey, 2001). Its arrangement is identical to that of a print model: regardless of the fact that it is housed in the digital environ-

---

In some exhibits, you see the progression of a painting: a sketch, a study, another study, then a canvas partially painted ... re/iterations until what appears as the culminating version.

ment, it does not participate in the environment, and the student resembles her print cousin. She is the invention of print.

But other digital portfolios enact another re-mediation, this one less print portfolio than digital gallery. Like a gallery, a digital portfolio has a central entry point, which for portfolios is typically called a portal. Like a gallery, the digital portfolio includes verbal text and image and audio text, using the one modality to explain and juxtapose the others. Like a gallery, the digital portfolio makes multiple contexts a part of the display, which in the case of portfolios means linking internally to the student's own work, linking externally to multiple worlds outside the student's own purview to show multiple and complex relationships. The readership for a digital portfolio is, likewise, multiple, as are the ways of processing the portfolio. Often, there is an implied linear path, but that may be interrupted by peripheral links that themselves take one to the nooks and crannies of the digital portfolio gallery. In the terms of linguistics, digital portfolios can right branch, and they right branch again; they left branch, and they left branch again. Cumulatively and literally, the right and left branches produce a textured literacy that is different in kind than the thesis-and-support literacy of the print model. Depth of thought is created and demonstrated through multiple contexts: evoked verbally, evoked visually, evoked through internal links, evoked through external links. The arrangement of *this* portfolio, modeled on the gallery, thus provides for the invention of a different particular kind of student: one who can make multiple connections and who creates depth through multiplicity and elaboration, who can work in visual and verbal and aural modalities, who can offer a reader multiple narratives extending ever outward. It is the electronic text described by Richard Lanham in *The Electronic Word*: "No 'final cut' means no conventional endings, or beginnings or middles either. Interactive literary texts will ... require some basic non-Aristotelian adjustments" (Lanham, 1993, p. 7).

> Only final because nothing came afterward.
>
> —Myka Vielstimmig

If, then, the print portfolio is Aristotelian, the digital is post-Aristotelian. The digital portfolio seems gallery-like both within a single course, as student portfolios span temporal, spatial, and intellectual contexts, and beyond the single course, as students develop portfolios that span courses, that chart development over longer time, that from semester to semester provide *a continuing place* for students to compose. Indeed, the digital portfolio, located in multiple and multiple kinds of relationships, is a *digital composition*: a single, unified text through which various fragments rational and intuitive are related to each other, directly, associatively. Moreover, as students move from one curricular experience to another—from first-year composition to service learning assignment to the introduction to the major to the internship to the junior seminar to the capstone— they find in the portfolio a continuing site where experiences can be planned, articulated, interrogated, reflected upon, made sense of. Much as we see in a gallery, in the digital portfolio students continue a re/ iteration project. Students create multiple iterations of the portfolio, returning to the original, carrying forward some prose and reworking it, creating new images, raising new questions. Located both within the curriculum writ large and yet outside and between it—a key distinction I'll return to—the digital portfolio is the gallery canvas on which the student composes identity between, as it were, electronic drafts. And much as in a gallery, the various drafts are explained, interpreted, represented chronologically and juxtapositionally more than in a master narrative of progress uninterrupted; that is, a student may well plot a linear narrative of progress within this medium, but the medium itself invites other narratives, other arrangements, and thus other selves.

> **Because the web portfolio is a newer medium, criteria for evaluating them will emerge as the medium itself matures. Generally, excellent web portfolios will be characterized by the extent of the web, the creativity of the links, the meaningful coherence of the whole, the quality of the individual sites, the clarity of the overall design (its logic), the degree to which the rationale for particular links is explicit and sensible, the critical judgment apparent in the selection of external sites, and the overall aesthetic quality of the portfolio.**
> **http//www.stolaf.edu/depts.cis**

Like a print portfolio, the digital includes traces of earlier thinking: palimtext and palimpsest both. The palimpsest of multiple representations occurs through linking, which itself functions to provide multiple layers. Digital portfolios, because they are "spatial," inhabit three dimensions. They are quite literally and materially another *space of ideas*. Like maps, each link takes the viewer to something not quite captured-and thus the value of multiple layering.

> Because you can link externally as well as internally and
> because those links are material,
> you have more contexts you can link to,
> more strata you can layer,
> more you to invent,
> more invention to represent.

Digital portfolios, then, precisely because they are digital, privilege perspective and multiplicity and a representation of palimpsest. Or: that is the hope.

Which is not always realized, of course. As in the case of print, students may weave a narrative that is not supported by the "textual evidence." Students may not write well for either page or screen, and digital tends to require both. Students may produce links that literally don't link, or that don't create a substantial or significant relationship between the linked items. (And in fact, the linking may be the point on which the digital hinges: who decides if a link "works"? Or why?) The task of design may be overwhelming.

More generally, however, what this list of concerns demonstrates is that the medium is suggestive rather than deterministic. The virtues of the digital outlined here are more potential than realized, but this articulation demonstrates potential for a new identity, one not fully determined by medium, but possible within and through it.

Finally, I want to borrow from humanist geography to think in another way about digital portfolios. The concept of weaving is instructive here. The word itself derives from the Latin *texere*, meaning "to weave," which came to mean the thing woven (textile) and the feel of the weave (texture). But it also refers to a "weave" of an organized arrangement of words or other intangible things (context). A textile is created by bringing together many threads and, as such, represents ordered complexity. Language, too, is ordered complexity, and when we understand a word by its context we are discerning a pattern and filling in a gap, sewing together what is torn, extracting meaning not only from what is said but from the relationships this act of saying sets up with other statements, conditions, events, and situations (Adams, Hoelscher, & Till, 2001, p. viii).

Knowledge, in this metaphor, is created through relationships, which provide the center of the digital portfolio, the pattern of the intellectual weave. We see such complexity valued in models like that at St. Olaf College, where students create digital portfolios to represent their individual majors. It's knowledge as a function of the weaving of *ordered complexity.*

Multiple modes of coherence are possible: verbal, contextual, visual. Like the print portfolio, the digital is produced through the processes outlined in *Myths of the Paperless Office*, but those processes may be managed quite differently: how so (as story boarding, or as organic development of ideas) is an open question. They include design, of course: who will teach design and how, and how might this change what we do in the teaching of writing? Not least, what is the relationship of (this kind of) digital composition to the more familiar print composition that has defined the field for the last fifty years?

And from yet another vantage point, there are curricular issues associated with the digital that haven't surfaced with print portfolios or other forms of progressive pedagogy. As Lanham points out in *The Electronic Word*, the electronic medium provides a new place for students to work:

> Electronic text creates not only a new writing space but a
> new educational space as well. Not only the humanities
> curriculum, but school and university structures,
> administrative and physical, are affected at every point, as
> of course is the whole cultural repository and information
> system we call a library. (Lanham, 1993, p. xii)

Perhaps so, but if so, this new medium of portfolio may need to find a new curricular place within—but probably not inside of—the curriculum. The distinction is critical. Inside the curriculum is the place where students stay inside. In the aggregate, inside the curriculum is inside each of the disparate courses that compose a student's course of study. Inside the curriculum is the minimal portfolio submission. Because of institution's exigency, because of an exit requirement, let's say, or a rising junior hurdle, students put a portfolio together, submit it, and hope it suffices. Digitally, this portfolio takes the form of a "dynamically delivered, web-interfaced" system; like a standardized test, it asks that students fill up the predigested slots and comment reflectively on how satisfying it felt. The new place cited by Lanham is the digital portfolio created *within and beyond* the curriculum, and *this place* is likewise a new curricular place. If the curriculum is one text and the extracurriculum another, this portfolio is intertextually curricular, itself an exercise in palimpsest. It asks students to write *for the screen* as well as *for the page*; to create relationships between and among linked material, as between and among experiences; to update it as a habit of mind; and to represent learning in part by exploring the connections the digital environment invites.

Or: so digital portfolios are developing at several places across the country. As they do, it behooves us to be intentional, to understand that these portfolios, like their print cousins, bring with them opportunities and challenges.

Among them:

Where will students do this work—and why? Will they, like students at LaGuardia Community College, complete portfolio assignments in several "portfolio courses" as part of their graduation requirements? Will students periodically work on their digital portfolios as part of the advising process, as at Alverno College? Will students complete portfolios as a capstone experience in a self-designed major, as at St. Olaf? Will students do all of the above?

As program portfolios are developed, will they be "thematized" as artifacts of local culture? The LaGuardia model, for instance, invites students to represent both their home culture as well as their school culture, which makes particular sense given that a majority of students (and of faculty as well) are immigrants; they speak in two cultures already; the portfolio model welcomes that. The Clemson general education model may well include the theme of the "higher seminary of learning," given that this is part of its mission, and other initiatives (like an orientation reading program) are being built around that idea, too.

Will students work on their portfolios in some new physical space, a studio of some kind, as at Clemson University?[9]

What effects will these portfolios exert? Embedded in an interdisciplinary yearlong first-year seminar at Portland State, digital portfolios are cited as one reason the retention rate, from first year to second, has more than doubled in the last four years, from 30+% to 67%: is the power of connecting, within the intimate context of a yearlong themed seminar, this powerful?[10]

What are the exhibits that will most help students? Are they the same as we see in print? Different? What is the role that the concept and processes of composition will play in these portfolios, especially if we define the digital portfolio not as a templated drag-and-drop online assessment, *but as a new kind of composition*?

What is the relationship between intellectual connections and digital linking?

Does the *kind* of linking matter? There are many ways to categorize links, from the simple dichotomy of internal and external to the kinds of classification offered by Scott DeWitt and Kip Strasma and by Emily Golson. Does one kind of link lead to greater learning? Does one set of links, either of one special type or of a certain mix, characterize more sophisticated learning?

What will students tell us about the learning in digital portfolios?[11]

What will teachers need to learn in order to teach the digital portfolio? How can this learning be supported?

If digital portfolios call for a new definition of composition, how will that affect graduate programs? How will that affect the labor of composition, both in terms of our "work" and in terms of the qualifications for those who teach composition?

How will we read digital portfolios? As we navigate these texts, at what point is the arrangement we-as-readers plot sufficiently different one person to the next that we are creating different texts? When (if ever)/ Is such difference a problem?[12]

What are the values associated with digital portfolios? Will the values we associate with print portfolio suffice, will we need new criteria, or will the criteria themselves be remediated?

How/Will the digital portfolio change teaching, learning, and the academy itself? Will we continue to move to a visual rhetoric only, or will we, in mainstream composition classes, begin to incorporate media, not for the sake of teaching writing but for the sake of teaching media? As important, what role, if any, will we teachers of composition play?

The answer to the previous question depends in part on the answer to this: who is the digital composer, and where inside/outside the curriculum does she or he learn this composing?

Digital portfolios operate on the "felt edge" (R. Bass, personal communication, June 7, 1997) between technology and portfolio, in a space that could be productive, that, alternatively, could be Foucaultian, given the impulse of the portfolio to collect, the impulse of technology to collect and systematize. How do we navigate this felt edge without harming others, without getting hurt ourselves?

> When the blackbird flew out of sight
> It marked the edge
> Of one of many circles

Wallace Stevens' poem "Thirteen Ways of Looking at a Blackbird," a highly associative poem, speaks to what and how we know. The blackbird's *mark[ing] the edge/ Of one of many circles* suggests a plurality of possibility. "Each sense of the blackbird defines an intelligible circle, the 'meaning' of which exists only until the blackbird crosses its horizon" (Leggett, 2000). In other words, the existence of the world isn't in question, only an existence outside the perspective of the perceiver. Digital portfolios seek to represent exactly this-the perspective of the perceiver-over time, in space, aesthetically, intuitively, intellectually. These representations are themselves practices, which, as Todd May reminds us, are constitutive in ways we don't always appreciate. Much like Donald Schon and Lee Schulman, May suggests that what we know and what we hold dear are created through practice. He also understands practice as social and thus ethical. Like the rhetoricians of ancient Greece, May looks to language—to that ordered complexity—for the means of helping people move beyond information to understanding, possibly to wisdom. Through practice, we compose identity, task by rhetorical task, moment by reflective moment.

Identity is itself a composition. The relationship between identity and the digital portfolio is reciprocal, hence the importance of both print and digital. Enabling different arrangements, they permit different inventions, invite different representations. We understand fairly well the value of the one, print, but we are only beginning to chart the potential of the digital. For those of us who teach and learn composition, charting this potential may define us even more than it will define our students, and for all of us, we should, in Cindy Selfe's terms, pay attention.

Our future will be shaped as we do.

ACKNOWLEDGMENTS

I am indebted to several colleagues: Barbara Cambridge and Pat Hutchings for inviting me to the MLA session where I gave an early version of this paper; David Booth of St. Olaf College for inviting another version, and whose work inspires much of my own thinking; Todd Taylor who provided encouragement, suggestions, and (best of all) questions; Donna Winchell and Shane Peagler for their work with me on the Clemson project; reviewers Bill Condon and Gill Creel for their helpful readings and recommendations; and Marilyn Cooper for her thorough reading and able advice.

NOTES

1. Of course, as I suggest later in the chapter, a digital portfolio doesn't guarantee that this won't happen, either.

2. It's interesting that the syntax cues us as to the issue: is a fuller representation achieved, or do we achieve a fuller representation?

3. As the example of the x-rays for diagnosis makes clear, the issue of how we represent is not merely a theoretical point.

4. For a discussion of this point regarding delivery, see Martin Jacobi's "Delivery: A Definition and History," in Kathleen Blake Yancey (Ed.) (2006), *Delivering College Composition*, Heinemann.

5. My argument here is similar to Richard Lanham's in that I see the potential of digital technology to radically alter the delivery of education as well as its substance. As I explain later, the digital portfolio is one specific site for such education.

6. The idea that we refashion what came before is not, of course, limited to technology: see, for example, Harold Bloom's *The Anxiety of Influence* (1985), which traces the influence of earlier canonical poets on later ones, as well as the recent historical scholarship on Adams and Jefferson. Interestingly, as I suggest regarding technology, this influence often back-ends as well, so that it's more in the nature of a dialogue than patriarchal influence. See, for example, the recent MOMA exhibit on Picasso and Matisse, which argues a kind of call-and-response relationship between the two artists, much as was the case with Adams and Jefferson.

7. Often portfolios are read communally, for programmatic purposes, in the case of high-stakes assessment, and occasionally for other purposes, i.e., principally for formal and summative assessment. This is different than having a portfolio on the Web that invites responses outside of the sphere of the classroom and the teacher and that is intended to speak to a myriad of readers, as Joe Harris suggested in his interview for "New Media Live" (Taylor & Halbritter, 2003).

8. As Bill Condon notes, the verbal coherence, (merely) a single intelligence in Howard Gardner's term, is an intelligence worth exercising.

9. Clemson's Class of 1941 Studio for Student Communication (http://www.clemson. edu/1941studio) provides a single curricular and physical space for work in communication across the curriculum, including continuing and cumulative portfolio work.

10. T. Rhodes, personal communication, June 2003.

11. At least two studies across the country have explored student reaction to the creation of digital portfolios, one produced by the University of Washington, which tracked what students learned in freshman interest groups in fall 2002; and another produced by Clemson University in 2002, which interviewed students about what they had learned across the curriculum and what they saw as the value of a digital portfolio.

12. As Bill Condon suggested when he reviewed this manuscript in July 2003, all readings are different: "I'd raise the specter of Fish and ask when two readers are not experiencing different texts." Point taken, and one I've addressed about print in print (e.g., *Reflection in the Writing Classroom*). At the same time, it seems to me, but certainly remains to be documented, that readings of print portfolios tend to differ by degree, while those of the Web-sensible can (and will) differ by kind, given the variety of navigational possibilities they offer. Just as the arrangement possible for a writer provides for invention of self, so too the arrangement of texts provides for the invention of the digital composition.

REFERENCES

Adams, P. C., Hoelscher, S., Till, K. (2001). Place in context: Rethinking humanist geographies. In P. C. Adams, S. Hoelscher, & K. Till (Eds.), *Textures of place* (pp. xiii-xxxiii). Minneapolis: University of Minnesota Press.

Allen, M., Frick, J., Sommers, J., & Yancey, K. (1997). Outside review of writing portfolios: An on-line evaluation. *WPA: Writing Program Administration* (Spring), 64-88.

Barton, B., & Barton, M. (1993). Ideology and the map: Toward a postmodern visual design practice." In N. Blyler & C. Thralls (Eds.), *Professional Communication* (pp. 49-79). Newbury Park, CA: Sage.

Belanoff, P., & Dickson, M. (Eds.), (1991). *Portfolios: Process and product.* Portsmouth, NH: Boynton/Cook.

Bloom, H. (1985). *The Anxiety of influence: A theory of poetry*. Oxford: Oxford University Press.

Bolter, J. D., & Grusin, R. (2000). *Remediation*. Cambridge, MA: MIT Press.

Cambridge, B. (Ed.), (2001). *Electronic portfolios: Emerging practices in student, faculty, and institutional learning*. Washington, DC: American Association of Higher Education.

Conference on College Composition and Communication Guidelines for the Ethical Treatment of Students and Student Writing in Composition Studies. (2000). The National Council of Teachers of English. Retrieved from http://www.ncte.org/cccc/resources/positions/ethicalconduct

Davidson, M. (1995). Palimtexts. In M. Perloff (Ed.), *Postmodern genres* (pp. 75-95). Norman, OK: University of Oklahoma Press.

de Certeau, M. (1984/1988). *The practice of everyday life*. Berkeley: University of California Press.

DeWitt, S., & Strasma, K. (Eds.). (1999). *Contexts, intertexts, and hypertexts*. Cresskill, NJ: Hampton Press.

Dickens, C. (1950). *David Copperfield*. New York: Modern Library.

Freed, R. (1993). Postmodern practice: Perspective and prospects." In N. Blyler, & C. Thralls (Eds.), *Professional Communication* (pp. 196-215). Newbury Park, CA: Sage.

Gardner, H. (1993). *Frames of mind: The theory of multiple intelligences*. New York: Basic Books.

Geertz, C. (1983). *Local knowledge*. New York: Basic Books.

Golson, E. (1999). Cognition, meaning, and creativity: On reading student hypertexts. In L. DeWitt, M. Farr, & K. Strasma (Eds.), *Contexts, Intertexts, and Hypertexts* (pp. 155-77). New York: Hampton Press.

Jacobi, M. (2006). Delivery: A definition and history. In K. B. Yancey (Ed.), *Delivering college composition: The fifth canon*. Portsmouth, NH: Heinemann.

Lanham, R. (1993). *The electronic word: Democracy, technology, and the arts*. Chicago: University of Chicago Press.

Leggett, B. J. (2000). On thirteen ways of looking at a blackbird. In C. Nelson (Ed.), Modern American Poetry. Retrieved from http://www.english.uiuc.edu/maps/poets/s_z/stevens/ blackbird.htm

May, T. (2001). *Our practices, our selves*. University Park, PA: Penn State University Press.

McLuhan, M. (1964). *Understanding new media*. Cambridge, MA: MIT Press.

Schon, D. (1983). *The reflective practitioner*. New York: Basic Books.

Schulman, L. (1996, January). Course anatomy: The dissection and transformation of knowledge." Presented at the AAHE Faculty Roles and Rewards Conference in Atlanta, GA.

Selfe, C. (1999). Technology and literacy: A story about the perils of not paying attention. *CCC 50*(3), 411-436.

Sellen, A., & Harper, R. (2001). *The myth of the paperless office*. Cambridge, MA: MIT Press.

Stevens, W. (2003). "Thirteen ways of looking at a blackbird." In I. Lancashire (Ed.), *Representative Poetry Online*. Retrieved from http://eir.library.utoronto.ca/rpo/ display/poem2018.html

Taylor, T., & Halbritter, S. (2003, March). *New media live*. Paper presented at the Annual Convention Conference on College Composition and Communication in New York City.

Tinberg, H. (2002). Starting where students are, but knowing (and letting them know) where we want to take them. *TETYC, 30*(1), 5.

Truer, P., & Jensen, J. (2003). Electronic portfolios need standards to thrive? *EDUCAUSE Quarterly, 26*(2), 34-41.

Van Bruggen, C. (1997). *Frank O. Gehry Guggenheim Museum Bilbao*. New York: Guggenheim Museum.

Vielstimmig, M. (1998). Not a cosmic convergence: Rhetorics, poetics, performance, and the web." *Kairos: A Journal of Rhetoric, Technology, and Pedagogy, 3*(2). Retrieved from http://english.ttu.edu/kairos/3.2/features/myka/cosmic4.htm

Wickliffe, G., & Yancey, K. B. (2001). The perils of creating a class web-site: It was the best of times, it was the .... *Computers and Composition, 18*(3), 177-186.

Yancey, K. B. (2004). Looking for sources of coherence in a fragmented world: Notes toward a new assessment design. *Computers and Composition, 21*(1), 89-102.

Yancey, K. B. (1998). *Reflection in the writing classroom*. Logan, UT: Utah State University Press.

Yancey, K. B., & Weiser, I. (1997). *Situating portfolios*. Logan, UT: Utah State University Press.

CHAPTER 2.

THE HYPERMEDIATED TEACHING PHILOSOPHY EPORTFOLIO PERFORMANCE SUPPORT SYSTEM

Rich Rice
Texas Tech University

The teaching philosophy assignment is a staple of professional development. Oftentimes, however, students new to the genre imbalance the theoretical and the practical, rendering lessons learned and what can eventually serve as an effective bridge between school and workplace, instead, an inauthentic representation of teaching praxis. Teaching students how to compose balanced teaching philosophy statements by using hypermediated comments and hyperlinks to artifacts in support of theory offers opportunities to create more effective teaching philosophy spaces.

The teaching philosophy assignment is a staple of professional development. It is a regular in English Education and Composition Theory courses. It serves as a reflective space for preservice and practicing teachers alike, exploring theoretical underpinnings and making clear ideological knowledge-making. The teaching philosophy can be used as an ePortfolio's reflective essay for the purpose of working with colleagues, for grant proposals, for job application dossiers, and for promotion and tenure, linking artifacts which support extensive claims. And like a modern palimpsest which is scraped and re-tooled again and again, the teaching philosophy can take on numerous revisions throughout the experiential maturation of the reflective practitioner (Zubizarreta, 1997, 2004). Oftentimes, however, students new to the genre imbalance the theoretical and the practical, rendering lessons learned and what can eventually serve as an effective bridge between school and workplace, instead, an inauthentic representation of teaching praxis.

Teaching students how to compose balanced teaching philosophy statements by using hypermediated comments and hyperlinks to artifacts in support of theory, what is often called a practical theory approach to composing, can offer opportunities for deeper reflection. The approach follows the *College Composition and Communication* call for "a changed understanding of the relationship between performance and composition," in particular (Fishman et al., p. 241). In one article in this *CCC* issue from 2005, "Performing Writing, Performing Literacy," in particular, written in part by Andrea Lunsford, specific performance techniques, such as flashback as it relates to portfolios, are examined as tools composition can use. In fact, the introductory reflective essay to a portfolio, as a sort of performance, can serve as an invaluable tool. Writing is performance, and performance is writing: a situated rhetorical positioning (see Manis, 2009). We all want students and workplace employees to reflect over what they're doing in meaningful ways in order to improve individual performance to impact larger systems productively. This is the purpose of an ePortfolio, generally, as well. But just as most definitions of ePortfolio include multimodality, so too can traditional assignments. Consider this definition: an ePortfolio is "a collection of digitized collection of artifacts including demonstrations, resources, and accomplishments that represent an individual, group, an organization, or institution. This collection can be comprised of text-based, graphic, or multi-media elements archived on a website or any other electronic media" (Lorenzo & Ittelson, 2005). What if this is the basic definition of a teaching philosophy statement as well?

A quick look at the teaching philosophy statement assignment from The Teaching Center at Washington University in St. Louis demonstrates how such enhancements improve effectiveness and clarity. This website is clear and well-considered, and was featured in *The Chronicle of Higher Education* in 2010. The teaching philosophy statement is defined as "a one- to two-page document that provides a clear, concise account of your teaching approach, methods, and expertise" (Fisher, 2012). Writers are encouraged to identity why, what, and how one teaches as well as how one measures teaching effectiveness. Accordingly, the teaching philosophy statement "should include *concrete examples* of specific course topics, assignments, assessments, and strategies drawn from courses that you have taught or are or prepared to teach, or from past mentoring and advising experiences" (emphasis theirs). But in the same paragraph the assignment quickly morphs into a teaching portfolio, because demonstrating a range of teaching expertise and fleshing out the philosophy with supporting documents such as syllabi, assignments, assessments, and graded papers is simply impossible to do well in a page or two. What is needed are not concrete examples, but specific yet malleable examples.

Teaching statements must demonstrate teaching performance, which is necessarily malleable according to shifting content and audiences, and hypertextual content is critical in showing flexible performance. These are not the same documents or assignments, however. The latter is much more dynamic. Reticence to move toward native hypertextual composing with this assignment, because one- to two-page statements required in job applications is critical to the process of selecting viable applicants for interviewing, gives an incomplete view of the teacher. In fact, the type of information that could be revealed more accurately from a hypermediated teaching philosophy statement (a teaching portfolio) could be shared at the point of application instead of interview as an electronic performance support system quite efficiently (see Rosenbloom, 2008; see also Wright, 1980, on teaching writing for the digital Generation Me).

Here are other well-informed discussions about what should go into teaching philosophy statements. Please review them online in their entirety. But note the complexity of what should go into a brief statement, even when the genre and medium provides obvious limits. Rachel Narehood Austin (2006) offers career advice in *Science Careers*, emphasizing commitment rather than creativity on teaching philosophy statements. She says they should be tailored to the institution to which one is applying, identifying specific courses, drawing upon experiences as a student and scholar and human being, all the while avoiding promising too much. Lee Haugen (1998) in the Center for Excellence in Learning and Teaching at Iowa State University recommends starting with teaching objectives, highlighting how one does what one preaches, identifying effective teaching practices, and then closing with why teaching is important. James M. Lang (2010) in *The Chronicle of Higher Education* asks us to consider how to write a statement different than everyone else's. Avoid the generic at all cost. He says relate best practices, make distinctions that connect to specific sorts of classes one is applying to teach, provide specific examples, and reference sources to support claims. Teresa Mangum (2009) in *Inside Higher Ed* says relate teaching and learning objectives clearly, balance theory with evidence of practice, use personal examples and anecdotes which are reflective of relevant theory, and present a sort of "love story of an intellectual life." Avoid clichés. Oh, and include life experience. Forster reflective practice through ePortfolios, as T. Sporer and K. Bredl (2011) suggest. Similarly, Gabriela Montell (2003) in *The Chronicle of Higher Education* warns against rehashing one's CV, advises avoiding "empty" statements, and suggests adopting a tone of humility while emphasizing student-centered teaching. And Nancy Van Note Chism (2012) through The Ohio State University's University Center for the Advancement of Teaching offers teaching philosophy statements across the curriculum which value unique and contextual approaches. All great advice and helpful stories that adds to portfolio teaching lore (Carney, 2002). All more possible to do well by demonstrating teaching performance *through* the teaching philosophy statement, which in result could strengthen systems of hiring.

PERFORMING THROUGH DOCUMENTS

Research on electronic performance support systems is directly relevant. For instance, in *Electronic Performance Support Systems: How and Why to Remake the Workplace Through the Strategic Application of Technology*, Gloria J. Gery (1991) points out that the most common problem in organization redesign for improvement is a denial or refusal to admit the truth, such as perceiving what workers simply want to perceive, avoiding problematic circumstances, explaining data with "yes, but ..." responses, covering up the unacceptable, and reviewing information superficially (p. 3). Little is lost in translation when thinking about how this works specifically with teachers. In philosophy statements, generally, writers will often refuse to admit that they simply can't reach every student as effectively as they wish. They will imply that their classroom management and assessment skills work perfectly every time. They don't highlight problems in their own philosophies which are difficult to address, and how they've addressed them. They don't mention that adequate resources are critical to their effective teaching. They can't include all of the great advice above. And they don't often reference their work and cite their own action research as practical evidence to support theoretical claims about their own teaching.

Productive support systems, however, embrace what Gery calls the "performance zone"; this is a *kairoic*, rhetorical space where an employee's workplace skills are honed to match varying workplace situations. According to Gery, "individual employees and entire organizations can systematically work and achieve in the performance zone" (p. 13). And this is done through retooling old paradigms, and through re-envisioning how we justify and resist change, because the goal of any electronic performance support is to enable people to perform in a system. Teaching philosophy essays are designed to demonstrate theories of performance, but instead of asking a teacher to simply *tell* it, those writing such essays must compose transactionally in the dialogic context of various teaching situations and capabilities to *show* it. Otherwise, there can be relatively little demonstration of the transfer and application of teaching praxis in the intended audience's context. The inexperienced teacher will try another approach or make specific, yet often implausible, examples when something doesn't work in order to generate the same outcome. But more experienced communicators, Gery suggests:

> [C]ommunicate dynamically in relation to the situation
> and to the needs and to each other's capabilities. In the
> best situations, this process is fluid, complementary, and
> energizing. Learners maintain or increase their motivation as
> skill, knowledge, and confidence increase. Masters, teachers,
> or coaches increasingly understand what's necessary and what
> works—and they anticipate the needs of the learner and
> avoid unproductive paths. (p. 32)

Thus, the ideal performance zone or most effective teaching philosophy essay is one which demonstrates situated change just-in-time; sound principles on-demand at any time and in any place. Good teaching, perhaps deceptively simple, is flexible teaching, and the traditional genre of the teaching philosophy essay as represented by traditional print exposition offers limited opportunity to demonstrate flexibility and affordances of change on-demand. In other words, text-only teaching philosophy statements, like print-only portfolios, offer relatively little rhetorical and situational maneuvering opportunity, which is quintessential to good teaching performance. See also Light, Chen, and Ittelson (2012) on building faculty buy-in, training, and support systems (pp. 109-120), and their analysis of Virginia Tech's ePortfolio system, which is also analyzed by Zaldivar, Summers, and Watson in this collection).

As technological affordances change what we can do with what we have, value-added situated teaching philosophy statements with hypermediated metareflections is a more dynamic composition. Philip Auslander (1990) offers a useful analogy in *Liveness: Performance in a Mediatized Culture*, when he discusses relationships between television, cinema, and the theater: "the television image was frontal and oriented toward the viewer in much the same way as a performance on a proscenium stage would be. This was reflected in the actors" playing [toward the camera]" (p. 21). Traditional essay writing in general, and the traditional teaching philosophy essay specifically, is akin to early television or theatrical performances that are performed with a specific audience-seated-in-the-near-distance in mind. But new technologies, new audiences, and new teaching situations with new media call for more realistic or "live" or enlivened performance, simulation which embraces practical theory and "re-directable" application. Auslander analyzes what liveness means in terms of legal (re)presentation as an extension of a performer's identity having value (pp. 148-149). In fact, that new media is what Kember and Zylinski (2012) refer to as life itself in *Life after New Media: Mediation as a Vital Process*. When writers share a teaching philosophy statement, but do not address varied situations to which it can be applied, which is critical in today's post-process classrooms, or the hidden ideologies from which the teaching approaches are rooted, the performance is mediated by static text rather than dynamically performed to create realistic identity and voice. It is not owned, in other words, as an inhabited "thirdspace," something Carl Whithaus discusses in this collection of essays. Ultimately, a teaching philosophy is not intended to be a live performance, although readers who analyze teaching philosophies do so with the intention of envisioning a teacher—live—performing in front of students.

Let's look at this another way. In 2002 Lee-Ann Kastman Breuch published "Post-Process 'Pedagogy': A Philosophical Exercise" in the *Journal of Advanced Composition*. She considers Sid Dobrin's, Thomas Kent's, Joseph Petraglia's, and Irene Ward's theories about post-process, dialogic pedagogy which philosophize the potential of divergent teaching praxis. Kastman Breuch reasons that, like realistic performance through teaching philosophy statements, post-process theory should not remain a theoretical endeavor but a "*how-centered*" approach to teaching emphasizing what we do with content:

> It means becoming teachers who are more in tune to the
> pedagogical needs of students, more willing to discuss ideas,
> more willing to listen, more willing to be moved by moments
> of mutual understanding. It means, in sum, to be more
> conscientious in our attempts to meet the needs of students
> in their educational journeys. (p. 122)

An educational journey involves contextualizing teaching approaches according to changing student demographic, according to changing technological affordances and experiences, and according to changing programmatic or systematic influences and requirements in syllabus development and assessment measurements. The movement from product to process in order to provide more learning opportunities for unique students was an obvious move in the history of composition instruction, but oftentimes we create approaches to assignments and specific genre which, in effect, render processes a product. Instead, to move from emphasizing what to how, such genre must adopt opportunity to massage or contextualize or re-center writing given new audiences for which we must invoke and perform, in order to recognize value in many dynamic and revolving processes.

Kastman Breuch, in fact, cites Ward (1994) and Kent (1999) who describe a "functional dialogism" writing pedagogy, emphasizing internalized audiences, and increased dialogues between students/teachers, between students/larger communities, and between students/subject matter. More dialectical engagement, formally, enables writers to gain insight into multiple perspectives (p.

103). And this emphasis of functional infrastructure is critical to Shepherd and Goggin's (2012) more recent work, calling for us to pay attention to technological as well as social infrastructures. What if scoring guides for assessing teaching philosophy statements helped identify the value of increased dialectical performance? In "Employee Performance Management: Policies and Practices in Multinational Enterprises," Dennis Briscoe and Lisbeth Claus (2008) define performance management this way: "[T]he system through which organizations set work goals, determine performance standards, assign and evaluate work, provide performance feedback, determine training and development needs, and distribute rewards" (p. 15). They go on to investigate performance management in global and organizational contexts, but applying their definition in the context of hypermediated teaching philosophy essays demonstrates functional dialogism and Bartholomae's (1988) concept of inventing the university as well. Light, Chen, and Ittelson (2012) highlight ePortfolios as global bridge tools, as do many theorists, pointing out that "today, most students can expect to explore cultures and have life experiences, and world views that are different from other people they meet, learn and work with. Valuing the 'other,' therefore, is a central contemporary competency. ePortfolios can provide a way for students to document their experiences with other cultures whether this is through experiential learning in their own community, or through study abroad experiences" (p. 59).

For instance, traditional text-only based teaching philosophy essays don't match the goals and objectives of the writer with work goals of institutions because such complex and specific goals are difficult to squeeze into a short philosophy statement. Yet, any rhetorically effective document works to match goals. A hypermediated teaching philosophy can link to or metareflect over such goals of a variety of types of institutions to demonstrate realistic application. The traditional genre can theorize about how performance standards can be met in the future, whereas much like an ePortfolio, hypermediated philosophies can link to teaching videos and documentation outlining ways in which performance standards have actually been met. Further, as a system, a hypermediated teaching philosophy can demonstrate process or how work has been assigned and revised and resubmitted based on evaluative feedback on materials produced as well as teaching performed, which enables readers to see what training the writer has effectively received as well as may still need. And beyond the scope of a traditional teaching philosophy are artifacts deserving of rewards which demonstrate effective praxis. An electronic portfolio performance system, then, and a hypermediated teaching philosophy as a reflective essay beginning, outlining, and defining a portfolio, can be considered part of such a performance management composition, enhancing an individual's performance with the ultimate purpose of improving an organization's performance.

NETWORKED WRITING SYSTEMS

More recently, in *PostComposition*, Sid Dobrin (2011) provides an overview of what he calls the (e)state of composition/theory. He traces the social-construction of Stephen North's knowledge-making principles, through David Smit's *The End of Composition Studies*, which emphasizes the spreading and integration of writing instruction with disciplines outside English Studies. Smit's (2004) work identifies interdisciplinary venues as the true purpose and future direction of writing instruction, that "research and scholarship in composition studies have reached a certain limit in their ability to formulate fundamental paradigms, models, and theories about the nature of writing" (p. 9), suggesting that the best writing is therefore always already bridging into disciplines and situations beyond the composition classroom (see also Batson, 2011 in the *International Journal of ePortfolio*). In addition to questioning the (e)state space that composition studies occupies, Dobrin points out we must teach students how to occupy space authentically: "Writing requires space. Writing requires the material space onto/into which writing is inscribed, and it requires cultural, historical, political space to occupy. In both of these instance, writing sets up occupancy within or saturates a particular space" (p. 56). Without space content can't move; it can't find power, it can't occupy. And as Dobrin continues, "content is limited by capacity. Content limits space, limits possibility. Content is subject matter, the matter of the subject, denoting both power of the subject over the matter/the content and the makeup of the subject" (p. 57). What is required is beyond socially-constructed transactional rhetorical spaces; writing with voice, today, according to Dobrin, must make use of the "hyper-circulatory, networked condition of writing" (p. 57). These are the minds of the future (Gardner, 2007). See also Ira Shor's (1996) discussion of negotiating authority in critical pedagogy.

The hypermediated teaching philosophy is a genre exemplifying this new type of system of writing performance within disciplines operation. Lee Rainie and Barry Wellman (2012) call this a networked condition or process of networked individualism as well in *Networked: The New Social Operating System*. They raise the idea, following Sherrie Turkle, just like the medium and the message is the message, that the virtual and the real are the real. Turkle's (2012) latest book, in fact, is called *Alone Together: Why We Expect More from Technology and Less from Each Other*. These writing lives of students exist only in as much as they are both real and imagined, or in-text and hyper-connected to future application or situation. According to Rainie and Wellman, "In-person encounters" are not the only "meaningful form of social connection"; emails, texts, Facebook® posts, tweets, and more are just as significant and natural (p. 119).

The multilayered processes of layered and interwoven media forms and narratives must be demediated in a sort of hypermediated pedagogy in order to make sense as Kember and Zylinska (2012) write in their chapter "Face-to-Facebook, or the Ethics of Mediation: From Media Ethics to an Ethics of Mediation" (pp. 153-172). Similarly, composing a teaching philosophy statement which is not dialogically performing connections to artifacts intended to be used in the audience's own environments, renders teaching philosophy statements incomplete. Byron Hawk (2011) underlines this point in "Reassembling Postprocess: Toward a Posthuman Theory of Public Rhetoric," which is a chapter in a collection by Dobrin, Jenny Rice, and Michael Vastola called *Beyond Postprocess*. Hawk begins with Kent's post-process assumptions that writing is public, interpretive, and situated but connects them to networked identity and performance to argue that "the subject of writing is the network that inscribes the subject as the subject scribes the network" (p. 75). Accordingly, to create documents with identity is to define and enliven the public sphere as a networked, integrated loop. This dialogic connection between an individual's view of teaching and how it can connect and adapt within an organization is also referred to as a romantic social epistemic bringing together the individual and the socially-constructed (Gradin), "newly mediated" convergences (Atwan, 2002), networked individualism (Rainie & Wellman, 2012), "smart" timeliness and the ability to move quickly in dynamic and interconnected ways (Rheingold, 2002), intelligent growth (Kahn & Hamilton, 2009), networked and symphonic selves (Cambridge, 2010), and even "glocalized" thinking (Jay, 2010).

It is clear we are experiencing an epistemological shift in knowledge creation to an individuated expression from a personalized perspective that accrues reliability through being distributed through networked spaces or distributed visualities. As such, I want to turn now to an early draft of my own teaching philosophy statement, in print form, and ask my readers to consider how best to hypertextualize and metareflect over what it's saying in your own audience. How might I better situate it beyond the print genre? I use my own teaching philosophy statement because I know it best, because I know it has been reworked many times, but I see many problems in it because it is not designed to demonstrate performance in a system. My interests, too, have now expanded given many technological affordances, and my interests in glocalization and intercultural communication and mobile media in networked society and other trends (see Figure 1; see also Reese & Levy (2009) on ePortfolio trends and uses).

I use some of the techniques advised by experts on teaching philosophy statements mentioned earlier, such as being specific, demonstrating a love for teaching, referencing some ideas by citing specific theorists, pointing out tools

I use to measure my own teaching effectiveness, etc. I outline three ideas which shape my philosophy, as an attempt to recognize how quickly this document would be read if I were to use it to support a job application. I point out, right away, that my philosophy evolves, and then I highlight that throughout in terms of flexibility, connecting to different types of learners, and seeking interconnections between language and learning and contexts. As far as teaching philosophy statements go, it's fairly fluent. But there is a lot missing because of the genre itself, and because this draft was written in 2001.

If I could include hyperlinks and metareflections, I would link to student traditional and multimodal assignments, to edited video clips of me working with students, to comments on student writing, to a series of syllabi which look at synchronizing assignment sets, to other materials I have written. Doing so would be a true ePortfolio performance support system. This would not be a CV, but present how I see myself as an integrated scholar, working to connect teaching, research, service, and grant writing with changing needs and directions of the department I work in over time. That network of connections, an individual within a system, cannot be separated from my teaching, and is now what I would like to present to others if I were seeking a job or demonstrating how teaching works to other colleagues or students. I would walk readers through a student experience in one of my classes, making my teaching philosophy statement itself a sort of portfolio of portfolios. How do the approaches in this paragraph provide a stronger augmented reality to my teaching philosophy statement? If you were my audience, what else would I need to include, and could that best be included in text or through a network of ideas? Others in this collection, as well as C. S. Johnson (2006), regarding online portfolios in technical communication, offer suggestions.

In what ways does such an augmented reality support my own professional development? Certainly my philosophy of teaching grows over time through transitional phases in my own understanding of how my philosophy relates to effective teaching and accurate presentation of my own teaching performance, but my teaching performance work is directly rooted to my philosophical foundation (Heath, 2004). Darren Cambridge (2010) and Helen Chen (2009) highlight the significance of lifelong learning and assessment portfolio models with regard to mediated self-representation and managed interaction, reinforcing this point specifically. According to Cambridge, "Symphonic eportfolio composition, done iteratively through more intensive reflection at points of transition, helps authors find coherence and establish commitments that are informed by and have the potential to influence day-to-day decision making" (p. 186).

The teaching philosophy statement as a one- to two-page document—similar to how the essay is a genre created largely for assessment purposes—is a genre that should be expanded to embrace, much like ePortfolio performance support systems, individual identity *and* rhetorically situated networked spaces. The technology affords it, and hypermediated teaching philosophy statements fulfill in large part the purpose of the genre. Such documents can be short enough for readers who are making quick judgments of the theory presented in the document, but integrated enough for readers who want to see teacher performance in more practical ways. Simply put, the genre enables students to better demonstrate how specific reading, writing, and thinking ideas and values can be directly connected to real contexts.

REFERENCES

Atwan, R. (2002). *Convergences: Message, method, medium.* Boston: Bedford/St.Martin's.

Auslander, P. (1999). *Liveness: Performance in a mediatized culture.* New York: Routledge.

Austin, R. N. (2006). Writing the teaching statement. *Science Careers.* Retrieved from http://sciencecareers.sciencemag.org/career_magazine/previous_issues/articles/2006_04_14/writing_the_teaching_statement. doi:14633728089694563528.

Bartholomae, D. (1988). Inventing the university. In E. R. Kintgen, B. M. Kroll, & M. Rose (Eds.), *Perspectives on literacy* (pp. 273-285). Carbondale & Edwardsville, IL: Southern Illinois University Press.

Batson, T. (2011). Situated learning: A theoretical frame to guide transformational change using electronic portfolio technology. *International Journal of ePortfolio, 1*(1), 107-114.

Briscoe, D. R., & Clause, L. M. (2008). Employee performance management: Policies and practices in multinational enterprises. In A. Varma, P. S. Budhwar, & A. DeNisi, *Performance management systems: A global perspective* (pp. 15-39). New York: Routledge.

Cambridge, D. (2010). *Eportfolios for lifelong learning and deliberative assessment.* San Francisco: Jossey-Bass.

Carney, J. (2002). Campfires around which we tell our stories: Confronting the dilemmas of teacher portfolios and new technologies. Retrieved from http://helenbarrett.com/campfires.htm

Chen, H. L. (2009). Using eportfolios to support lifelong and lifewide learning. In D. Cambridge, B. Cambridge, & K. B. Yancey (Eds.), *Electronic portfolios 2.0: Emergent research on implementation and impact* (pp. 29-35). Sterling, VA: Stylus.

Chism, N. (2012). Writing a philosophy of teaching statement. *Ohio State University*. Retrieved from http://ucat.osu.edu/teaching_portfolio/philosophy/philosophy2.html

Dobrin, S. (2011). *PostComposition*. Carbondale, IL: Southern Illinois University Press.

Fisher, B. (2012). Writing a teaching philosophy statement. *Washington University in St. Louis: The Teaching Center*. Retrieved from http://teachingcenter.wustl.edu/writing-teaching-philosophy-statement

Fishman, J., et al. (2005). Performing writing, performing literacy. *College Composition and Communication, 57*(2), 224-253.

Gardner, H. (2007). *Five minds for the future*. Boston: Harvard Business School.

Gery, G. J. (1991). *Electronic performance support systems: How and why to remake the workplace through the strategic application of technology*. Cambridge, MA: Ziff Institute.

Gradin, S. (1995). *Romancing rhetorics: Social expressivist perspectives on the teaching of writing*. Portsmouth, NH: Boynton/Cook.

Haugen, L. (1998). Writing a teaching philosophy statement. *Iowa State University*. Retrieved from http://www.celt.iastate.edu/teaching/philosophy.html

Hawk, B. (2011). Reassembling postprocess: Toward a posthuman theory of public rhetoric. In S. I. Dobrin, J. A. Rice, & M. Vastola, *Beyond Postprocess* (pp. 75-93). Logan, UT: Utah State Press.

Heath, M. (2004). *Electronic portfolios: A guide to professional development and assessment*. New York: Linworth Learning.

Jay, P. J. (2010). *Global matters: The transnational turn in literary studies*. Ithaca, NY: Cornell University Press.

Johnson, C. S. (2006). A decade of research: Assessing change in the technical communication classroom using online portfolios. *Journal of Technical Writing and Communication, 36*(**4**), 413-431.

Kahn, S., & Hamilton, S. J. (2009). Demonstrating intellectual growth and development: The IUPUI ePort. In D. Cambridge, B. Cambridge, & K. B. Yancey (Eds.), *Electronic portfolios 2.0: Emergent research on implementation and impact* (pp. 91-96). Sterling, VA: Stylus.

Kastman Breuch, L. M. (2011). Post-process "pedagogy": A philosophical exercise. In V. Villanueva, & K. L. Arola. *Cross-talk in comp theory: A reader* (3rd ed). (pp. 97-125). Urbana, IL: NCTE.

Kember, S., & Zylinska, J. (2012). *Life after new media: Mediation as a vital process*. Boston: MIT Press.

Kent, T. (1999). *Post-process theory: Beyond the writing-process paradigm*. Carbondale: Southern Illinois University Press.

Statement of Teaching Philosophy
–Rich Rice

My teaching evolves with my reading of theoretical and practical texts, with my continuing experience with traditional and nontraditional K-16 teachers and students in the classroom, with my professional development activities, and with my growing awareness of work in other disciplines. There are some core values, however, that make up who I am as a teacher. For instance, in order to teach literacy, it is my view that writing teachers must expand students' ways of seeing as readers and writers. As Patricia A. Sullivan suggests in "Charting a Course in First-Year English," encouraging students to be "more active and reflective participants in the various cultures that comprise the world" is vital. To do this, students need to learn how to use both personal voice and academic discourse to convey knowledge to authentic audiences. They also need to learn how to use *ethos, pathos,* and *logos* to become savvy surveyors of rhetorical situations. Further, because of our society's reliance on computer technology, students must pay attention to and become functionally literate with communication and presentation tools. Fundamentally, three ideas shape my philosophy:

> *"Teaching procedures have to harmonize with evaluative theories. More precisely, one's philosophy about what writing is for leads to a theory of what constitutes good writing. That philosophy, in turn, leads to a concept of pedagogical goals, and the goals lead, in turn, to classroom procedures."*
>
> *–Richard Fulkerson, Composition in Four Keys*

      (1) I believe in the value and power of language;
      (2) I believe that flexible, effective teaching involves reflection, reflexivity, and action; and
      (3) I believe in connecting students' learning to something they know or value.

I work to help students recognize the value and power of language to make meaning in various subcultures. Meaning making is a social act, the process of getting an image from a writer's head to a reader's head. Assembling words into sentences and paragraphs requires a writer to organize concepts into a form that others can understand. It is in this act of assembly that learning takes place. Consequently, I prompt students to use writing as a crucial step toward comprehension. Students in my first-year composition courses, for example, write critical responses of different flavors to at least three class readings. They consider how their own literacy has developed and they look at the roles writing may play in their academic, social, and work lives. They reflect on their own experiences, interview others, and consult both primary and secondary research sources. My students also learn about language by writing about the activities they're undertaking. They use peer, tutor, cyber-tutor, and teacher response to compose multiple drafts, and then they produce digital portfolios to interconnect learning artifacts and writing processes. This is the subject of my dissertation and action research.

Writing is an inherently technological activity. Whether we use pencil and paper, a printing press, or a networked writing environment, we must use a set of tools in order to write. The tools we write with can have a profound impact on *how* and *what* we write. The advent of hypertextual forms of writing offer some striking illustrations of this point. The criteria for measuring the effective organization and development of an email message or Web site, for instance, differ from the criteria for the effective organization and development of a ten-page printed essay. Likewise, our habits for reading differ in each medium. And face-to-face, hybrid, and distance education environments impact how and what we can write as well. I want my students to understand this. I integrate a variety of flexible technological tools in my teaching, including intranet learning environments, multimedia presentations, digital texts and online journals, digital cameras and scanners, online writing labs, and synchronous and asynchronous exchange programs. I celebrate and embrace what some teachers consider to be chaos in their own classrooms, enabling me to provide more individualized, empowering, and *kairotic* instruction.

Flexible, effective teaching involves reflection, reflexivity, and action. Donna Qualley defines reflexivity in *Turns of Thought*: "Reflexivity is a response triggered by dialectical engagement with the other—an idea, theory, person, culture, text, or even an other part of one's self." I believe in moving from self-reflection to reflexivity to action in my teaching, and I believe in teaching my students this recursive process as well. As Duncan Carter and Sherrie Gradin point out in their new reader, *Writing as Reflective Action,* when we engage an "other" we reflect on the subject, but we also examine, critique, and change. This is why I often share and think through my teaching ideas with my colleagues, and why I often invite them physically or virtually into my classroom. Further, my students keep dialogue journals to engage the other, and to see their thinking process manifested in writing. I am proud of my students: many of them have used my assignments to create pieces of writing that have cultivated significant changes in their communities.

This relates to my third point about my philosophy of teaching: what and how I teach must connect students' learning to something they know or value. This follows educational principles of schemata networking, and Joseph Campbell's ideas about the cycling journey from the known to the new. I accomplish this in a few ways. My students routinely shape the direction the class takes based on their interest in current events or experiences in their lives. Students often bring in readings, for instance, or they ask that I find readings on specific subjects for them. To a certain degree, we negotiate the purpose and scope of each assignment; or I provide various assignment options so that each student *can* find each assignment personally meaningful. Oftentimes I create virtual peer-groups that include my students and students from culturally-diverse cities, such as New York and Portland, Oregon. Or I invite experts from the community or work place to participate in online discussion. Further, my students take an active role in figuring how their work will be assessed. I treat every assessment component as an opportunity to learn.

My teaching philosophy values the interconnectedness of language, learning, and context as elements that inform both writing practices specifically and learning experiences in general.

Figure 1. Philosophy of Teaching Statement.

Lang, J. M. (2010). 4 Steps to a Memorable Teaching Philosophy. *The Chronicle of Higher Education.* Retrieved from http://chronicle.com/article/5-Steps-to-a-Memorable/124199

Light, T. P., Chen, H. L., & Ittelson, J. (2012). *Documenting learning with ep-ortfolios: A guide for college instructors*. San Francisco: Jossey-Bass.

Lorenzo, G., & Ittelson, J. (2005). An overview of institutional e-portfo-lios. *EDUCAUSE Learning Initiative*, 2005. ELI Paper 1. Retrieved from http://www.educause.edu/ir/library/pdf/ELI3001.pdf

Mangum, T. (2009). Views of the classroom. *Insider Higher Education*. Re-trieved from http://www.insidehighered.com/advice/academic_career_con-fidential/mangum10

Manis, S. (2009). Writing as performance: Using performance theory to teach writing in theatre classrooms. *Theatre Topics, 19*(2), 139-151.

Montell, G. (2003). How to write a statement of teaching philosophy. *The Chronicle of Higher Education*. Retrieved from http://chronicle.com/article/How-to-Write-a-Statement-of/45133

Petraglia, J. (1999). Is there life after process? The role of social scientism in a changing discipline. In T. Kent, *Post-process theory: Beyond the writing-process paradigm* (pp. 49-64). Carbondale, IL: Southern Illinois University Press.

Rainie, L., & Wellman, B. (2012). *Networked: The new social operating system*. Boston: MIT Press.

Reese, M. and Levy, R. (2009). *Assessing the future: E-portfolio trends, uses, and options in higher education* (Research Bulletin, Issue 4). Boulder, CO: EDU-CAUSE Center for Applied Research.

Rheingold, H. (2002). *Smart mobs: The next social revolution*. New York: Basic Books.

Rosenbloom, S. (2008, January 17). Generation me vs. you revisited. *The New York Times*. Retrieved from http://www.nytimes.com/2008/01/17/fashion/17narcissism.html

Shepherd, R., & Goggin, P. (2012). Reclaiming 'old' literacies in the new lit-eracy information age: The functional literacies of the mediated workstation. *Composition Studies, 40*(2), 66-91.

Shor, I. (1996). *When students have power: Negotiating authority in a critical pedagogy*. Chicago: University of Chicago Press.

Smit, D. W. (2004). *The end of composition studies*. Carbondale, IL: Southern Illinois University Press.

Sporer, T., & Bredl, K. (2011). Fostering reflective practice through e-portfolios in higher education. In *Proceedings of world conference on e-learning in cor-porate, government, healthcare, and higher education 2011* (pp. 1720-1724). Chesapeake, VA: AACE.

Turkle, S. (2012). *Alone together: Why we expect more from technology and less from each other*. New York: Basic Books.

Ward, I. (1994). *Literacy, ideology, and dialogue: Towards a dialogic pedagogy.* Albany, NY: State University New York Press.

Wright, W., Jr. (1980). Teaching writing in the age of narcissism. *The English Journal, 69*(8), 26-29.

Zubizarreta, J. (1997). Improving teaching through portfolio revisions. In P. Seldon (Ed.), *The teaching portfolio* (2nd Ed.) (pp. 37-45). Bolton, MA: Anker.

Zubizarreta, J. (2004). *The learning portfolio.* Bolton, MA: Anker.

CHAPTER 3.

THE SOCIAL EPORTFOLIO: INTEGRATING SOCIAL MEDIA AND MODELS OF LEARNING IN ACADEMIC EPORTFOLIOS

Lauren F. Klein
Macaulay Honors College, City University of New York

As recent research by danah boyd, Nicole Ellison (2007), and Caroline Haythornthwaite (2005) has shown, social network sites have attracted millions of users. The academy has begun to recognize and incorporate opportunities the reconfigured social space of the web affords for "identity formation, status negotiation, and peer-to-peer sociality" (boyd, 2007, p. 119). Even more recently, industry professionals have begun to embrace social network sites for the "web-based social values" that they encourage in their employees (Hamel, 2009, ¶ 17). In each of these contexts, however, users continue to view social network sites as distinct from sites such as ePortfolios, which present professional work to a public audience.

These days, the business world is atwitter with talk of social media. In a 2009 *Wall Street Journal* article, management consultant Gary Hamel mapped out the transformations to the workplace that must take place should businesses hope "to attract the most creative and energetic members" of the "Facebook Generation." "Gen F," Hamel explains, will "expect the social environment of work to reflect the social context of the Web" (¶ 1). Meanwhile, in the academy, where the Facebook® eneration is currently being trained, the environment continues to reflect a division between traditional approaches to learning and the "social context" of Web 2.0. Blackboard, a course management system with significant market share, has only begun to include aspects of social media in its online learning environment (Gerben, 2009). The majority of ePortfolio systems, including eFolio and TaskStream, offer carefully template-based solutions to displaying student work, with few options for sociability. I argue for the pedagogical benefits of social media in terms of opportunities for connection, communication, and collaboration. ePortfolio systems can emphasize social media alongside professional presentation encourage students to develop individual voices and produce a range of content. This content, which can be translated across media and contexts, puts students' intellectual leadership, analytical ability, and personal creativity on display.

SOCIAL MEDIA DEFINED

The term social media denotes a set of Internet-enabled environments and practices through which people connect, communicate, collaborate, and share. At present, these environments include social network sites such as Facebook® and MySpace®, social bookmarking sites such as Delicious® and Digg®, media tagging sites including YouTube® and Flickr®, blogging and micro-blogging sites such as Twitter®, and wiki-based sites such as Wikipedia (see Duffy, 2008). However, rather than define social media as a set of websites, social media is best understood in terms of the modes of interaction that it facilitates and the methods by which its content is produced (see Sweeney, 2008).

The concept of social media inverts Marshall McLuhan's (1964) famous phrase, "The *medium is the message*." In the case of social media, the method is the message. Three unique characteristics associated with social media and the idea of the medium is the message emerges in relevant literature: the ability to forge relationships between individuals and within communities; the ability to communicate, collaborate, and share ideas within these communities; and the organic, egalitarian nature of the ideas themselves. The first characteristic, the ability to forge relationships, is best modeled by popular social network sites. These sites provide opportunities for interpersonal connection in what boyd (2007) characterizes as "networked publics," which include both real-life friends and "latent ties" (Haythornthwaite, 2005). Social network sites make use of the mediated nature of online interaction to bring pre-existing groups online and to bring new groups together.

The second characteristic of social media, the ability to communicate, collaborate, and share ideas, can be observed in blogs, on wikis, and in social bookmarking and tagging sites (Richardson, 2006). While these sites encompass a diverse collection of media, including text, photography, video, and web links, they are similar in their orientation toward a single community. Each individual is considered a member of the site, and as such, contributes his or her own content to a collective whole. This creates an online forum for the participation in what Bruffee (1962) memorably describes as the "conversation of mankind."

Finally, in order to grasp the egalitarian nature of the ideas and content produced through social media, it may be helpful to consider user-generated sites like Wikipedia and meme-spreading sites like Twitter. As Hamel (2009) explains, on sites such as Twitter® "all ideas compete on equal footing" (¶ 4). Similarly, on Wikipedia it is consensus, not credential, which functions as the arbiter of value and truth. While the networked, collaborative, and non-hierarchical nature of social media signifies a conceptual departure from most traditional modes of research and representation, the methods associated with social media foreground new models for integrating interpersonal interaction with uninhibited production of ideas. Schnurr (2013), too, discusses relevant identity construction categorize based on social construction and interaction principles in ways that relate to methods for learning (pp. 122-127).

SOCIAL MEDIA IN THE ACADEMY: METHODS FOR LEARNING

What are the benefits of social media for the academy? One needs only to look at the (online) evidence in order to see the benefits of users having an opportunity to connect, communicate, and collaborate. Moreover, the egalitarian nature of content associated with social media meshes seamlessly with pedagogical models for empowering student voices. Incorporating social media into classroom activities and research assignments also increases opportunities for the cross-contextual "movement" that has been recognized by Jamie Bianco (2007), among others, as a powerful tool for learning. Rethinking the major components of social media within the context of the academy reveals the ways in which social media can enhance a range of traditional learning objectives.

CONNECTION

Scholarly discussions about the role of technology in the academy often center on creation of virtual classrooms and online environments for distance learning. In these discussions, scholars distinguish between the digital, online world and the so-called "real world" (see the CCCC position statement on teaching, learning, and assessing writing in digital environments). The unique ability of social media to forge both on- and offline can play an important—and as yet unmet—role in connecting the physical world to the virtual one. Within communities formed through social media, as Moxley and Meehan observe, "students can write documents for tangible audiences, which can often lead to a greater sense of accountability on the part of the author" (2007, ¶ 1). In addition to these benefits, the ability to connect with others through online communities also begins to address the counterproductive, "counter-pointed" relation between the forms of writing that are used in- and outside of the academy (Yancey, 2004).

COMMUNICATION AND COLLABORATION

Teachers have debated the pedagogical value of collaborative learning for decades, but social media provides a new model and new tools for communication and collaboration. In 1984, Kenneth Bruffee theorized a relation between conversation and analytical thought and to that end began to introduce collaborative, conversation-based pedagogical strategies into his classroom. He admitted mixed results, concluding only that "understanding both the history and the complex ideas that underlie collaborative learning can improve its practice and demonstrate its educational value" (p. 636). Because of the rapid spread of social media tools, teachers should rededicate themselves to collaborative learning; now that technology has caught up to theory, teachers can put ideas about process-oriented writing, procedural authorship, and critical multimedia literacy into practice (Jones & Lea, 2008).

STUDENT-GENERATED CONTENT

Empowering student voices is a frequently-mentioned objective in the field of Composition and Rhetoric (see Geraldine de Luca, Peter Elbow, and others). Within the context of social media, this objective gains not only a technological framework, but also a conceptual one (Warner, 2009). Students, more so than teachers, are comfortable in the credential-less environment of the Web. When teachers frame assignments in this new social context, students become more inclined to express themselves in their own voices rather than in the register of "clarity" they believe is required of them in the academy (Minh-ha, 1991, as cited in Bianco, 2007, ¶ 13). In addition, the polyphony of voices that emerges from this social context confirms the "active role" of writing and other forms of expression in "producing different theoretical discourses and creating specific social identities" (Giroux, 1992, p. 221). Such attention to professional discourses is highly useful, as Schnurr (2013) points out: "discourse and profession-specific ways of using language create, reflect and reinforce those activities, knowledge and skills that charaterise a specific profession" (p. 14).

CROSS-CONTEXTUAL MOVEMENT

Another benefit of introducing social media to the academy is an extension of what Bianco (2007) identifies as "cross media movement." She describes a learning environment in which "digital objects are produced such that compositional intertextuality folds into and/or unfolds across composited cross mediation, resonant through particularized and distributed fields and domains"— media that is capable of moving across and between different contexts, both online and off (¶ 22). By adapting Bianco's conception of "cross media movement" to social media's methods and modes of representation, we arrive at a conception of cross-contextual movement that underlies the work that we do at the Macaulay Honors College of the City University of New York to develop, promote, and sustain our social ePortfolio system.

THE MACAULAY EPORTFOLIO COLLECTION: A CASE STUDY

HISTORY AND TECHNICAL OVERVIEW

The Macaulay ePortfolio Collection was introduced fall 2008 to incoming students at Macaulay Honors College, CUNY. Students were presented with the concept of an ePortfolio through a *cabinet of curiosities* metaphor conceived by Joseph Ugoretz, Director of Technology and Learning at Macaulay. We encouraged students to place "artifacts" of their thinking, their learning, and themselves on display in their own ePortfolios. We emphasized that the work that they engaged in might consist of a range of formats—research and essays to be sure, but also conversations, quotations, photos, and other online artifacts. In the same way that a curiosity cabinet, during the sixteenth through eighteenth centuries, was arranged according to the owner's individual organization scheme, we impressed upon each student that ePortfolios must reflect a sense of self.

We chose WordPress Multi-User (WPMU) as the platform for our ePortfolio system. WPMU began as a personal web-publishing platform—that is to say, a blogging platform—although it has since expanded to support a wide range of applications. WPMU integrates an updateable blog with standalone pages that are all created and edited through a personal "dashboard," where students can enter text and other media via an easy-to-use visual editor. Students customize the look and feel of individual ePortfolios by selecting from a set of pre-designed "skins," by adding new skins, or by editing preexisting ones. They can invite other students to contribute to collaborative ePortfolios in a variety of roles, and can allow or disallow comments on any page. Individual ePortfolios can be private, password-protected, or open to the public (the default). Students can have additional functionality via WPMU plug-ins, such as the ability to embed video or a calendar, or include an RSS feed. WPMU is also free and open-source (FOSS).

When we selected WPMU as the technical platform for our ePortfolio system, we believed that the blog-style format would encourage students to create and curate a range of multimedia content for public display. We hoped that the social context of the WPMU platform would facilitate the connection, communication, and collaboration associated with social media. We saw the WPMU system as a method of encouraging creative expression and cross-contextual movement. In addition, we hoped that the self-managed aspect of the WPMU system would engender a sense of ownership and empowerment in each student.

In spring 2009 we introduced the Macaulay Social Network, powered by the WPMU BuddyPress plug-in. BuddyPress allows each student to create a profile associated with his or her ePortfolio. Through our social network, users can create profiles, befriend other users, join groups, and view other users' posts and comments. In this way, our ePortfolio system now adheres to boyd and Ellison's (2007) definition of a social network site. Although we designed the Macaulay ePortfolio Collection with social media in mind, the overlay of the Macaulay Social Network implements an explicitly social mode of interacting with others within an otherwise conventional ePortfolio system.

The following four examples demonstrate the advantages of incorporating an ePortfolio system with a social setting, not only in terms of the ideas outlined above, but also in terms of new opportunities for personal reflection, interpersonal conversation, professional presentation, and intellectual growth.

EXAMPLE: "CULTURAL ENCOUNTERS"

One reason for our decision to use WPMU as our ePortfolio platform was that our students were already familiar with WordPress from their experiences with various course blogs and websites.[1] When Roslyn Bernstein decided to replace her course blog with a class-wide ePortfolio, the transition was seamless; students could use the same editing interface they had used in previous courses with the added benefit of a single login screen for all their ePortfolios, both personal and class-related.

Bernstein shaped the course ePortfolio, "Cultural Encounters," around a multimedia collage project. For the assignment, students were asked to create individual, themed collages that expressed a personal "cultural encounter." They were encouraged to use a range of physical materials, including found objects, and were then required to write a short essay describing their collage. Each collage was scanned and put on the course ePortfolio alongside the accompanying critical essay.

One student created a collage containing artifacts from his upbringing in communist China. It includes cutouts from his elementary school textbooks, images of school supplies, and drawings of significant items from his childhood, such as the red scarf he wore to indicate his membership in the Chinese Communist Party (see Figure 1). In his written analysis, the student described the artifacts in the collage as "permanent reminders to me that I lived a life which many people today in America have never experienced." In his essay, expressing a sentiment of difference, the student provided a detailed rationale for including each of the artifacts, assuming that his classmates would require additional context with which to interpret the experiences of his childhood in China. However, in the comment section of the ePortfolio page, his classmates reflected on the collage in ways that expressed both identification with and admiration for his work. A Russian student wrote, "I could relate to this because of the red scarves that my parents also had to wear in the Soviet Union." Another student, palpably affected, praised the "emotion and symbolism [that] were embodied in that report card" that the student from China included.

This single ePortfolio page—the scanned collage, the written analysis, and the comments below—models many of the benefits of social media in terms of opportunities for connection, communication, and collaboration. Although no single aspect of the collage assignment is explicitly social, its placement on the course ePortfolio site contributes Moxley and Meehan's "tangible audience" to an otherwise personal project. Initially a document of a life apart, the student's collage became a means of connection. Sure enough, as other students began to post their collages on the site, a conversation developed. Empowered by their own experiences and bolstered by their online interactions with others, the students of the "Cultural Encounters" ePortfolio demonstrated a deep level of analytical ability as well as a creative engagement that moved across media and contexts. This creative engagement was confirmed by the frequency with which students involved in the "Cultural Encounters" project reposted their collage projects on their own ePortfolio sites. These students have recognized that their collages, placed within the social context of the Macaulay ePortfolio Collection, represent not only their personal histories, but also their collective future. These are the minds of the future (Gardner, 2007).

EXAMPLE: "AWAY AND ABROAD"

"Away and Abroad" is a more explicitly social instance of a collaborative ePortfolio (see Figure 2). The site, designed by Joseph Ugoretz functions as an aggregator of content posted on the personal ePortfolios of students studying abroad. When a student writes a blog post on or uploads a photo to his or her individual ePortfolio, the content becomes immediately viewable on the "Away and Abroad" site. Initially conceived as a site to showcase the diversity of students' experiences studying abroad, the ePortfolio quickly became a social hub for the students themselves.

A recent visit to the "Away and Abroad" front page reveals one student's photos of graffiti near the Gare du Nord in Paris, another student's written reflection entitled "An American in China," a third student's link to a *New York Times* article about international urban planning, and a fourth student's blog post about hamburgers. Clicking through to each of the students' individual ePortfolios reveals a range of topics and formats. The photographer's site takes the form of a blog, with frequent short updates about his life in Paris. The student in China, along with a detailed personal profile, has charted his semester-long itinerary to the day. His blog posts, each a carefully composed meditation on life abroad, are tagged and cross-referenced so that they can be viewed by topic, location, or medium of composition.

Study abroad ePortfolios are noteworthy for their diversity of structure, content, and tone. Abrami and Barrett (2005), in their pioneering study of uses for ePortfolios, distinguish between "process portfolios," which document learning processes, and "showcase portfolios," which demonstrate skills and knowledge attained. With the open-ended WPMU platform, Macaulay students can decide for themselves—at any point in time—about the primary use and the intended audience of each ePortfolio. In the case of the study abroad ePortfolios, some students, like the student in Paris, opted for more flexible, process-oriented ePortfolios. The student in China, like many others, conceived of his site as showcase for both scholarly and personal growth. Common to both sites—and to the study abroad ePortfolios as a whole—is the knowledge (or perception) of an audience, and the belief that the experience of traveling abroad is worthy of documentation. With no prompting from any classroom assignment, each student engaged in substantial analysis of differences between life at home and abroad. Through written reflections, digital photos, and—in some cases—short films, students demonstrated critical multimedia literacy, the ultimate learning objective of many college-level courses (see Clive Thompson's discussion in *Wired* on the new literacy, 2009).

An additional, unanticipated outcome of the "Away and Abroad" site was the conversation that developed between students studying abroad in different countries and between the students studying abroad and those about to depart. After recounting a harrowing night at a youth hostel in Tokyo, one student received a comment from a friend who had had a similar experience at a hostel in Rome. Another student, preparing to leave for his own semester abroad, left a comment on the student in China's ePortfolio, asking how much he should be prepared to spend on food. A third student in Argentina received a comment from a classmate at home: "It's so wonderful to read your impressions thus far. I can almost taste the steak and other more mysterious foods!" In the process of documenting their experiences abroad, these students engaged in additional, unexpected forms of connection and communication. By producing content that not only moves across contexts, but also moves across continents, the study abroad students provide tangible evidence of the advantages of the social ePortfolio.

EXAMPLE: "ALTERMANIA"

One student's personal ePortfolio exhibits ways in which social media has begun to shape how students present themselves to future employers. Consider "Altermania," the ePortfolio of Tyler, a college sophomore (see Figure 3):

The front page announces: "Tyler is a student in the Macaulay Honors College at CUNY Hunter. He's pretty into creative multimedia production and his inherited tie collection. For the future, Tyler aspires to get into the design/guerrilla marketing business and create things like this, this, and this." (The links lead to graphic design and marketing companies whose work he admires). On the right-hand navigation menu, links lead to Tyler's contact information and résumé as well as examples of his audio, video, and graphic design work. A tag cloud provides an additional method of navigating his ePortfolio. In place of a traditional mission statement or employment objective, Tyler describes his career aspirations in his own voice (see Amarian & Flanigan, 2006). His self-description mimics a profile on a social network site, but Tyler, a member of the Facebook Generation, considers his casual tone appropriate to describe his professional goals. His tone exemplifies the new "social context" of our Internet-infused society (see Zhang, Olfman, & Rachtham, 2007).

In his design portfolio, which can be accessed by following a link from the navigation menu, Tyler includes a similarly conversational narrative that describes his involvement in a marketing campaign for an arts event. He provides a scanned version of a "submission-garnering flyer," an embedded promotional video that he created to publicize the event, a screenshot of the Facebook® event page, and photographic evidence of his own guerilla marketing campaign: "I set the default home page on every computer to the [promotional] video," he explains. Tyler uses the same conversational voice in each of his reflections on the various components of the campaign. Through the content of his ePortfolio, Tyler demonstrates his marketing skills, but through the tone of his descriptions, he demonstrates himself. As Tyler intuits, in the increasingly social context of the Web, skills and personality play an equal part in professional presentation and future success.

EXAMPLE: "A DESIGN A DAY"

By exploring Tyler's profile on the Macaulay Social Network, one discovers that he is involved in a second, collaborative ePortfolio. "A Design A Day," developed in partnership with another student, Phoebe, documents a challenge to "create one new work or learn one new graphic design technique [or] principle per day." This ePortfolio, intended as an informal record of the students' whimsical challenge, consists of each day's completed design followed by an explanation of how one or the other accomplished the effect. The ePortfolio functions as a collaborative "progress portfolio," as a means of communication between the two students, and as a technical reference for other aspiring designers (see Figure 4).

In this ePortfolio, Tyler and Phoebe embrace the flexibility of the WPMU system in order to upload, comment on, and converse about a range of media. The self-managed nature of the system, in addition, allows the two students to demonstrate their personal creativity, professional engagement, and intellectual leadership. In the future, this ePortfolio might be integrated into each student's individual ePortfolio, accompanied by a narrative that conveys the ideas behind the project and the skills they each acquired. In this way, "A Design A Day" demonstrates the possibilities for a productive synthesis of social media and professional presentation while facilitating acquisition of skills, collaboration between peers, and public display of knowledge.

THE SOCIAL EPORTFOLIO: A NEW CONCEPTION OF PROFESSIONAL PRESENTATION

The above examples demonstrate how social media enhances opportunities for connection, communication, and collaboration and provides opportunities for showcasing a range of student-generated content when integrated into a traditional ePortfolio environment. From the perspective of potential employers, the social ePortfolio can supply additional evidence of skills and qualities valued in the workplace: analytical ability, intellectual leadership, and creativity, which are often difficult to discern in other presentations of student work.

Figure 1. "Childhood" by Jack.

ANALYTICAL ABILITY

The social ePortfolio encourages commentary and reflection. Because of the blog-style format, students often frame their work within narratives that can account for weakness in early work or express ideas for improvement. One student, in the process of constructing her ePortfolio, apologized to the public for her inexperience. "I am very excited to begin sharing my work with you," she wrote. "You will have to excuse me as I take some time to get acquainted with all of the available features." In her admission, she expresses her desire for a higher quality level for her site and additional knowledge about the publishing platform. Commentary like this can provide valuable information to potential employers about students' thought processes as well as their ability and desire to continue to learn. In the case of this student, as she began to post her work on her ePortfolio, her self-analysis continued. In this way, the social ePortfolio facilitates commentary and reflection, offering potential employers a glimpse of a particular student's analytical ability and capacity for self-reflection.

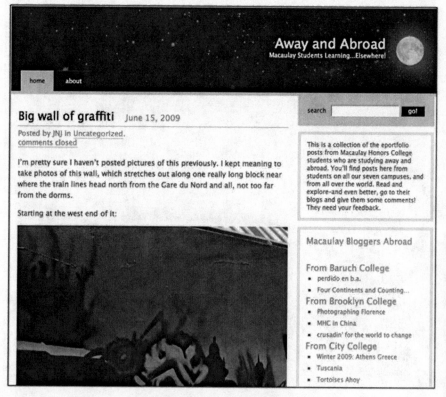

Figure 2. The "Away and Abroad" Study Abroad ePortfolio.

INTELLECTUAL LEADERSHIP

In terms of presenting a student's intellectual *ethos* to future employers, the benefits of a social ePortfolio system extend beyond showcasing techniques of analysis and reflection. Because they offer opportunities for communication and collaboration, social ePortfolios allow students to demonstrate intellectual leadership in a variety of contexts. Through the conversations that take place in the comment section, students provide evidence of their ability to convey their own ideas and accept others' criticism. One student, after posting a link to an article he had written for his campus newspaper, received a comment from a fellow student suggesting that he might revise his critique. The conversation continued, culminating with a comment from a professor that validated the student's original angle as well as the commenter's concerns. This evidence of the student's ability to engage in constructive dialogue with peers and superiors might provide future employers a window into the student's workplace personality and intellectual *ethos*.

CREATIVITY

The flexible format of the social ePortfolio allows students to showcase more than intellectual leadership; it provides a forum in which they can pursue multiple ideas. Because social ePortfolios encourage students to rapidly produce and display content in a context of peer comment and review, students can test out a variety of approaches to exhibiting their work. At Macaulay, students have created ePortfolios that document short-term events, such as attending the 2009 Presidential Inauguration or organizing a school-wide movie night; or ePortfolios that persist through long-term commitments, such as a semester spent abroad or a summer involved in community service. Students can choose to adapt these event-based ePortfolios into cumulative, showcase sites, or they can simply begin again. The Macaulay ePortfolio Collection, infused with an *ethos* of openness and experimentation, encourages each student to pursue a range of projects and ideas. Some projects culminate in polished, public-facing ePortfolios while others remain fragmentary and unfinished. But with each project, students demonstrate—to their peers and to future employers—their enthusiasm for learning and their willingness to pursue creative ideas.

CONCLUSION

Gary Hamel is not alone in identifying the value of social media for workplaces. In a recent article for *Business Week*, Stephen Baker and Heather Green (2008) describe the changes to workplace environments and practices that social media will affect. "Blogs are not a business elective," they declare, "They're a prerequisite" (¶ 2). Significantly, they draw upon academic constructs—the "elective" and the "prerequisite"—in order to convey the urgency of adopting the blog as a new business practice. In their symbolic language, Baker and Green underscore the fundamental interconnection of social media and models for learning. Indeed, social media and models for learning influence each other; incorporating social media into academic practices not only enhances traditional learning objectives, but also introduces new methods and skills with which to prepare students for productive roles in the workplace.

The case study of the Macaulay ePortfolio Collection demonstrates the myriad benefits associated with integrating social media into ePortfolio systems. In terms of opportunities for connection, communication, and collaboration, so-

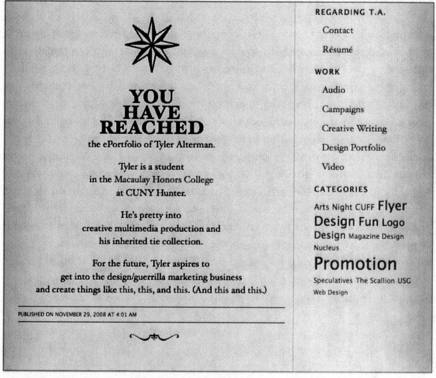

Figure 3. "Altermania" the ePortfolio of Tyler.

cial media supplies an exceptional technological and social framework for interaction. Furthermore, situating student ePortfolios within the social context of the Web fosters authentic student voices and facilitates student-centered social content. This content in turn may provide potential employers with evidence of students' analytical ability, intellectual leadership, and capacity for creativity, productivity, and growth.

As businesses move to embrace the social environment of the Web as a new model for professional interaction, the academy must not only follow suit, it must innovate. As Baker and Green make clear, academic models of learning continue to hold influence in the workplace. With the scholarly support of professors and the technical knowledge of students, the social ePortfolio can become a valuable tool for producing productive members of the business world—confident in their abilities, experienced in their methods, and positioned to enter the workforce with intellectual energy and entrepreneurial drive.

ACKNOWLEDGMENTS

Many thanks to Jeff Drouin, my colleague at Macaulay Honors College, CUNY, for his assistance throughout this project, and in particular his comments on the "Cultural Encounters" ePortfolio included in the case study. My analysis of the site incorporates many of his compelling ideas. Additional thanks goes to Joe Ugoretz, Director of Technology and Learning at Macaulay, for his continued encouragement and support.

WEBSITE LIST

- WordPress Multi-User: http://mu.wordpress.org
- BuddyPress: http://buddypress.org
- The Macaulay ePortfolio Collection: http://macaulay.cuny.edu/eportfolios
- The Macaulay Social Network: http://macaulay.cuny.edu/eportfolios/social
- Childhood-Cultural Encounters: http://macaulay.cuny.edu/eportfolios/bernstein08/2008/12/21/childhood/#more-1157
- Away and Abroad: http://macaulay.cuny.edu/eportfolios/abroad
- Altermania: http://macaulay.cuny.edu/eportfolios/ty274
- A Design a Day: http://macaulay.cuny.edu/eportfolios/adesignaday

NOTE

1. I owe a debt to Jeff Drouin, my colleague at Macaulay Honors College, for his thoughts on the "Cultural Encounters" ePortfolio. Many of the ideas included in this analysis derive from our conversations about the site.

REFERENCES

Abrami, P. C., & Barrett, H. (2005). Directions for research and development on electronic portfolio. *Canadian Journal of Learning and Technology.* Retrieved from http://www.cjlt.ca/index.php/cjlt/rt/printerFriendly/92/86

Amarian, S., & Flanigan, E. (2006). *Create your digital portfolio: The fast track to career success.* Indianapolis: JIST.

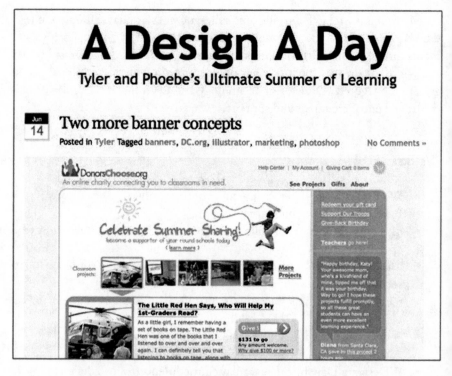

Figure 4. "A Design A Day" by Tyler and Phoebe.

Baker, S., & Green, H. (2008, June 20). Social media will change your business. BusinessWeek. Retrieved from http://www.businessweek.com/bwdaily/dnflash/content/feb2008/db20080219_908252.htm

Bianco, J. (2007). Composing and compositing: Integrated digital writing and academic pedagogy. *Fibreculture 10*(3). Retrieved from http://journal.fibreculture.org/issue10/issue10_bianco.html

boyd, d. (2007). Why youth (heart) social network sites: The role of networked publics in teenage social life. In D. Buckingham (Ed.), *MacArthur Foundation Series on digital learning—youth, identity, and digital media volume* (pp. 119-142). Cambridge, MA: MIT Press.

boyd, d., & Ellison, N. (2007, October). Social network sites: Definition, history, and scholarship. *Journal of Computer-Mediated Communication, 13*(1). Retrieved from http://jcmc.indiana.edu/vol13/issue1/boyd.ellison.html

Bruffee, K. (1984). Collaborative learning and the "Conversation of Mankind." *College English, 46*(7), 635-652.

Conference on College Composition and Communication. (2004). *CCCC position statement on teaching, learning, and assessing writing in digital environments.* Retrieved from http://www.ncte.org/cccc/resources/positions/digitalenvironments

Duffy, P. (2008). Engaging the YouTube® Google-eyed generation: Strategies for using web 2.0 in teaching and learning. *The Electronic Journal of e-Learning, 6*(2), 119-130.

Gardner, H. (2007). *Five minds for the future.* Boston: Harvard Business School.

Gerben, C. (2009). Putting 2.0 and two together: What web 2.0 can teach composition about collaborative learning. *Computers and composition online,* (Fall 2009). Retrieved from http://candcblog.org/Gerben

Giroux, H. (1992). Language, difference, and curriculum theory: Beyond the politics of clarity. *Theory into Practice, 31*(3), 219-227.

Hamel, G. (2009). The Facebook generation vs. the Fortune 500. *The Wall Street Journal, 2009, March 24.* Retrieved from http://blogs.wsj.com/management/2009/03/24/the-facebook-generation-vs-the-fortune-500

Haythornthwaite, C. (2005). Social networks and Internet connectivity effects. *Information, Communication, & Society, 8*(2), 125-147.

Jones, S., & Lea, M. R. (2008). Digital literacies in the lives of undergraduate students: Exploring personal and curricular spheres of practice. *The Electronic Journal of e-Learning, 6*(3), 207-216.

McLuhan, M. (1964). *Understanding media: The extensions of man.* Cambridge, MA: MIT Press.

Moxley, J., & Meehan, R. (2007). Collaboration, literacy, authorship: Using social networking tools to engage the wisdom of teachers. *Kairos: A Journal of Rhetoric, Technology, and Pedagogy, 12*(1). Retrieved from http://kairos. technorhetoric.net/12.1/binder.html?praxis/moxley_meehan

Richardson, W. (2006). *Blogs, wikis, podcasts, and other powerful web tools for classrooms*. Thousand Oaks, CA: Corwin.

Schnurr, S. (2013). *Exploring professional communication: Language in action*. London: Routledge.

Sweeney, C. (2008, September 10). Twittering from the cradle. *The New York Times*. Retrieved from http://www.nytimes.com/2008/09/11/fashion/11Tots.html?pagewanted=all

Thompson, C. (2009, August 24). Clive Thompson on the new literacy. *Wired*. Retrieved from http://www.wired.com/techbiz/people/magazine/17-09/st_thompson

Warner, A. (2009). *ePortfolios: Enhancing student self-authorship and student assessment*. Workshop conducted at the AAC & U Integrative Learning: Addressing the Complexities Conference in Atlanta, GA.

Yancey, K. (2004). Made not only in words: Composition in a new key. *College Composition and Communication, 56*(2), 297-328.

Zhang, S., Olfman, L., & Rachtham, P. (2007). Designing ePortfolio 2.0: Integrating and coordinating web 2.0 services with ePortfolio systems for enhancing users' learning. *Journal of Information Systems Education, 18*(2), 203-214.

SECTION 2: CONSTRUCTING THE BRIDGE

[Performance Management] is usually described as the system through which organizations set work goals, determine performance standards, assign and evaluate work, provide performance feedback, determine training and development needs, and distribute rewards.

—Briscoe & Clause, "Employee Performance Management: Policies and Practices in Multinational Enterprises," in Varma, Budhwar, & DeNisi's *Performance Management Systems: A Global Perspective* (2008), p. 15

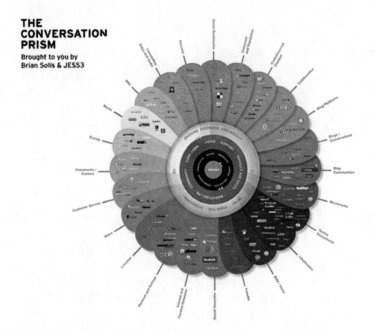

THE CONVERSATION PRISM
Brought to you by
Brian Solis & JESS3

Brodie, "The Conversation Prism,"
http://theconversationprism.com

CHAPTER 4.

EPORTS: MAKING THE PASSAGE FROM ACADEMICS TO WORKPLACE

Barbara J. D'Angelo
Arizona State University

Barry M. Maid
Arizona State University

The apparently "age old" discussion of whether to teach tools or rhetorical skills in technical communication courses seems to naturally come to a head when faced with the creation and assessment of capstone ePortfolios. This only makes sense when ePorts are viewed as the passageway from demonstrating proficiencies in meeting academic program outcomes while also meeting entry skill levels into the workplace. Technical Communication and other applied programs are constantly being pressured by different stakeholders, both internal and external, to teach specific software tools. One of the challenges Technical Communication program directors have faced is to make sure we include appropriate and assessable technology outcomes into our program outcomes; we need to sustain ourselves as an academic program and yet still meet workplace needs.

And we are here as on a darkling plain
Swept with confused alarms of struggle and flight,
Where ignorant armies clash by night.

—Matthew Arnold, "Dover Beach"

Though clearly out of context, perhaps this quotation from Matthew Arnold really does sum up the seemingly ever-present dissonance between academic and practicing technical communicators. Both groups are somewhat naïve as to the conditions and needs of the other. As a result, they often almost operate in the dark with regard to the other. As academics many of us believe that all

73

we teach needs to be grounded in good theory that can then be implemented into best practices. We are concerned with "how" and "why" not with "what" and "how to." On the other hand, practitioners seem to be (from an academic's perspective) obsessed with how to get things done and what they need to know. They are champions of knowing specific tools and creating necessary "bodies of knowledge."

Thus, those of us who teach in, design, and administer academic programs in technical communication are faced with a dilemma. How can we prepare our students with a solid academic background that is often seen as too theoretical and out-of-touch with the workplace while still making sure they have the skills to compete in what is often a very tight job market? For us, in the Technical Communication (TC) Program at Arizona State University (ASU), the answer lies in creating a set of program outcomes that can be accepted by both worlds. We then assess our graduating seniors for their proficiency in those outcomes by means of an electronic portfolio.

When we developed the program in Multimedia Writing and Technical Communication (now just Technical Communication) at ASU, we were primarily concerned with meeting academic-based outcomes. A set of outcomes appropriate for a technical communication program was built on the Writing Program Administrators' (WPA) Outcomes Statement (OS). The original statement was revised so that technology outcomes were present. Those outcomes were then modified to include information outcomes as well. That story has been told elsewhere (see D'Angelo & Maid, 2004; Maid, 2004).

Although the original WPA Outcomes Group discussed incorporation of technology into the WPA OS, debate about the responsibility of first-year composition to teach technology outcomes or competencies resulted in the adoption of it without them. However, debate related to inclusion of technology outcomes continued and a new WPA group met at the 2005 WPA Conference in Alaska to begin discussion about how technology could be incorporated in the document (Yancey, 2005). In 2006, the group drafted a revision of the WPA OS to incorporate both technology and information literacy (IL); a revised draft was presented and adopted at the 2007 WPA Conference in Tempe, Arizona.

The revision incorporates outcomes for composing in electronic environments as a fifth category rather than as outcomes integrated into the original WPA document so that the existing categories, already accepted and adopted by both rhetoric and composition and other fields, not be disrupted. The outcomes included in the new section relate to the use of technology as tools to compose and for research as well as to rhetorical strategies related to both print and electronic texts. Thus, technology is incorporated both as tools and within rhetorical contexts while IL is embedded as the use of technology to access information.

It is important to understand this context for our integration and use of technology outcomes as a foundation for our approach. We integrated technology as a construct for programmatic learning and assessment prior to the development of the revised WPA OS section (see Albert and Luzzo, 1999, for more on perceived barriers in career development). Because our approach to integrating technology was holistic, integrating constructs where appropriate in each of the original OS's four sections, rather than adding a separate section, our approach to assessment is also holistic so that students' use and learning of technology is evaluated as part of a whole rather than as discrete skills. Specifically, the TC Program at ASU has the following outcomes that can be considered to be technology outcomes:

- Understand the role of a variety of technologies/media in accessing, retrieving, managing, and communicating information
- Use appropriate technologies to organize, present, and communicate information to address a range of audiences, purposes, and genres
- Use appropriate technologies to manage data and information collected or generated for future use
- Understand and apply legal and ethical uses of information and technology including copyright and intellectual property.

Like all the other program outcomes, we ask students to demonstrate proficiency with these outcomes in their senior capstone electronic portfolio. See Hakel & Smith, 2009; and Edwards & Burnham, 2009 for more information regarding institutional assessment and outcomes-based ePortfolio work. However, unlike the other outcomes, students will not be able to even complete an electronic portfolio unless they have a certain level of technical proficiency. Purposefully, we chose not to use any kind of canned portfolio software where students can easily dump content into a template. Rather, we expect our students to be capable of making choices about the best possible tools to present their portfolio. Once they've made the choice, we expect they will be proficient in that tool. We clearly resist the notion that it is the responsibility of an academic unit to train anyone in software proficiency. While those skills are useful, and often necessary, we feel it is not the kind of skill one gets academic credit for mastering.

On the other hand, we do feel it is important for students to understand what tools are capable of doing. That means, when given the option, they should be able to pick the most appropriate and most effective tool. For example, it is relatively easy to create a brochure using today's word processing software. The question becomes, however, is that the best tool to create a brochure? The answer may not always be the same. We would hope our students would know the capabilities and the limitations of both word processing and desktop publishing software to make an informed choice.

Yet, despite our beliefs, the question of relevance of our outcomes to practitioners remains. Using comment from portfolios and a survey of practitioners helps us answer this question. In 2006, Scott Crooker, a student enrolled in the Master of Science of Technology program at ASU, asked how practitioners viewed our program outcomes. That ended up being the research question for his master's thesis where he surveyed members of the Phoenix Chapter of the Society for Technical Communication about the program outcomes (Crooker, 2006). In the light of this research, we began to rethink how our academic technical communication program prepared students for real jobs by addressing how our outcomes were perceived by practitioners.

TOOLS OR THEORY

Those of us who have been teaching writing courses from technical communication to first-year composition have been faced with the "Do you teach the tools" question for decades. At its most basic level, this question is raised because the assumption is that students are not capable of using digital tools unless they are specifically trained to do so. This assumption is reinforced by the huge software training industry and exacerbated by organizations that refuse to give employees access to tools necessary for their jobs until they have undergone prescribed training. And, of course this perspective is reinforced by the numerous certification and assessment tools promoted by the software/technology industry, ranging from Microsoft certifications to more academically-based tools such as Educational Testing Services' (ETS) iSkills test.

While we can certainly understand the desire to make sure people are well-trained, the reality is that if the same demands were placed on how people should be trained to write before they are allowed to do corporate writing, everyone would be trained in endless grammar, punctuation, and mechanics drills before being allowed to open a new word-processing document. It may be the only reason Human Resource types aren't demanding that is because of their faulty assumption that English is fixed and never changes so they don't realize that English version 1930 is different from English version 2009.

Though it's easy to try to dismiss the tool-centric people, it is also expedient to try to understand them. We suspect they have a legitimate point of view, though one that doesn't necessarily align with what most of us see as our primary mission as technical communication educators. In framing this issue we have chosen to do so as if we were consultants coming into an organization from the outside. In that scenario, one of our first questions would be, "What is your core mission?" Looking at academic programs, it seems that our mission is to prepare our students to have successful careers, writ large, throughout their entire lives. On the other hand, hiring managers prefer people who will have successful careers, writ small, within the particular constraints of an organization. Both points of view are reasonable, but often conflict.

Another way to understand these points of view is with a football analogy. Every spring as professional football teams prepare to draft college players, endless time and energy is spent on finding which player best fits the needs of a team. The assumption is usually that in the highly specialized world of professional football, filling specific needs is the best way to excel. The old Dallas Cowboys had a different philosophy. They simply wanted to draft the best player available—assuming that talented players would find ways to be productive and successful. In many ways, this is no different than when academics recruit faculty. In most instances departments look for faculty who can teach or research in highly defined specialties—instead of just looking for the most talented candidate available. That's exactly what hiring managers in the industry are doing when they try to recruit technical communicators and require that candidates must know SuperSoftware, ver. 7.65.

The assumption, especially in tight job markets, is that the quicker a new hire can actually get to work, the more money the company will save. After all, hiring new people is expensive. In addition, in many workplace cultures, being perceived as having software skills tends to lend status. Software skills also appear to be more quantifiable (though this may be completely subjective and illusory) than the other kinds of skills technical communicators must necessarily possess. As a result, the kind of results "rePorted" by Clinton Lanier (2009) in a recent issue of *Technical Communication* should not be unexpected.

Lanier describes the results of an analysis of 1,399 technical writer job postings for the types of skills and experience required, resulting in the following categories: experience, technical knowledge (specific computer or markup languages, subject expertise, or foreign language), technical writing specific knowledge (formats and genres), technologies/tools, several software categories, and project management skills. Interestingly, he included rhetorical skills such as audience analysis within the broad category of technology/tool knowledge but broke out specific types of software knowledge as separate categories. Lanier found that employers require some type of subject matter experience 33% of the time. In addition, he found that 16% of ads required proficiency in online help software, 20% in specialized software tools, 24% in graphics software, and 34% in publishing software. In comparison only 17% required basic technical writing skills (in which Lanier categorizes audience analysis/writing for specific audiences). He believes his results challenge assumptions that teaching tools is unimportant. However, he places less emphasis on analyzing the project management category, which includes communication skills, collaboration, analysis, and others, despite the finding that 32% of postings call for interpersonal and collaborative skills. Lanier's lack of emphasis on project management seems to be based on the belief that the communication category is vague and hard to define or plan within a curriculum (2009). Lanier's findings, however, contradict earlier analysis of survey findings by Rainey, Turner, and Dayton (2005) in which they found that despite an emphasis on technology skills, managers were more concerned with employees' ability to be able to adapt and learn new software quickly. Rainey acknowledges the tension between technical skills and other "soft" skills such as collaboration and people skills that pervades the field and the often contradictory evidence gained from industry; this tension clearly continues as evidenced by Lanier's findings.

Indeed, the tension between academic and industry perspectives has been a constant theme within technical communication, with certification acting as another indicator. Turner and Rainey (2004) review the history of debate surrounding certification. While these authors advocated for a mechanism for certification to codify bodies of knowledge for technical communicators and to identify the ethical and professional responsibilities of technical communicators, certification still remains an object of debate which is constantly revisited in the literature and within professional and practitioner societies (Hart, 2008; Rosenberg, 2008). Clearly this debate and conversation impact on curriculum. There are a limited number of hours within a degree program, thereby constraining what can be taught. Some have attempted to address and frame technology skills by contextualizing them within the literacy debate. In this perspective, technical or tool literacy becomes one of several literacies advocated for in technical communication education (Breuch, 2002; Cargile Cook, 2002; Nagelhout, 1999). Lastly, this debate has importance because what is taught and how we teach is impacted by assessment and the methods we use to evaluate student learning. Certification, for example, is a type of assessment; yet, it is often correlated with quantifiable mechanical skills of tool use. For academic programs such as ours, assessment is more broad-based to incorporate a more holistic range of outcomes.

BRIDGING THE ACADEMIC/WORKPLACE GAP?

From the beginning, we used ePortfolios to assess whether our students are meeting program outcomes. Electronic portfolios are a common method of assessing student writing, including technical communication. Students enroll in a capstone course during their semester of graduation in which they review outcomes and the scoring guide which faculty use to evaluate portfolios and work together to draft, revise, and finalize portfolios. Students select and use examples of their work as evidence for claims made in a persuasive cover statement to demonstrate their learning and growth in the context of program outcomes.

As mentioned earlier, we do not mandate a specific application or technology for students to use to submit their portfolio. Since the portfolio itself is an artifact, we believe that the students' choice of technology and application is a demonstration of their achievement of outcomes. Of the 32 portfolios submitted since fall 2006, 27 were websites and 5 were PowerPoint files. The same criteria and scoring were used to evaluate all portfolios regardless of the application used to submit them. Though we do not explicitly address issues related to technology with evaluators, we expect that they assess the portfolio based on its achievement of outcomes. Since the portfolio itself is an artifact, we expect rater scoring is influenced by how the portfolio is constructed and how the student uses the selected software to present their argument about achieving outcomes. We would be surprised if the use of an application to present the portfolio did not influence rater scores since a portfolio which contradicted claims made by the student would undermine their argument for achieving outcomes, resulting in lower scores. For the fall 2008 and spring 2009 semester, one of our adjunct faculty, who is a practitioner, became one of our portfolio evaluators. These evaluative comments give us an added perspective on our students and curriculum. Part of our scoring process asks evaluators to add formative feedback for the student. Some of the comments, included below, indicate how students bridge the academic-workplace in their use of technology:

> I was struck by your comment in your statement conclusion where you noted that there is "an ever growing demand for communication to bridge the juncture where human interaction meets technology ... That beautifully describes where we are in 2008. And as a Technical Writer in 3G Technologies, and as an Instructor at ASU, I am pleased to welcome you into this exciting profession."

> Your final project, your group evaluation of projects, was a nice evaluation of products. This is what technical writers do! ... Your portfolio showcased a nice array of applications.

> Your portfolio is fun and appropriately tells a framed story.

> You have a strong voice and your use of technology places you in an expert category.

Not all was well, of course. Other comments included:

> I'm not seeing a wide-range of technologies here. I don't see any mention of flash, for example, or other tools. And I would have liked to have seen evidence of your web site.

> PowerPoint is a powerful tool. You didn't use any graphics. The words were not placed on the page with thought to design. Your Portfolio did not have a professional look and feel. It should be the culminating artifact of your MWTC experience.

Of course, comments to individual students may or may not be representative of overall student achievement, of their ability to use technology, or of the relevance of those outcomes to the workplace. However, these comments do indicate that students are learning technologies and tools and trying to adapt them for their work to varying degrees. As part of an overall program assessment strategy, since spring 2008 we have asked graduating students to complete a short survey about the capstone course and about their experiences in the TC Program. A link to an anonymous online survey is sent to students after graduation and grades are posted to allow students (now alumni) to provide us with information they are not able to present in their portfolios.

Lack of direct instruction in tools or software is the most common negative comment, with three out of six suggesting that some type of tool learning be incorporated into the TC Program in some way. For example, one student recommended that students be required to take an exploratory course to learn basic software tools or that the TC Program partner with companies to provide online training or workshops for students. Two other respondents recommended that students be required to take a web- or multi-media design course. This focus on tools is, perhaps, not surprising from students who are either currently practitioners or who are searching for a job and faced with meeting requirements related to specific software applications in job ads. Certainly the perspective of these students is consistent with that of Lanier. If we take job ads as guiding criteria for making decisions about curriculum, then teaching of tools would seem to be paramount (Zhang, Olfman, & Rachtham, 2007). However, as we have seen in the conversations over certification and literacies, the evidence for teaching of tools is not consistent (Jones & Lea, 2008).

Another indication of how we are bridging the gap between academic and workplace needs is an analysis of the results of a master's student survey of Phoenix Chapter STC members, including students of the TC Program, to determine the relevance of TC Program outcomes to practitioners as knowledge areas and skills (Crooker, 2006). Crooker's thesis has provided us one way of understanding how our outcomes meet practitioner needs. Out of a sample of 167, Crooker analyzed 46 submitted surveys (40 from practitioners, 6 from ASU students with industry experience). Although he surveyed chapter members on all outcomes, we focus here on his results related to technology outcomes only. Breaking out these outcomes, Crooker found that the majority of respondents found technology outcomes to be essential for technical communicators. He sums up his results at the end of his thesis by saying:

> This study found that the specific educational outcomes designed for the technical writing curriculum at ASU are considered up-to-date and are generally regarded as relevant to professionals who have current experience in the field of technical communication. This means that, according to professional technical writers and technical communicators, ASU's technical writing program seems to be teaching material that is essentially on track with the current educational needs of college students. (p. 61)

In many ways the strongest indictment that Crooker's study had of the program was of what he implied was academic jargon in the outcomes. He pointed out that many of the practitioners were uncomfortable with the word "genre" and suggests we use language more appropriate for a lay audience in the future (Crooker, p. 60). In the midst of the discussion about certification and defining a body of knowledge, we find it strange that practitioners, who we assume might need certification, if it is ever created, would be uncomfortable with using the professional language of the field. This appears stranger when we assume that one of the skills that would necessarily be part of any body of knowledge would be identifying the appropriate level of discourse for any particular audience. Surely, anyone proficient in technical communication would be a member of the technical communication discourse community. We recognize the reality that the tools controversy is never going to go away. We also know that there are many technical communication positions where practitioners will have to be proficient in specific tools. However, not all technical communicators write help files. If they don't, do they really need to be proficient in Robo-Help? If they never write a document longer than twenty-five pages, do they really need FrameMaker skills? In fact, it would probably be healthy for the field if it recognized that technical communicators worked in many industries—not just software.

Finally, we have tried working with the local STC chapter that has graciously allowed students to attend software-training workshops, which they sponsor at a discounted price. We have also had a program alumnus volunteer to give software-training workshops. Despite the hue and cry for the training, very few people used the opportunities. We understand timing and money may be a factor. We hope to have online modules developed that may help students in the TC program. In addition, the TC Program requires students to take 12 hours in related area courses from outside of the TC curriculum. This requirement is intended to allow students to take courses that match their interests and job- or career-paths. Many of our students take advantage of tool-centric courses offered by ASU's College of Technology and Innovation, for example, while others enroll in courses in other programs to enhance the skills and knowledge areas that best match their career plans.

Ultimately, we feel that the tools controversy is more of perception than reality. The reality is that students preparing for careers as technical communicators do need to possess certain abilities. We feel the outcomes our students demonstrate in their capstone ePortfolios demonstrate proficiency with those skills. This same skill-set is confirmed by practicing professionals in Crooker's thesis. In addition, the fact that our students must submit an electronic portfolio using tools of their choice, tells us that they are capable of learning and utilizing appropriate digital tools. We believe the perception that only people who are trained in specific software tools can be successful technical communicators is specious. Yet, our job as technical communication educators is sometimes a balancing act between that perception and reality.

REFERENCES

Cargile Cook, K. (2002). Layered literacies: A theoretical frame for technical communication pedagogy. *Technical Communication Quarterly, 11*(1), 5-29.

D'Angelo, B. J., & Maid, B. M. (2004). Moving beyond definitions: Implementing information literacy across the curriculum. *Journal of Academic Librarianship, 30*(3), 212-217.

Edwards, T. S., & Burnham, C. (2009). The promise of eportfolios for institutional assessment. In D. Cambridge, B. Cambridge, & K. B. Yancey (Eds.), *Electronic portfolios 2.0: Emergent research on implementation and impact* (pp. 87-90). Sterling, VA: Stylus.

Hakel, M. D., & Smith, E. N. (2009). Documenting the outcomes of learning. In D. Cambridge, B. Cambridge, & K. B. Yancey (Eds.), *Electronic portfolios 2.0: Emergent research on implementation and impact* (pp. 133-135). Sterling, VA: Stylus.

Hart, G. J. S. (2008). Why certification by STC won't work. *Intercom*, *55*(7), 11, 13.

Lanier, C. R. (2009). Analysis of the skills called for by technical communication employers in recruitment postings. *Technical Communication*, *56*(1), 51-61.

Maid, B. M. (2004). Using the outcomes statement for technical communication. In S. Harrington, K. Rhodes, R. Overman-Fischer, & R. Malenczyk (Eds.), *The outcomes book: Debate and consensus after the WPA Outcomes Statement* (pp. 139-149). Logan, UT: Utah State University Press.

Nagelhout, E. (1999). Pre-professional practices in the technical writing classroom: Promoting multiple literacies through research. *Technical Communication Quarterly*, *8*(3), 285-299.

Peckham, I. (2006, August 14). Tech outcomes [Online discussion comment]. Retrieved from http://lists.asu.edu/cgi-bin/wa?HOME

Rainey, K. T., Turner, R. K., & Dayton, D. (2005). Do curricula correspond to managerial expectations? Core competencies for technical communicators. *Technical Communication*, *52*(3), 323-352.

Rosenberg, N. (2008). Certification: Why we need to begin. *Intercom*, *55*(7), 11-12.

Turner, R. K., & Rainey, K. T. (2004). Certification in technical communication. *Technical Communication Quarterly*, *13*(2), 211-234.

Yancey, K. B. (2005, July 12). Re: The technology and outcomes discussion at the WPA. [Electronic mailing list message]. Retrieved from http://lists.asu.edu/cgi-bin/wa?A2=ind0507&L=WPA-L&P=R46003&I=-3

Zhang, S., Olfman, L., & Rachtham, P. (2007). Designing ePortfolio 2.0: Integrating and coordinating web 2.0 services with ePortfolio systems for enhancing users' learning. *Journal of Information Systems Education*, *18*(2), 203-214.

CHAPTER 5.

WHAT ARE YOU GOING TO DO WITH *THAT* MAJOR? AN EPORTFOLIO AS BRIDGE FROM UNIVERSITY TO THE WORLD

Karen Ramsay Johnson
Indiana University-Purdue University Indianapolis

Susan Kahn
Indiana University-Purdue University Indianapolis

As liberal arts students on a campus where professional programs predominate, senior English majors at IUPUI are often uncertain of the value of their degree post-graduation. Creating a culminating reflective electronic portfolio in the Senior Capstone Seminar in English helps them develop a sense of accomplishment and take a broader perspective on their learning. Carefully scaffolded reflection within the ePortfolio prepares them for the transition to post-graduate life by prompting them to envision and articulate how they will apply their learning to new contexts as professionals and citizens in a globalizing world.

As English majors on a campus dominated by professional programs, our students are constantly asked the above question by their fellow students, their friends, and often their parents and other family members. Many are asking themselves the same thing when they begin the English Senior Capstone Seminar that we team teach. One of our main objectives for the course is to offer students a sense of the options available to them as English graduates. Equally important, we want our students to gain confidence in the value of their educational experiences as liberal arts majors, both for their future careers and for their lives beyond work.

The English Capstone at IUPUI is intended as a culminating experience for English majors that enables them to demonstrate their academic achievements and supports them as they make the transition to careers or further study. In our institutional context, these goals present particular challenges. Our mostly first-generation students enter college largely for the purpose of gaining entrée to the professional world, and the vast majority choose professional and pre-professional majors. While some of our Capstone students have made a conscious decision to major in the discipline they are most interested in, regardless of professional consequences, and others plan to pursue a graduate or post-baccalaureate professional degree, most begin the course with some anxiety about the utility of their degree in English. We have even had students tell us that their parents actively disapprove of their choice of major. On a predominantly professional, first-generation campus, we thus face the special challenge of helping humanities majors construct a bridge between their academic studies and their life beyond the academy. To meet this challenge, we use IUPUI's electronic portfolio as a site for students to present and reflect on their educational accomplishments.

CONTEXTS

THE UNIVERSITY: AN URBAN RESEARCH INSTITUTION

Our institution, Indiana University-Purdue University Indianapolis (IUPUI), is an urban research university, with over 30,000 students and some 21 schools. Professional education, particularly in the health and life sciences, is a strong component of the university's mission; the campus is home to the state's only medical school and the nation's largest nursing school. Approximately one third of our students are in graduate/professional programs. Professional schools dominate at the undergraduate level as well. Among the 15,300 undergraduate students who had declared a major in 2009, only about 3,550 chose to pursue studies in traditional liberal arts and sciences disciplines. Indiana has typically had low educational attainment in comparison to other states and IUPUI students' family backgrounds reflect this trend: in 2008, only 19 % of undergraduates reported that both parents had completed college; 55 % came from families where neither parent had a bachelor's degree. Almost all students commute to campus.

While student demographics have changed over the years, with more undergraduate students entering directly from high school, the average age of students in the School of Liberal Arts is 26. About 40% are 25 or over, while 33% are part-time students. English majors offer a slightly more traditional profile, with 44% over the age of 25 and 31 % part-time students. A majority of seniors began their higher education at another campus and some have transferred more than once. Many undergraduates already have families of their own and most work while attending college. With all of these commitments, our students—in contrast to traditional undergraduates—often do not view higher education as the main focus of their lives. And because so many are transfers who have taken time off from college and/or changed majors at least once, they may perceive their undergraduate education as a set of fragmented, unrelated experiences. Another challenge for us in the Capstone is thus to help students "connect the dots" among their courses and out-of-class learning experiences, so that they can see their education as a meaningful and coherent whole.

THE DEPARTMENT OF ENGLISH: A MULTIFACETED DEPARTMENT

The English Department's Capstone seminar began about ten years ago, when the department experimented with replacing its tracks with a single English Studies major in which students were required to take a common introductory course, the Capstone seminar, a range of courses across the tracks, and a set of electives. Four years ago, in response to a recognition that many students still wanted to specialize in a track, we reinstated the tracks, while incorporating an individualized program as a sixth track The department's nearly 300 majors are now divided primarily into five tracks: Literature, Linguistics, Writing and Literacy, Film Studies, and Creative Writing. Each track then established its own introductory course, but we have retained the common Capstone. Students in each track are still required to take two to four major-level courses in other tracks, so the Capstone has the secondary purpose of reaffirming the interconnection of the tracks. Currently, Literature and Creative Writing offer students the option of taking a senior seminar rather than the Capstone Seminar, but most students continue to choose the Capstone.

THE CAPSTONE COURSE DESIGN

For the sections of the English Capstone that we team teach, we want students to achieve these outcomes:
- Integrating learning across courses and disciplines (and for many students, across work and academic experiences) and making sense of disparate experiences, so that their education adds up to more than just a set of disconnected courses or requirements completed.
- Articulating what they have learned and gained from their studies in English and the liberal arts in terms meaningful to potential employers and other audiences.
- Using evidence to substantiate claims about the skills and abilities they have developed; for example, simply announcing that one is an effective

writer and researcher, without pointing to evidence and providing some analysis of that evidence, is inadequate.

- Gaining insight into their own learning processes, so that they feel empowered to take control over their learning outside formal educational settings.
- Developing confidence in the value of a liberal arts/English degree. As we have noted, for our professionally oriented student population, this can be challenging.

With these outcomes in mind, we have designed the current iteration of the course around two main components, which we call "Professional Development and Career Planning" and "English in the World and Global Citizenship." These components are intended to focus students' reflections on the future, while encouraging them to consider how they have developed over the course of a liberal education as potential professionals and as active citizens at both local and global levels. The structure of the ePortfolio learning matrix that students develop mirrors these two components, with one major section devoted to career and a second section to "English in the World" (see Figure 1).

Both of the main components of the course are scaffolded by assigned readings, guest speakers, and online and in-class discussions. Some readings and speakers directly address the value of a liberal arts education to the world of work today. For example, a 2006 *New York Times* op-ed article by Thomas Friedman, "Learning to Keep Learning," argues that the 21st-century workplace demands professionals who can learn continually, think creatively, work with ideas and abstractions, and integrate concepts across disciplines—the kinds of abilities fostered by study in the liberal arts (2006, December 13). Guest speakers include not only School of Liberal Arts career placement staff, but graduates from the Department of English, often recent students in the course, who discuss their job search strategies and the ways in which their studies in the liberal arts generally and English specifically proved relevant to a diverse array of work experiences. Similarly, for the "English in the World and Global Citizenship" theme, students read an essay by philosopher Martha Nussbaum that speaks to the importance of imagination and empathy—capacities closely linked to one another, in Nussbaum's argument—for effective citizenship and action in the world (Nussbaum, 2005). Speakers on this theme include senior faculty members and administrators from liberal arts fields who are involved with issues of civic engagement and international affairs.

THE PROFESSIONAL DEVELOPMENT AND CAREER PLANNING COMPONENT

For this component of the course and the ePortfolio matrix, students are asked to collect several pieces of past work, or "artifacts," that exemplify key career skills they have developed in the course of their education and work experience and that are related to one of IUPUI's general education outcomes (called the Principles of Undergraduate Learning or PULs) and an outcome for their chosen track in the English major. These examples might represent a student's best work or might demonstrate the evolution of an ability or skill over a period of time. Students also create a résumé and cover letter, in consultation with career professionals in the School of Liberal Arts. Finally, they develop a career reflection that includes analysis and evaluation of their portfolio artifacts in relation to their selected PUL and track outcome, as well as discussion of areas they need to strengthen or continue developing. Students who have identified a specific career interest write the reflection with an eye to the abilities and skills needed for success in that career. For the many students who have not decided on a career path, the artifacts, résumé, and reflection can address the development of abilities and skills key to effectiveness in any professional field. We have found that the scaffolding provided by the readings, speakers, online forums, and discussions helps students to develop a vocabulary for discussing their learning in terms that are relevant to potential employers. Additional scaffolding is supplied by a series of reflection prompts. (See Appendix, Activity 1 for a list of the prompts we used for the Career and Professional Development reflection in Spring 2010.)

THE ENGLISH IN THE WORLD AND GLOBAL CITIZENSHIP COMPONENT

The main assignments for the English in the World and Global Citizenship component are the Senior Project and the English in the World reflection essay. The Senior Project includes a project plan, a complete early draft of the project, an annotated bibliography, and the final project, which the students present to the whole class at the end of the semester. Because our students come from all of the tracks in the major, they have their choice of project topics, but each project must contain a research component. Students can also opt to do a group senior project, though most choose the individual option. For the reflective essay in the ePortfolio, students are then asked to draw on the project, as well as other portfolio artifacts, to consider how their studies in English and in their particular tracks have shaped their identities in "the world"—e.g., as members of a particular community or culture, as global citizens, or as lifelong learners able to contribute to society in particular ways. (See Light, Chen, and Ittelson, 2012, and Steinberg and Norris, 2011, for more extended discussion of how ePortfolios can help to advance development of a "civic" identity. A list of the prompts we used for this section of the portfolio in Spring 2010 can be found in the Appendix, Activity 2.)

THE CAPSTONE PORTFOLIO

This year, we began using a two-part portfolio process that culminates in a webfolio. The process is based on the portfolio tools available in our university's learning management system, Sakai, known as Oncourse at Indiana University. Beginning in 2005, Kahn and Sharon Hamilton designed and refined a matrix system, in which students practice a kind of integrative thinking that Kahn and Hamilton have called "matrix thinking" (Hamilton & Kahn, 2009). In the current iteration, we use a simple two-cell matrix (see Figure 1), which both continues the dual focus that is characteristic of matrix thinking and serves as a training ground to prepare students for what Helen Chen terms "folio thinking" (Chen, 2009). Using the Principles of Undergraduate Learning and at least one goal from those emphasized by their tracks within the English major, students collect artifacts, save and revise reflective commentary, and create a storehouse for their potential webfolio materials.

For the webfolio, students can opt to use a platform within Oncourse or other web development software of their choice. Each student is required to include four specific sets of materials: an introductory welcome page, an up-to-date résumé, the senior capstone project, and their two reflective essays. They may organize these materials in any configuration that they prefer. They can also add extra pages to highlight specific skills, interests, or causes and organizations that they support. Some students choose to add their course portfolios to other websites that they maintain or to which they belong. (The appendix includes screen shots from webfolios created with Oncourse Presentation Maker.)

STUDENT LEARNING IN THE CAPSTONE PORTFOLIO EXPERIENCE

PREPARING STUDENTS TO REFLECT

Simply asking students to "reflect" on a piece of work or on an experience is unlikely to yield results that are meaningful to them or to the faculty members who read those reflections. We want students' reflections to contribute to their accomplishments of the outcomes for the course and we gear our preparations for reflection to those outcomes.

We begin preparing students to reflect by discussing what we mean by "reflection" and what we hope they will achieve as a result of reflecting. A particularly helpful tool has been a document titled "Development in Reflective Thinking" (see Appendix, Table 1), originally created as a descriptive rubric at

Alverno College and later adapted by Sharon Hamilton for IUPUI (Hamilton & Kahn, 2009, p. 96). The document, which we distribute to and discuss with our students, describes characteristics of "introductory," "intermediate," and "advanced" reflective writing. For example, in "introductory"-level reflections, students tend to narrate "what I did" to create a piece of work, to make general claims of competence or mastery without evidence, to repeat evaluators' judgments, and to state assumptions without explaining or questioning them. "Advanced"-level reflections, by contrast, exhibit characteristics associated with higher-order thinking skills: analysis of thought processes (i.e., metacognition); use of evidence to support arguments; questioning of assumptions and awareness that assumptions are shaped by culture and individual experience; ability to self-assess; high-level conceptual thinking; and synthesis of ideas from multiple disciplinary and experiential frameworks.

Keeping in mind that most reflections do not fall neatly into one developmental category, here are two brief reflection excerpts that serve, respectively, to illustrate some of the characteristics of "introductory" and "advanced" reflection:

> **Example 1:** Second in this section is my outline for a graphic novel titled *What Good Men Dream*. This was my first at-

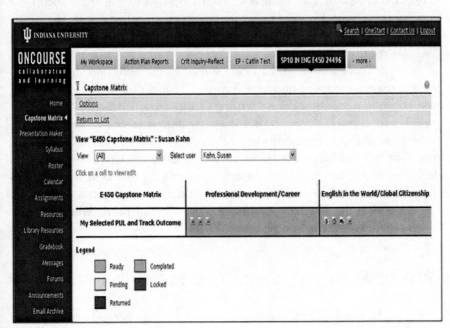

Figure 1: English Capstone Matrix.

tempt at writing anything like this. Over the course of the semester every student worked on an outline for a story and at the end we polished it and presented the full outline with a few sample pages. Mine went very well and the teacher was pleased with it.

Example 2: "Afternoon at Grandma's House" was my first attempt at writing a form poem. I chose the sestina because of its difficulty, and I was very pleased with the way that my piece came out. I found that I had a little difficulty keeping the line lengths consistent as the piece went along, but I focused on keeping my language compact and precise. Wordiness is something I struggle with, so this was a real challenge to me.

After discussing the "Development in Reflective Thinking" document with the class, we spend part of a class session working in small groups to evaluate several reflections written in past sections of the class. While the students' conclusions do not always agree with our own, this exercise provides the opportunity for students to see several examples of reflections written at varying levels of intellectual maturity and sophistication and to discuss and defend their judgments about the effectiveness of each. To avoid giving the students the impression that there is one "right" way to approach reflection or that we are looking for writing that adheres to a specific formula, we try to provide more than one example of "advanced" reflection.

Now students write a rough draft of their career reflection, using one or more of the questions or prompts we provide. Thoughtful prompts are essential to supporting students' reflective writing (Zubizarreta, 2009, pp. 11-13). Our prompts are derived in part from the course outcomes and in part from the observations in the "Development in Reflective Thinking" document. In the next class, we break up into groups of two or three to critique one another's drafts, using a review form that we created based on "Development in Reflective Thinking." Each student receives at least one and, ideally, two written and oral critiques of the first draft. At this point, we ask students to write the "final" version of their career reflections.

OUTCOMES OF EPORTFOLIO DEVELOPMENT

Do students achieve the outcomes we seek for the ePortfolio and the class as a whole? It depends. Kahn notes that in earlier iterations of the class, where students were asked to develop a much more extensive ePortfolio in lieu of the traditional senior project, they were given more practice in writing reflections and the reflections showed greater sophistication. At the same time, too much reflective writing can make reflection seem routine, a rote exercise. We have yet to find the ideal balance between more traditional class work and portfolio development—and perhaps this balance is different for each class and even each student.

Many students, however, do find the combination of readings, speakers, consultation with a career placement professional, and development of the ePortfolio helpful in enabling them to articulate more clearly to themselves and others the value of their English degree, both to the workplace and to life beyond the workplace. In particular, reviewing a body of past work created over time and then reflecting on it can be powerful; students who have kept examples of early work done in college often note that they had not realized the extent of their intellectual growth since they were freshmen. One student writes:

> I no longer see what I have to offer as an English job hunter
> in mere terms of degree possessed and years of experience ...
> I look at what I have to offer in a larger context. Beyond the
> essentials in my résumé that I share with all other graduates, I
> now see capacities in critical thinking, communications, and
> multi-project analyses. All these capacities can be supported
> with the creative and scholarly material in my matrix.

Some students show visible growth in their capacity to reflect on their own learning and experiences over the course of the semester. A student whose first reflection in the semester was broadly focused, with only a few references to professors and courses and brief statements of what she learned in each, had, by semester's end, developed the ability to connect her years of work (often with troubled youth) to her own background of growing "up poor even by poor people's standards," and her English major to her future:

> Beyond my own hunger for the kind of learning that I can
> only get from sitting among a group of other learners and
> hashing issues out, I want to share it. I want to bring that
> opportunity to people in shelters who are just too bone-tired
> to do more than sit in a circle and talk about life and the shit
> it throws at you .... I feel like it's my role in life to be some
> sort of liaison between those who want, and the knowledge
> they want to obtain but don't quite know how to get it.

Another student, who had served in the military in Iraq and returned to school to complete a double major in English and Political Science, makes powerful connections among several liberal arts disciplines as she writes about the development of her critical thinking skills:

> IslamY107.doc exemplifies my ability to be a critical thinker because I had to put forth significant effort to separate my emotion from the facts and research. This skill was one of the first skills taught to me in college. I believe that objectivity and rationality are at the core of every serious student—this paper shows me that I can be a serious student. Every class that I have taken in political science, English, and philosophy has emphasized the importance of looking past the surface of things. Additionally, my education in the liberal arts has taught me that there is much more to things than what my emotions tell me there are. There is an entire world of people out there, each person possessing a uniqueness of mind and emotional experience. There are several cultures and societies that need to be taken into consideration before my own. My emotions are only central to my own experiences, and my critical thinking skills allow me to leap outside of my own experiences.

Cathy, a middle-aged, middle-class wife and mother, came to IUPUI when her children reached high school age; as she writes, when she graduated from high school, she "did not have the parental support to be anything other than a wife." She credits her Capstone project with clarifying her life's purpose: "After contemplating my final project, I have discovered that the works I researched are a direct reflection of who I am and my place within society." Now, she says, she wants "to help others achieve a college education and experience for themselves [a] transformation [like the one that she experienced]."

As these four students illustrate, the diversity of our student body, especially in terms of age, class, and life circumstances, guarantees that their experiences of reflection and of its outcomes will also be different. Another common category of student at our university is the one who begins at a traditional liberal arts college or university and becomes disillusioned. Ted, who is from a well-educated family on the west coast, dropped out of a liberal arts college to work for Americorps and for several non-profit ventures. Perhaps the most sophisticated thinker in our sections of the Capstone, he began the class with the sense that his education would give him nothing more than a necessary credential.

Yet even he acknowledges in his final reflection that his training has come to shape his thinking. After a semester of reading, reflecting, and interacting with guest speakers and students, Ted had arrived at a somewhat better place; talking with guest speakers and fellow students about work that might advance his ideals, he became more active in class discussion and in on-line forums and e-mail exchanges. His second reflection supplements the theme of work learning and focuses on a series of obviously successful course experiences; for example, he integrates his English training with his work in a computer science course:

> Even when I tried to study other disciplines I found myself still thinking within the Liberal Arts mindset. The clearest example of this was a paper I wrote about Charles Babbage during my Fundamental Computer Science Concepts course. While looking at the history of computing, as it is commonly taught, I noticed some interesting narrative gaps and accepted assumptions. My paper focused only on assumptions made by present historians looking back at Babbage, but the impulse for the paper was some fundamental errors I noticed in the way the history of computing is told. As I mentioned, there are many assumptions made about what Charles Babbage intended to produce (given that he produced very little), but even worse the entire narrative stems from an idea of technological determinism—that is technology advanced the way it did and when it did because it was bound to. While a common way of viewing any topic within history (e.g., WWII was inevitable because of WWI) it is only one view, and completely ignores the idea of contingency—that is just because something has occurred does not mean that it was certain to occur.

ISSUES EMERGING THROUGH ASSESSMENT

While we are gratified when students make visible progress in their thinking and integrative skills or arrive at important insights over the course of their Capstone experience, some issues have been difficult for us to resolve:

- It is difficult to devise instructions and prompts that work for a wide range of students. While the diversity of our student body is, in most respects, one of IUPUI's greatest strengths, it can be hard to address all levels of preparedness at the same time. For example, while weak students cannot begin to reflect without very precise instructions and insecure students need the reassurance that such instructions provide, strong students tend to find them limiting. In one section particularly, while discussing the reflection prompts and examples, the stronger students pointed out that it is easy to see what is "right" to say. They viewed the "good" sample reflection as one in which the writer was saying what he or she knew the instructor wanted to hear, parroting the language of the PULs and the rubric, and engaging in what they saw as a relatively mindless exercise of finding examples. Although the bad example was visibly poorly written and lacking in any serious thought, even the strongest students viewed this writer as "honest," because he or she was not trying to please the instructor. To a great extent, this resistance diminished as the semester progressed, but we would prefer to have a range of prompts that can be geared to individual needs.

- Because many of our students have significant work experience (often full-time work), they can experience a bifurcation of identity, in which their student selves seem distanced from their identities in the work place. Thus, unlike traditional students, they need to see a direct connection not only between their work and their courses, but also between academic and professional reflection. A vivid example of this need appears in the reflections of our recent student, Jay. Jay dropped out of his first college to take a full-time job with a web-based company; he has had enormous success in his job, including being selected as the company's "first ever employee of the month, standing out beyond others as a hard-working, ambitious employee always ready to take on new challenges." Thus, he has become convinced that "most of my skills for the 'real-world' have been honed in the real world." For Jay, integration of his academic and workplace learning was not a meaningful goal, and Jay is not alone. Some of our students continue to view education purely as a credential, either because, like him, they have been successful without it or because they have "learned," either from poor teachers or from parents, that the main goal is to have the diploma. Thus, they tend to undervalue reflection in an academic setting, because they view it specifically as an academic process.

- On the other hand, for other students, inflated ideas about the value of a baccalaureate degree can inhibit the reflection process. As we have noted, a large percentage of our students are first-generation college students, and they often have an unrealistic view of what a college education means. They rightly view college graduation as a major accomplishment, but, because they have known very few college graduates as they grew up, they may believe that the degree credential itself will enable them to move directly into the job of their choice. They also, however, continue to underrate their own accomplishments. They need to recognize that, valuable though their college experience is, their earlier experience must also figure into their examined life, as Plato called it; they must learn to see how their pasts inform their presents and their futures.

ADDRESSING THE ISSUES

The most immediate issues that we need to address stem from some students' lack of familiarity with the process of writing reflective essays; we have noticed over time that almost all of the second essays are far better than the first ones. Accordingly, we have reformatted the reflection process to allow for more specific reflections and more individual input. Our next iteration of the course will follow this process:

- Have students do a reflection early in the semester, to be revised and expanded near the end of the semester.
- On the first or second day (or first day after drop/add), have students explain what they think reflection means and how they think that one should go about writing a reflective essay on one's education as an English major.
- First artifact: Write a short (2-3) page reflection specifically on that piece, using PUL and track goal.
- Second artifact: Write a short (2-3) page reflection specifically on that piece, using PUL and track goal.
- First Reflection: Write a 4-5 page reflective essay referring to those artifacts and reflections.
- Students will then make a list of the main points in that essay in a word processing program or in a blog; as the semester progresses, they will keep notes (checked periodically) on what new ideas they have about those points or on others that they add to the list: a reflective journal. For students who have trouble doing this, we will offer specific journal topics related to readings, guest speakers, and the individual student's track and career goals.
- Students will create a skills résumé (can be in addition to a standard résumé).
- Students will write a short reflective essay for the Senior Project.

- Second Reflection (revision of Reflection 1): As the last assignment, students will revise the first reflective essay, adding new ideas from the journal and referring to the skills résumé, senior project, and project reflection for more ideas (7-10 pages).

We also want to address the issues specific to students who have difficulty integrating the academic and work aspects of their lives, but we believe that all of our students will benefit from understanding that electronic portfolios, with their central component of reflection, are increasingly important not only to higher education, but also to employers. Thus, we are in the process of identifying two or three companies in Indianapolis that use electronic portfolios and requesting information on the purposes for which they are used, the guidelines that are given to employees preparing them, and samples of exemplary portfolios. If possible, we will also have a company representative who is involved in the process visit our class.

CONCLUSIONS

As the above discussion suggests, our versions of the English Capstone Seminar and the Capstone portfolio remain works-in-progress, particularly when it comes to helping students reflect in more meaningful ways. In the most recent iteration of the course and portfolio, however, our meshing of the matrix format developed by Kahn and Hamilton with the webfolio proved largely successful, in our opinion. The matrix continues to be enormously helpful to the students because of the scaffolding it enables us to provide, but they are, not surprisingly, more engaged and stimulated by the experience of creating Web pages. This holds true even for students who are not normally frequent technology users. An added benefit is that they are easily able to envision a potential employer visiting their webfolios; many students say that they expect to maintain and update their webfolios regularly. While the materials included in the webfolio are still informed by matrix thinking, the webfolio adds new levels of integration and provides students, professors, and other site visitors with a highly individualized, immediately engaging, and visually exciting representation of student work and reflection.

We are immensely grateful to our students who, over the years, have shared their time, work and thoughts with us; we especially thank those who have allowed us to share their work with our readers. The English Capstone has been at least as powerful a reflection experience for us as it has for them. Indeed, our experience of reflection has reaffirmed for us the vanity of "conclusions." Even in the process of writing this essay, we found ourselves entertaining new ideas about how we might refine the course, and we welcome any comments or suggestions that our readers may offer.

REFERENCES

Barrett, H. (2004). Electronic portfolios as digital stories of deep learning: Emerging digital tools to support reflection in learner-centered portfolios. Retrieved from http://electronicportfolios.org/digistory/epstory.html

Batson, T. (2010). ePortfolios, Finally! *Campus Technology*. Retrieved from http://campustechnology.com/Articles/2010/04/07/ePortfolios-Finally.aspx?Page=1

Cambridge, D., Cambridge, B., & Yancey, K. (Eds.). (2009). *Electronic portfolios 2.0: Emergent research on implementation and impact*. Sterling, VA: Stylus.

Chen, H. L. (2009). Using eportfolios to support lifelong and lifewide learning. In D. Cambridge, B. Cambridge, & K. B. Yancey (Eds.), *Electronic portfolios 2.0: Emergent research on implementation and impact* (pp. 29-35). Sterling, VA: Stylus.

Cohn, E. R., & Hibbitts, B. J. (2004). Beyond the electronic portfolio: A lifetime personal web space. *Educause Quarterly, 27*(4). Retrieved from http://www.educause.edu/EDUCAUSE+Quarterly/EDUCAUSEQuarterlyMagazineVolum/BeyondtheElectronicPortfolioAL/157310

Friedman, T. (2006, December 13). Learning to keep learning. Retrieved from http://select.nytimes.com/2006/12/13/opinion/13friedman.html?_r=2

Heinrich, E., Bhattacharya, M., & Rayudu, R. (2007). Preparation for lifelong learning using ePortfolios. *European Journal of Engineering Education, 32*(6), 653-663.

Jones, S., & Lea, M. R. (2008). Digital literacies in the lives of undergraduate students: Exploring personal and curricular spheres of practice. *The Electronic Journal of e-Learning, 6*(3), 207-216.

Kahn, S., & Hamilton, S. J. (2009). Demonstrating intellectual growth and development: The IUPUI ePort. In D. Cambridge, B. Cambridge, & K. B. Yancey (Eds.), *Electronic portfolios 2.0: Emergent research on implementation and impact* (pp. 91-96). Sterling, VA: Stylus.

Light, T. P., Chen, H. L., & Ittelson, J. (2012). *Documenting learning with eportfolios: A guide for college instructors*. San Francisco: Jossey-Bass.

Nussbaum, M. (2004). Liberal education & global community. *Liberal Education 90*(1). Retrieved from http://www.aacu.org/liberaleducation/le-wi04/le-wi04feature4.cfm

Siemens, G. (2004). ePortfolios. *Elearnspace: Everthing elearning.* Retrieved from http://www.elearnspace.org/Articles/eportfolios.htm

Steinberg, K.S., & Norris, K.E. (2011). Assessing civic mindedness. Diversity & Democracy: Civic Learning for Shared Futures, 14(3), 12-14

Yancey, K. B. (2009). Reflection and electronic portfolios: Inventing the self and reinventing the university. In D. Cambridge, B. Cambridge, & K. B. Yancey (Eds.), *Electronic portfolios 2.0: Emergent research on implementation and impact* (pp. 5-16). Sterling, VA: Stylus.

Zubizaretta, J. (2009). *The learning portfolio: Reflective practice for improving student learning* (2nd ed.). San Francisco: Jossey-Bass.

APPENDIX A

Activity 1: Prompts for Career and Professional Development Reflection

As you write your reflection, please focus your thinking on one of IUPUI's Principles of Undergraduate Learning and one of the outcomes for your track within the English major. You might consider some (but probably not all) of the following questions:

- How is your classroom learning of your selected PUL and English outcome related to work and career issues? How have these learning experiences contributed to your development as a professional?
- How do your chosen artifacts demonstrate your ability to apply your selected PUL and English outcome to your professional work? (Or how did creating these artifacts contribute to your professional development?) Do they show a trajectory of professional development? If so, how?
- If you have selected a career, how does your choice of major specifically relate to the requirements of this profession?
- In what ways do you need to improve to prepare further for your career?
- Be sure to provide a well-supported critical analysis of your selected artifacts in the context of PUL and English outcome and to use the artifacts to exemplify your insights.
- Also be sure to specify which PUL and track outcomes you're addressing and to use the examples as evidence for your claims.

You might find it helpful to think of your reflection as either an extended argument (with your work samples as evidence) or as a narrative about your learning over time (again citing your work examples or specific aspects of them as evidence).

Activity 2: Prompts for English in the World and Global Citizenship Reflection

Your "English in the World" matrix cell should demonstrate the ways in which your studies in English and in your particular track have shaped your identity in "the world"—e.g., as a member of a particular community or culture, as a global citizen, as a lifelong learner able to contribute to society in particular ways, or in relation to some other aspect of the world beyond your college education. If they're relevant, please also consider courses in other disciplines and work or intern experiences. Think of our capstone seminar as a bridge between your education and your life in "the world." As you select examples of past work to upload, consider how the skills and values you've acquired from your studies in English and other disciplines will influence and support you as an individual, family and community member, and citizen of and in the world. Questions to think about when you write your reflection (remember you shouldn't try to respond to all of these—pick one or several and organize your reflection around those):

- In what ways do your artifacts/work examples and senior capstone project demonstrate your ability to identify and question assumptions (your own and others)?
- In what ways do your artifacts and senior capstone project demonstrate awareness of who you are as a citizen of a local culture and global society?
- What else do your artifacts and senior capstone project demonstrate about your strongest skills as you move from your education (or this stage of it) to the rest of your life?
- Can you identify specific aspects of your major that have shaped your self-concept and aspirations? For example, has your major (or track) influenced how you see yourself as a local and global citizen? In what ways are these influences reflected in your artifacts and senior capstone project? (If you're a double major, you may consider both majors.)
- Do your artifacts, culminating in your senior capstone project, show a trajectory of development as a learner in relation to your PUL and track outcome? As a citizen? If so, how?
- How is your choice of major related to the abilities necessary for lifelong learning? How do you need to improve those abilities? Cite evidence from your artifacts and senior capstone project.

Be sure to provide a well-supported critical analysis of your selected artifacts, including your senior capstone project, in the context of PUL and English outcomes and to use the artifacts to exemplify your insights.

Table 1: Development in Reflective Thinking

Areas of Development	Introductory	Intermediate	Advanced
Ability to self-assess • observing own performance • using feedback & evidence • finding & analyzing patterns • making judgments	• global judgments w/o evidence • sees performance same as assignment (did what was told) • repeats judgments of evaluators • sees feedback as affirmation and evidence • narrates process (did this; did that) • observes rather than infers	• applies disciplinary constructs • demonstrates deeper understanding of concept • uses feedback to expand understanding • recognizes connections, links, and relationships, such as cause & effect • makes inferences (relates judgments to evidence)	• observes intentional changes as a basis for higher learning • probes own work and understanding • uses multiple and interdisciplinary frameworks to understand • makes connections, applications, and uses to move forward
Awareness of how one learns • concepts and misconceptions • knowledge Construction • metacognition	• limits concept development to the terms given in the assignment • sees feedback as external and not subject to analysis • sees knowledge construction only within terms of the assignment • employs personal theories largely without explanation or analysis	• sees feedback as a means to understanding links between current and future performance • notes changes in own patters of performance; • sees knowledge construction as integrating known and new knowledge • applies theories or broader frameworks to discussion of learning	• integrates feedback and past performance to construct future learning plans • uses growing awareness of knowledge structures to envision future learning • understands own performance as a learner and transfers learning strategies to multiple contexts

• Developing life-long learning skills • developing identity as a learner • transferring learning to other contexts • understands learning as a lifelong process	• confuses performance and feedback with identity as a learner • uses generalized notions of success or effectiveness as basis for reflection • global self-evaluations minimize connections between performance and reflecting on performance	• self-identifies as a learner, constructing meaning within experience, now and in the future • questions personal assumptions and recognizes multiple perspectives • identifies challenges, demonstrating positive attitude and confidence, using self-assessment as a basis to improve	• sees own identify as a learner, employing internalized construction of effectiveness • questions assumptions to construct intellectual commitments, aware of multiple perspectives • situates personal narrative in larger intellectual/professional frameworks, transferring learning to new situations

Derived from a model of "Developmental Perspectives on Reflective Learning"
Alverno College 2004. Sharon J. Hamilton 2005. Reprinted with permission.

APPENDIX B. WEBFOLIO SCREEN SHOTS

Figure 2. Webfolio Screen Shot 1.

Driven - Dedicated - Passionate

A professor once told me to drop his class. He said I wouldn't do well. I didn't drop his class. Instead, I worked hard, and I got an "A."

I am not the typical student. I am not going to graduate in four years, not even close. I don't live in a dorm on campus and ride a bike to class everyday. Actually, I have taken closer to ten years. Looking back on my education, I do not regret taking longer than the average student. I am grateful I chose this path. Throughout my educational career I have pursued valuable career opportunities that both enriched my educational and my professional experience.

This site is dedicated to my learning experiences at IUPUI. Among the fascinating facts you will learn about me, you'll also find:

-Samples of my latest and greatest works

-My professional resume

-An explanation and copy of my senior project

Browse at your leisure!

My Path to becoming an English Major

I am often questioned as to why I chose to become an English major. I normally respond with an equally puzzled stare. "Why not become an English major," I will reply. We all have our strengths, and I think it is important to recognize these. I began as a business major, but the courses looked really boring. Then, I looked at the courses in the English department, and said, "Wow! These look fun." Over the past 20 years, I had gotten to know myself well and realized I needed to be interested in the courses if I intended on actually graduating. My passion for writing and learning the humanities drove me to finish my degree.

Even though it took me several years to graduate, I never once thought about quitting. I am a very driven person who does not consider failure to ever be plan b, c, or even d. And, while I know my strengths, I am still always ready for a good challenge.

Figure 3. Webfolio Screen Shot 2.

CHAPTER 6.

CAREER EPORTFOLIOS: RECOGNIZING AND PROMOTING EMPLOYABLE SKILLS

Karen Bonsignore
New York City College of Technology

New York City College of Technology "City Tech," which is part of the City University of New York (CUNY), began its ePortfolio Project with Title V grant funding in 2001. The project was institutionalized when grant funding ended in 2006. Since it began, the City Tech ePortfolio project has provided well over 5,000 students from many departments within the college the opportunity to prepare a Career ePortfolio to be used to showcase their professional development and academic skills in the form of a digital résumé. The Career ePortfolio enables students to store their work, document what they have learned in college, and demonstrate how college has prepared them for a career.

CAREER EPORTFOLIO DEFINED

A Career ePortfolio is a specific type of portfolio that is created by students to showcase their best academic work and unique attributes that may not be demonstrated on a traditional résumé or during an interview. A Career ePortfolio may include artifacts such as an introduction or homepage, various academic examples, a statement of professional goals, work experience, internships, and a résumé. The Career ePortfolio is a dynamic document that can be viewed from any Internet-enabled computer or stored on other digital storage devices. An ePortfolio website address can easily be sent to multiple prospective employers both locally and around the world. In the case of a graduate applying for a job, detailed information about the student is not always easily added to a pen and paper résumé, but may be included effectively in an ePortfolio. For example, a student can post actual examples of their papers, artwork, engineering designs, budgets, reports, architectural drawings, advertising brochures, and PowerPoint presentations to demonstrate their skills (Zhang, Olfman, & Rachtham, 2007). They can also emphasize skills that are relevant to their career objectives.

In addition to creating a dynamic document for employment and graduate school, students write a brief reflective statement about their professional goals. The professional goals statement may be short term such as when they graduate or long term, 5 to 10 years after graduation and they have gained experience, or it can be a combination of the two. Goals also may include pursuing an advanced degree or gaining additional experience in related fields or a desire to move into management or their own business. Students are encouraged to demonstrate how they intend to contribute to their chosen field.

Students producing a Career ePortfolio are encouraged to be creative, but choose design elements such as colors, backgrounds, graphics, and fonts that show their work at its best. Discussion regarding principle elements of design, as well as rhetoric and purpose, is critical in such portfolio design. The goal of a Career ePortfolio is to present professional and academic information in addition to presenting a professional and creative image, demonstrating functionally literate skill sets. This is the type of development called for by scholars, recently, like Shepherd and Goggin (2012) in "Reclaiming 'Old' Literacies in the New Literacy Information Age: The Functional Literacies of the Mediated Workstation."

USING TECHNOLOGY TO ITS GREATEST ADVANTAGE

The City Tech Career ePortfolio project allows students to work with state of the art multimedia technology as they explore their career paths and professional development opportunities. This generation of students has been plugged into technology since the day they were born. They grew up with educational games, sophisticated software programs and the internet. They are comfortable communicating with computers, cell phones and through social networking. Creating a Career ePortfolio demonstrates that a student is able to use technology creatively and in a professional manner. The Career ePortfolio is an excellent way for students to "showcase" their best work to prospective employers, internships, and colleges. The Career ePortfolio allows students to build and share a dynamic résumé in a multimedia format. Students can share their Career ePortfolio with anyone connected to the internet anywhere in the world with a simple click of a mouse. Creating a Career ePortfolio allows students to take advantage of the 21st-century technology skills they are comfortable using. Students enjoy working with technology because they are comfortable with it. Although creating a Career ePortfolio may be new to most students, the learning curve required to create one is generally short because of students' previous technology and computer experiences.

STUDENT BUY-IN

Because students feel that the Career ePortfolio project is meaningful to their future when they graduate, as evidenced by many reflective statements, most enjoy working on their ePortfolios. Students understand that an ePortfolio is a way to help them stand out in a crowd of sometimes more than a hundred applicants applying for the same job. By including a professional goals statement as part of their ePortfolio, students are encouraged to think early in their academic career about their course work, graduate school, career path and professional development. Working with technology to create the ePortfolio is another plus that keeps students interested. The template system used at City Tech allows all students, from those who have only novice computer skills to students with the most advanced skills, the ability to create, update and maintain their ePortfolios. See the online version of this book for examples. All City Tech student ePortfolios are stored and maintained for no charge on the college server. This allows students to update their ePortfolio after graduation and provides storage of their documents. Many students take advantage of this feature by updating their ePortfolios after they have graduated and earned some work experience. Alumni ePortfolios remain on the server for five years after graduation.

WHO OWNS THE CAREER EPORTFOLIO?

A Career ePortfolio is the individual work of the student. Although it is stored on the college server, only the student may make changes to or delete his/her work. Collectively, the ePortfolios may be used for a single course, program or college-wide assessment purposes. Assessment will be discussed later in this chapter but it is important to note that the purpose of a Career ePortfolio is that it is student-owned for highlighting the student's best work and marketing his/her academic and career skills. Administration reserves the right to remove ePortfolios with questionable content. Any ePortfolio that is deemed inappropriate for posting on the Internet can be blocked from viewing until the student has been contacted and the ePortfolio has been revised. All students participating in ePortfolio program must sign a CUNY Computer User Contract. When students first start the ePortfolio project at City Tech, they sign a contract with a disclosure that their website may be seen by anyone with internet access. They are informed of the purpose of a professional "Career" ePortfolio and the repercussions of posting off-topic content. Students are encouraged not to post personal contact information because of the online aspect of the ePortfolio. Each student uses campus email instead of a personal email as contact information. The way ePortfolios are stored on the college server they are not easily found by search engines. The student generally must give their ITP web address to visitors or add it to a cover letter or résumé. Students are cautioned to always keep their ePortfolio updated and professional and follow the general rules of safety that apply to sharing information over the Internet.

Most Career ePortfolios are created as part of a single class project or a program including multiple courses. A Career ePortfolio may also be part of an academic club or society. In each cohort, a faculty member works with the students to mentor the online content. Students are encouraged to submit drafts to their professor before posting the final project. Similar to paper based assignments, ePortfolios may contain spelling and grammatical errors, which can be caught early if drafts are reviewed. Faculty often include the ePortfolio course requirements in the syllabus to guide students to produce a professional ePortfolio. Peer competition among the students in a class is a good way for the students to see other ePortfolios and improve their own work.

Generally, most students enjoy working on their ePortfolios. Today, students are more comfortable with online technology and want more computer enhanced learning assignments in their classes. This is no surprise since the current generation of students that have grown up with computers in their homes and communicate predominately through social networking. Being able to apply for a job or graduate school on-line seems natural to today's students. They embrace the technology as well as the purpose behind the ePortfolio.

Below is sample selection of students' comments on what they liked about creating their ePortfolio:

> Creating my ePortfolio allowed me to display my accomplishments on the web.

> It was something new to me and I enjoyed the challenge.

> My work can be posted online, so employers can see it.

> Once it's finished, I can forward the address to any employer, friend, or person of my choice. Also, I would have a chance to express myself in full and employers can learn more about me!

It gave me a chance to organize my skills and put them to use in a professional and technical way.

People can see my work around the world.

My ePortfolio helped me to organize my thoughts.

I realized that I want to continue with my career and I want to go on for my Master's degree.

The process itself (of creating the portfolio). I've never done anything like that before so it was fun.

It's already over, but we are lucky to have access to it in order to update.

This experience provided me with a chance to write about my thoughts, experiences and express my talents openly for others to share. It offered me a chance to allow people to see the real me.

I enjoyed creating my eVideo for my ePortfolio.

I was able to think about my long term goals.

I learned more about my industry and have a clearer understanding about where I want to be.

The ePortfolio project helped me think in depth about what I want to pursue as my career. It also made me analyze what I have accomplished and what I still need to accomplish.

ROLE OF FACULTY

Faculty are encouraged to develop clear *learning objectives* for the course/program and involve the implementation of the ePortfolio project into the course/program and the department's overarching *assessment* plan. Faculty are responsible for grading ePortfolios and using an electronic roster to view the student Career ePortfolios. When faculty are surveyed, they overwhelmingly responded that 1) they enjoy participating in the ePortfolio project, and 2) the ePortfolio project provides them with an additional way to assess their students' skills. Faculty new to the Career ePortfolio project should be supported with course preparation time, technology training and training in online pedagogy with details on the objectives of student Career ePortfolios.

If publishing a Career ePortfolio online so students can present themselves to employers is the main purpose, then the role of faculty is to partner with the students to help them develop their ePortfolio in a professional style. The process starts with clear instructions laid out in the syllabus so that the students know what will be expected and when assignment deadlines are due. Faculty should guide students to use professional backgrounds, colors, fonts, pictures and graphics. The style of the ePortfolio as well as the number and type of academic examples that are placed in the Career ePortfolio are important. Faculty who provide feedback throughout the process and ask for drafts before the final posting will receive a higher quality of work submitted. Generally, participation in the ePortfolio project is not "more work" for a faculty member, it is just different since they are grading the students' work or academic examples posted online rather than in paper formats. The same coursework or academic examples that were required before the ePortfolio are still a required part of the course, however, now the assignment has an online component. To simplify the grading process, many faculty use a Grading Rubric to score projects (Fox & DeLorenzo, 2009). A copy of an ePortfolio Rubric is included in the assessment section of this chapter. Faculty teaching ePortfolio content become facilitators in the learning process thereby fostering a transformation of the students from passive to active learners. Online and technology enhanced education is learner centered.

Creating an ePortfolio is a very creative process. Communication between faculty and students is paramount. Today, students want and expect faculty to be proficient with technology and incorporate it into their teaching. At the very least, students expect to be able to communicate with faculty via email, access online resources, have access to the Internet activities, and discussion boards. Electronic SMART classrooms are becoming more commonplace. The multiple uses of technology for teaching and learning are evolving and ePortfolio is a part of the advancement. The hands-on training of the ePortfolio creation is usually obtained in an ePortfolio computer lab with technology mentors not faculty. Since the creation of templates and online commercial products has made the technical part of creating the website easier, the website creation is secondary and the role of the faculty is to train the students regarding the content they place on their ePortfolio. Faculty are responsible for guiding the students and grading the ePortfolios. As for the grade given for the ePortfolio project, which is determined by the individual faculty member—the higher the grade value of the project, the more time the students will spend on their ePortfolio.

Selected faculty comments on what they liked about the ePortfolio project include:

> The ePortfolio project supported those students who may have never used a computer or attempted to access the internet. For those who had, it increased their computer skills. Many of my students were creative in their presentation of the ePortfolio. Some used sound, movement and other sophisticated graphics.

> In terms of the content, it challenged the students to perfect their writing skills since it is viewed in a public forum. The choice of content also encouraged them to make their decisions in terms of confidentiality and explanation of their career for the lay person to understand.

> For those who had yet to design a résumé, many students completed this ePortfolio exercise in their second year of college. Grammatical preciseness, attention to detail, layout and presentation were paramount for this type of assignment.

> When starting this project, I didn't see how the Career ePortfolio could be really useful for all students. But after the very first semester, I was excited to see how this project took to an absolutely new level the presentation of students. The projects and assignments of the course were presented in a structured and organized way, and were easy to read and analyze. Having ePortfolios to review together allowed us to have class discussions about the projects. The ePortfolio added a "human touch" to my courses: viewing and discussing portfolios with short biographies of the students, their goals and dreams was very moving, and allowed all of us to learn more about each other.

Students are educated for roles in industry and often seek recognition for their efforts from the eyes of "others"—clients, professors and/or peers. This makes perfect sense for their professional development but has a drawback, if, in the course of their education, they lose sight of the relationship between what they are learning and the value of their own creativity and critical thinking in choosing and developing content.

I cannot emphasize enough the insight and self-knowledge gained by these students in creating their ePortfolios. It was a new and valuable experience for them to consider a presentation in terms of WHO they are, WHERE they are on their journey, and WHAT they hope for. The project created self-awareness, and a new, healthy self-consciousness about their development over time and its validity as an achievement. In addition, the ePortfolio project gave my students the opportunity to hone their writing skills.

ALLOCATION OF RESOURCES/SUPPORT FROM ADMINISTRATION

Projects that use technology are usually costly. Students do not live in a 9 to 5 world. They expect access to technology all the time. They function in an international world with full access through the internet, and they want and expect services where technology works the way it is supposed to work. Administration not only must find ways to fund the growing need for technology on-campus and access off-campus, but also support student and faculty training. Faculty participating in ePortfolio projects must be supported with course preparation time/release time/reimbursement, technology training and support, professional development opportunities and technical resources. Training workshops for students and faculty as well as a dedicated ePortfolio computer lab are common things that are part of ePortfolio projects.

ASSESSMENT AND CAREER EPORTFOLIOS

ePortfolios allow faculty to assess work products and artifacts that are not easily graded or assessed with traditional methods. Assessment of student's ePortfolios will allow faculty to look at the larger picture. Regional accreditation agencies and the majority of professional program accreditation bodies now emphasize *student-learning outcomes* as the standards to be met. Accountability to funding sources and public use of data to inform decision-making guide the faculty. As the popularity of ePortfolio use grows, so does its use in assessment. See Barrett and Knezek (2003) for more infomration on issues related to assessment and accountability. Examples of types of assessment that can be done via ePortfolio projects include: 1) usage statistics, 2) rubric grades, 3) faculty surveys, 4) student surveys, and 5) student-learning outcomes. A common rubric can be used to assess student-learning outcomes and can be custom tailored for a course, department/program or the university. Using a grading rubric for ePortfolio is useful for individual courses as well as programmatic and college-wide assessment. Data collected over time will tell if students are improving in key areas. Additionally, weak areas can be identified and addressed. Comparative data is helpful to demonstrate trends among courses and departments within the institution (Goldsmith, 2007).

Table 1 below is a sample ePortfolio grading rubric. Students should be given a copy of the rubric with the syllabus. It is also helpful to have students grade their own or each other's ePortfolio using the rubric a few weeks before the final project is due as a form of self- and peer- assessment.

Table 1. ePortfolio Rubric

	Exceptional ___ points	Effective ___ points	Acceptable ___ points	Unsatisfactory ___ points	Non-Submit 0 points	Score
Response to ePortfolio Assignment	Followed all of the professor's directions; completed the assignment; added extra material.	Followed most of the professor's directions; completed the assignment.	Did not follow most of the professor's directions or failed to complete part of the assignment.	Disregarded professor's directions and failed to complete a significant part of the assignment.	Did not complete the ePortfolio assignment.	
Creative Use of Technology	Excellent use of graphics, sounds, e-mail, links, additional software and Internet resources.	Several resourceful sounds, graphics, and links used.	A number of uses of sounds, graphics and links.	No evidence of independent resources: monotonous presentation.	Did not complete the ePortfolio assignment.	
Attractiveness	Graphics, colors, font size attractive and easy to read: enhanced portfolio.	Graphics, colors, font size appropriate.	Graphics, colors, font size distracting or adds little to the portfolio.	Graphics, colors, font size distracting and difficult to read: detracts from the portfolio.	Did not complete the ePortfolio assignment.	
Professional Image	ePortfolio presents a excellent professional image.	ePortfolio presents an overall good professional image.	ePortfolio presents an overall acceptable professional image.	ePortfolio presents an overall non-professional image.	Did not complete the ePortfolio assignment.	

Grammar and Punctuation	Flawless grammar and punctuation.	Very few grammar and punctuation errors.	Some grammar and punctuation errors.	Several grammar and punctuation errors.	Did not complete the ePortfolio assignment.	
Personal Reflection	Excellent personal reflection demonstrated.	Truthful personal reflection demonstrated.	Some personal reflection demonstrated.	Little personal reflection demonstrated.	Did not complete the ePortfolio assignment.	
					Total:	___

Professional accreditation agencies recognize ePortfolios as a way to measure student performance. The Career ePortfolio is similar to other types of electronic portfolios, that is, reflective, course, and personal ePortfolios. However, the Career ePortfolio emphasizes the artifacts posted will be for a specific audience and the ePortfolio when finished will become public or will be published online. Career ePortfolios are an excellent way to measure student-learning outcomes. See Kenny et al. 2003, for more on perceived barriers to documenting outcomes with validity and reliability. A faculty member or a team of faculty, when measuring large number of student portfolios, can easily grade ePortfolio rubrics via a course roster (list of students) set-up in a simple word processing or Excel document. A roster cuts down on the time it takes to view portfolios. If a large sample is to be evaluated, the assessment team may grade every tenth or fiftieth portfolio rather than every ePortfolio. Taking a sample from a large cohort to measure English grammar and punctuation only, may be an accurate and quick way to use computer technology to measure the student-learning outcomes of students that have completed ePortfolios. The entire ePortfolio can be assessed or only a sample of features depending on the information needed.

OBTAINING JOBS USING CAREER EPORTFOLIO

Tracking the use of Career ePortfolios once students graduate from the institution has proved difficult for many programs offering ePortfolios. Like graduate surveys, it is extremely difficult to obtain hard data from alumni once they leave campus and enter the job market. We know of some individual success stories from students who used their Career ePortfolio with success to obtain both interviews and jobs by sending the link to their ePortfolio website to potential employers.

An ordered way to keep in touch with the students who become Alumni of the university is to transfer the Career ePortfolio over to either the Alumni Association or the Career and Transfer offices within the university to follow-up and store the ePortfolios on a server after students graduate.

SUMMARY

A major advantage of the Career ePortfolio is that students are able to market themselves to employers and graduate schools in a professional format that may give them an advantage over other candidates. The digital format of Career ePortfolios makes large assessment projects easier.

Sharing a Career ePortfolio is a way of sharing best practices or an individual's talent. Technology is used in such a way that both the students and faculty see the benefits of creating a Career ePortfolio. Since the Portfolio is in a digital form, it is easy to add artifacts that can personalize the website and make it easy to share. Creating a Career ePortfolio early allows students to identify professional goals and explore career options, which can help them focus their professional development while preparing them for the next phase in their professional career.

REFERENCES

Barrett, H., & Knezek, D. (2003). E-portfolios: Issues in assessment, accountability, and preservice teacher preparation. Retrieved from http://www.eric.ed.gov/ERICWebPortal/search/detailmini.jsp?_nfpb=true&_&ERICExtSearch_SearchValue_0=ED476185&ERICExtSearch_SearchType_0=no&accno=ED476185

Fox, R., & DeLorenzo, M. (2009). *Developing a professional teaching portfolio: A guide to success* (3rd ed.). Upper Saddle River, NJ: Pearson.

Goldsmith, D. J. (2007). Enhancing learning and assessment through e-portfolios: A collaborative effort in Connecticut. *New Directions for Student Services, 119*, 31-42. doi:10.1002/ss247

Kenny, M., Blustein, K., Chaves, A., Grossman, J., & Gallagher, L. (2003). The role of perceived barriers and relational support in the educational and vocational lives of urban high school students. *Journal of Counseling Psychology, 50*, 142-155.

Shepherd, R., & Goggin, P. (2012). Reclaiming 'old' literacies in the new literacy information age: The functional literacies of the mediated workstation. *Composition Studies, 40*(2), 66-91.

Zhang, S., Olfman, L., & Rachtham, P. (2007). Designing ePortfolio 2.0: Integrating and coordinating web 2.0 services with ePortfolio systems for enhancing users' learning. *Journal of Information Systems Education, 18*(2), 203-214.

SECTION 3: PRESENTING INTERACTIVE DESIGNS

As a thought experiment, we might consider how the concept of knowledge spaces fits in with or informs the academy. Thinking in terms of knowledge spaces and the academy as one, we can see the knowledge spaces of the academy in dialogue with other knowledge spaces outside the academy.

—Cambridge, Cambridge, & Yancey, "Moving Into The Future," in Cambridge, Cambridge, & Yancey, *Electronic Portfolios 2.0: Emergent Research on Implementation and Impact* (2008), p. 15

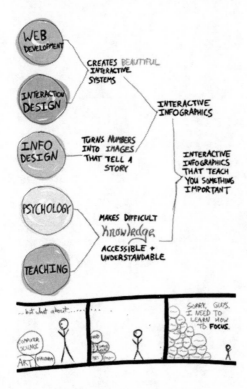

Bri Lance, "Beautiful Interfaces,"
http://www.bri-lance.net/category/personal

CHAPTER 7.

SHOWCASE HYBRIDITY: A ROLE FOR BLOGFOLIOS

Geoffrey Middlebrook
University of Southern California

Jerry Chih-Yuan Sun
National Chiao Tung University

Whether its origins are homegrown, open source, commercial, or common tool, defining an ePortfolio as a "digitized collection of artifacts, including demonstrations, resources, and accomplishments that represent an individual" (Lorenzo & Ittelson, 2005) has most often resulted in static Web pages or modified content management systems. Yet as new Web technologies emerge, there also arise new opportunities for ePortfolios to become much more dynamic. In particular, merging social media feature sets such as blogging into ePortfolios can help college students enhance their literacy skills, share information, build their reputations, and have an outlet for personal expression within a scholarly and professional online environment.

Even a cursory examination of the EDUCAUSE archives indicates there has been much work done on the opportunities and challenges that result from digital or Web-based portfolios in academe. It is known, for instance, that colleges and universities seeking to establish a student ePortfolio platform that demonstrates knowledge, abilities, and learning for a range of audiences and purposes, including impressing potential employers, are likely to face many of the implementation issues identified by George Lorenzo and John Ittelson (2005): hardware and software, support and scalability, security and privacy, ownership and intellectual property, assessment, acceptance, and long-term viability. Those campuses also confront the question of which ePortfolio vessel to utilize: homegrown, open source, commercial, or common tool. Such matters assume added significance if we heed Kathleen Yancey, Barbara Cambridge, and Darren Cambridge (2009), who assert that "eportfolios may be the most likely vehicle to help us make the transition to an academy of the future that is both relevant and authoritative."

We accept this potential for ePortfolios and so consider it encouraging that, according to the Campus Computing Project, over the past five years there has been a tripling of American institutions using them (Bass & Eynon, 2009). Nevertheless, for reasons that we will go on to argue, it is simultaneously disheartening to discover that most ePortfolios remain static Web pages or modified content management systems. But as new Web technologies appear, there are simultaneously new openings for ePortfolios to become significantly more vibrant. Particularly, joining social media feature sets such as blogging with ePortfolios can help students enhance their literacy skills and advance their scholarly and professional agendas online. However, the means for developing an ePortfolio system that permits student blogging and is, as Ali Jafari (2004) put it, "'sticky,' ... and is adopted by users" when it moves from concept to working system (p. 38), have thus far not been thoroughly addressed in the higher education literature. To help fill that deficit we discuss a project at the University of Southern California (USC) to implement a blog-based ePortfolio, or "blogfolio." Through an examination of educational blogging and blogfolios, followed by an assessment of challenges and outcomes, we take the position that if wisely put into effect, hybrid platforms represent a rich and flexible resource waiting to be wielded for the personal, intellectual, and vocational benefit of students.

THE DOMAIN OF EDUCATIONAL BLOGGING

As prelude to our argument for blogfolios, we first wish to make a case on behalf of blogging. It is obvious that the blogosphere is a flourishing cyber-realm, and while the many emphases of blogs not surprisingly differ, data from the Pew Internet & American Life Project (Lenhart & Fox, 2006) reveal that the most popular blogging topic, at least here in the United States, is one's own life and experiences. A self-referential use of weblogs certainly has merit; however, for those who are charged with guiding university students deeply into their majors and toward their careers, we are not convinced that an expressivist ambit, with the blog as personal journal, is where we ought to invest our pedagogical energies. Students are, in our estimation, better served if blogging is employed as a venue for developing their writing, critical thinking, and technology skills in conjunction with their disciplinary and professional identity. The New Media Consortium's Horizon Report (2008) declares that the "academy is faced with a need to provide formal instruction in ... how to create meaningful content with today's tools" (p. 6), and as we hope to demonstrate, this instruction can take place with blogs.

Jan Schmidt (2007) was undoubtedly correct when he observed that people utilize the blog format in a variety of contexts, and as such one "can speak about 'the blog' only in a very general sense" (p. 1410). Given this diversity, we would like to define our terms and establish the claims for what has come to be known as educational blogging. Aggregating the assertions of Stephen Downes (2004), Rebecca Blood (2002), the *EDUCAUSE Learning Initiative* (2005), the Support Blogging! site and other resources, our position, reinforced by years of classroom application at USC, is that educational blogging: helps students to find a voice and develop interests in a medium that appears to have life and longevity; motivates student engagement in conversations about their ideas and positions; provides students with an opportunity to consider the tenets of responsible writing, since there is at least in potential a wide and authentic audience; empowers students and stimulates the initiative to write; and engenders information sharing, reputation building, and personal expression. Evidence exists to bolster at least some of these declarations, as Amanda Lenhart (2008) and her co-authors discovered that pre-university teens who blog are "prolific writers online and offline" and recognize that writing is essential to their success in later life (p. v).

Given its promise, an increasing number of academicians understand the opportunities afforded by an educative use of the blog apparatus. For instance, Edward Maloney (2007) speaks of the "stars of the second-generation Web," among them blogs, which are consonant with "student-centered and active-learning models" (p. B26). In a related stance, Jean Burgess (2006) is convinced that blogs have the capacity to "contribute to a reconceptualization of students as critical, collaborative, and creative participants in the social construction of knowledge" (p. 105), and may moreover assist them in "developing literacies and competencies that are appropriate for the technological and social environments in which we all now work" (p. 106). To reinforce that point, Henry Jenkins (2006) and his colleagues see blogs as an important component in what they call "participatory culture," where access and mastery help to determine who will succeed or be left behind in school and employment (p. 3). The Jenkins team does not, in our estimation, exaggerate but rather captures the academic and career implications of social media (Jones & Lea, 2008).

A CALL FOR BLOGFOLIOS

Considering our position on educational blogging it is to be expected that we advocate embedding this dimension into an ePortfolio, with the outcome being a blogfolio, which Marco Antonio Mendoza Calderón and Joaquín

Ramírez Buentello (2006) define as a union with "the customization power of the weblog and the evidence showroom of an ePortfolio" (p. 495). Calderón and Buentello, though, are not alone in recognizing the potential of this aggregate resource. Lorraine Stefani, Robin Mason, and Chris Pegler (2007), for example, believe that combining blogs with ePortfolios "could be truly transformative for students" (p. 140), whereas Ittelson (2008) holds the view that "Web 2.0 applications and tools, such as blogs ... residing within ePortfolios ... is the basis of the next generation" (pp. 33-34). See also Gerben, 2009. These claims aside, before accepting that blogfolios do indeed represent a next generation, most readers would understandably like to see an instance of their deployment in a higher education setting. For this we turn to a joint endeavor at USC involving its Web Services, Center for Scholarly Technology, and Writing Program, using the Movable Type package and operating in part with funding from external and internal grants.

In the USC project, called "myPortfolio," undergraduate juniors and seniors enrolled in participating advanced writing courses are each provisioned a university branded and hosted blogfolio. James Farmer (2006) notes the importance of blogs as an indicator of digital identity, in part because bloggers "are not simply able to represent themselves through the content of their postings but also present much about themselves through aesthetic design, choice of media" (p. 98), and more. If one of the aims of the USC blogfolio is to help students manifest their higher-register selves, to establish and project a scholarly and professional persona online, then a simple but elegant interface possessing the institution's imprimatur is of no small consequence. That this matters has been shown in studies, reported by Barbara Warnick (2004), which divulge visitors to a site determine its credibility largely based on variables beyond the identity, affiliation, or aspiration of the author (p. 257), and are more influenced by "professionalism of design, usability, ... and other factors that operate as signs of trustworthiness" (p. 262).

Performing in this USC designed template, at the start of the semester each student decides on a distinctive area of inquiry that is a subset of his or her academic major or future profession, which will constitute the thematic parameters of their work in the course, and this information is stated in the student's sidebar profile. Before they begin to post, students are introduced to an array of award-winning blogs as well as to Schmidt's (2007) "selection, publication, and networking" rules (p. 1412). Students also receive orientation to a variety of Web search tools and techniques that offer the means to become a skilled and discriminating online researcher. Within their sites students publish hypertextual and multimodal posts on current and consequential phenomena in their fields and of their choosing that are interesting, important, and not obvious or already known. The entries fall into two categories: one where they initiate arguments with reference to and use of multiple online sources, and another where they locate and leave comments on blog posts, preferably written by people of stature, in their domain of inquiry. Along with publishing entries, students assemble a collection of sites and blogs, items of the highest quality in and greatest relevance to their areas, which they find and add as a sidebar link-roll, with the goal of making their own sites not just a repository of posts but also a resource for others.

As the above discussion indicates, USC is profoundly interested in having students assume a seat at the cyber-table and become active participants in the public conversations of their fields. This motive is found in Johndan Johnson-Eilola's (2004) observation on effective blogs as a professionalizing occasion: "They exist [in] complex rhetorical situations .... They make concrete intertextual connections and analyses. They provide interaction among multiple authors in a community" (p. 214), and they "require authors to read other texts, to analyze those texts, and to respond to those texts in writing" (p. 215). As Schnurr (2013) points out, "genres do not stand alone but tend to interact with other genres [creating] intertextuality and interdiscursivity" (p. 45). The blog stream, to be sure, is complemented in the USC template with a showcase ePortfolio component that is located in the sidebar of the site. Here students are offered two sections into which they may place their assets, academic work and extra-curricular experience. These artifacts, contextualized by an explanatory and reflective paragraph, may be text, audio, video, or image files intended to represent the aptitudes and aspirations of the students who produced them.

CHALLENGES AND OUTCOMES

While we hold that blogfolios have a powerful role to play in higher education, it is nevertheless necessary to address the challenges they face. Insofar as classroom blogging is concerned, obstacles include the provision of adequate training for teachers, the assessment of students' blogs, the creation of meaningful assignments, and the handling of potential information overload for students and faculty alike (Penrod, 2007, pp. 154-160). Taking these hindrances into account, we acknowledge that the objectives of developing students' literacy skills and nurturing their disciplinary and professional personae on a blog platform will be met incompletely. Pertaining to the part that the Internet plays in the construction of contemporary identities, Charles Ess (2005) argues that computer-mediated communication has caused neither a McLuhanesque "electronic global village" (p. 162), nor "its complete absence in the celebrated postmodern fragmentation and decentering" (p. 166). Instead the outcome is an agglomeration of what Ess refers to as "partial publics," a concept derived from Jurgen Habermas' notion of *Teilöffentlichkeiten* (p. 163); included among these partial publics, according to Ess, are scholarly and professional bodies, some of which conduct their Web-based interlocutions through blogs. Yet the research of Susan Herring and her co-authors (2005) indicates that though there is an "A-list" of blogs to which many link, refer to, and comment on, most blogs link to one another sparsely or not at all, with the implication being that the "blogosphere is [only] sporadically conversational" (p. 1).

Herring et al.'s (2005) findings notwithstanding, we maintain that educational blogging can produce at the very least an incipient sense of self in the discourses of one's field. Alexander Halavais (2006) is, we believe, accurate when he says that even bloggers who "might be classified as 'mumblers'—without obvious comments or readers ... are seeking a way of conversing with the world" (p. 118), and of enjoying the "intrinsic reputational rewards" that one may reap from blogging (p. 123). These rewards were observed by Jenkins (2007), who discovered that his students at the Massachusetts Institute of Technology "were making valuable professional contacts; some had developed real visibility ...; and a few received high-level job offers based on the professional connections they made on their blogs" (p. B9). A caution, however, must be sounded, as there are some in academe and the professional world who view blogs skeptically. The primary objections center on the consequences of an ill-conceived or intemperate post, which as Daniel Drezner (2006) phrased it, could become a "black mark that is difficult to erase" (p. B7). We acknowledge the consequences of careless entries, but such risks do not constitute, in our estimation, a sufficient case against the use of blogs for educative purposes.

With regard to ePortfolios, the potential difficulties are numerous. To put them in context, we evoke Jafari's (2004) steps to be followed in the development of an ePortfolio system: conceptual design, which involves functional and technical requirements; software design, where the concern is human and computer aspects; and implementation plan, comprised of business plan, daily operation, and software upgrade (p. 40). See also Shepherd and Goggin (2012). Along this path the needs and concerns of a variety of stakeholders, including students, faculty, administrators, and technologists must be addressed. That these steps are not always coordinated nor stakeholders always consulted is succinctly critiqued by among others Javier Ayala (2006), who points to the paucity of research on "integrating student voices into the dialogue of electronic portfolios" (p. 12). David Tosh, Tracy Penny Light, Kele Flemming, and Jeff Haywood (2005) explored the high cost of marginalizing the student voice, and concluded that unless students accept ePortfolios as "useful and worthwhile," these tools would be seen as simply "another hoop to jump through." As with our concession to the criticisms of educational blogging, we here allow that a successful ePortfolio is no easy undertaking. Nonetheless, if colleges and universities can convince students that growing numbers of prospective employers examine social networks like blogs to screen applicants (Wortham, 2009), and more than half of employers surveyed indicated an intention to use ePortfolios in the initial screening stage (Ward & Moser, 2008), then commitment would in all likelihood ensue.

Challenges assuredly exist, yet outcomes from the USC project are promising. One of our aims is for students to cultivate, as Teresa Acosta and Youmei Liu (2006) put it, "social capital" and "bridge the divide between the academy and society" (p. 23). Based on quantitative and qualitative data derived from course evaluations, student surveys, and student focus groups, it is evident that we have met with a high degree of success. Students indicate that their writing skills improve, and in apparent contrast with Gartner's "hype cycles," do not initially experience the importance and easiness of the blogfolio with over-enthusiasm followed by subsequent disappointment. Regarding the tool's usefulness, students express great willingness to share their work outside of the course, and many use their sites for applications to graduate and professional schools, jobs, and study-abroad programs (Martin-Kniep, 1999). One student captured it this way, "I had an interview for an internship and they asked about writing experience. I showed them my blogfolio and I got offered the job." It should in addition be remarked that our students are not working in a vacuum; Google Analytics logs disclose that almost half of the domestic visitors to the students' sites are from outside of California, and almost one-quarter of all visitors are from outside the United States.

CONCLUSION

It ought to come as no surprise that for students, who ostensibly belong to what Diana Oblinger (2003) and others have called the "millennial" or "net gen" or "digital native" population, "technology is assumed to be a natural part of the environment" (p. 38). However what may be surprising, and we think positive, are the results from an EDUCAUSE *Study of Undergraduates and Information Technology* (Salaway, Caruso, & Nelson, 2007). This research found that students have discretion and recognize "[t]echnology is an enabler of learning when [used] effectively" (p. 13), while "[p]oor use of technology ... detracts from the learning experience" (p. 14). We hope that our argument on behalf of blogfolios manifests the former as it affirmatively answers the question posed by Helen Chen: "Can we take advantage of some of these Web 2.0 technologies to create ... ePortfolio-related activities and reflective thinking" (Waters, 2007)? The advantage to which Chen refers resides at least partly in the recognition that blogfolios have the potential to stimulate students' enthusiasm, and facilitate the possibility of authentic and transactional participation in what Henry Farrell (2005) calls the blogospheric "carnival of ideas," where "the established, the up-and-comers, and the amateurs rub shoulders on a more or less equal footing" (p. B14).

At least one other study reinforced our findings that ePortfolios help students to "formulate career choices, facilitate entry into the workplace, facilitate entry into post-baccalaureate education, describe preferred career paths, [and] identify and develop skills and experiences relevant to achieving selected career goals" (Stephens & Moore, 2006, p. 527). When hybridized with educational blogging to create a showcase platform, the literature and our experiences at the University of Southern California lead to the conclusion that blogfolios can deliver significant personal, intellectual, and vocational benefits to students. Utilized in the manner here described, these digitized collections of artifacts not only serve as a valuable pedagogical tool, they may also contribute to the establishment of a deeper and perhaps durable scholarly and professional identity, or what Ittelson (2001) calls an "e-dentity" (p. 45), in the students who create them. Through the transferability of innovation, other institutions might at least want to consider this approach to technology in the service of mission-critical goals.

ACKNOWLEDGEMENTS

We would like to thank Candace Borland, Otto Khera, John Holland, and Kim Rothwell for their invaluable contributions to this project.

REFERENCES

Acosta, T., & Liu, Y. (2006). ePortfolios: Beyond assessment. In A. Jafari, & C. Kaufman (Eds.), *Handbook of research on ePortfolios* (pp. 15-23). Hershey, PA: Idea Group Reference.

Ayala, J. I. (2006). Electronic portfolios for whom? *EDUCAUSE Quarterly, 29*(1), 12-13.

Bass, R., & Bernstein, D. (2008). The middle of open spaces: Generating knowledge about learning through multiple layers of open teaching communities. In T. Iiyoshi, & M. S. V. Kumar (Eds.), *Opening up education: The collective advancement of education through open technology, open content, and open knowledge* (pp. 303-318). Cambridge, MA: MIT Press.

Bass, R., & Eynon, B. (2009, March 18). Electronic portfolios: A path to the future of learning. *The Chronicle of Higher Education*. Retrieved from http://chronicle.com/blogPost/Electronic-Portfolios-a-Path/4582

Blood, R. (2002). *The weblog handbook: Practical advice on creating and maintaining your blog*. Cambridge, MA: Perseus.

Burgess, J. (2006). Blogging to learn, learning to blog. In A. Bruns, & J. Jacobs (Eds.), *Uses of blogs* (pp. 105-114). New York: Peter Lang.

Calderón, M. A. M., & Buentello, J. R. (2006). Facilitating reflection through ePortfolios at technológico de Monterrey. In A. Jafari, & C. Kaufman (Eds.), *Handbook of research on ePortfolios* (pp. 486-495). Hershey, PA: Idea Group Reference.

Downes, S. (2004). Educational blogging. *EDUCAUSE Review, 39*(5), 50-70.

Drezner, D. W. (2006). The trouble with blogs. *The Chronicle of Higher Education, 52*(47), B7.

Educational Blogging. (2009). "Support Blogging!" Retrieved from http://supportblogging.com/Educational+Blogging

EDUCAUSE Learning Initiative. (n.d.). 7 Things You Should Know About ... Blogs. Retrieved from http://connect.educause.edu/Library/ELI/7ThingsYouShouldKnowAbout/39383

Ess, C. (2005). Moral Imperatives for life in an intercultural global village. In R. J. Cavalier (Ed.), *The Impact of the Internet on Our Moral Lives* (pp. 161-193). Albany, NY: SUNY.

Farrell, H. (2005). The blogosphere as a carnival of ideas. *The Chronicle of Higher Education, 52*(7), B14.

Farmer, J. (2006). Blogging to basics: How blogs are bringing online education back from the brink. In A. Bruns, & J. Jacobs (Eds.), *Uses of blogs* (pp. 91-103). New York: Peter Lang.

Gerben, C. (2009). Putting 2.0 and two together: What web 2.0 can teach composition about collaborative learning. *Computers and Composition Online*, (Fall 2009). Retrieved from http://www.bgsu.edu/cconline/theory.htm

Halavais, A. (2006). Scholarly blogging: Moving toward the visible college. In A. Bruns, & J. Jacobs (Eds.), *Uses of blogs* (pp. 117-126). New York: Peter Lang.

Herring, S. C., Kouper, I., Paolillo, J. C., Scheidt, L. A., Tyworth, M., Welsch, P., ... Ning Yu. (2005). Conversations in the blogosphere: An analysis "From the bottom up." *Proceedings of the thirty-eighth Hawai'i international conference on system sciences (HICSS-38)* (pp. 1-11). Los Alamitos, CA: IEEE. doi: 0.1109/HICSS.2005.167

Ittelson, J. (2001). Building an E-dentity for each student. *EDUCAUSE Quarterly, 24*(4), 43-45.

Ittelson, J. (2008). Know your ePortfolio. *Converge Magazine*, (Summer 2008), 32-35.

Jafari, A. (2000). The "Sticky" ePortfolio system: Tackling challenges and identifying attributes. *EDUCAUSE Review, 39*(4), 38-49.

Jenkins, H., Katie Clinton, C., Purushotma, R., Robison, A. J., & Weigel, M. (2006). Confronting the challenges of participatory culture: Media education for the 21st-century. The John D. and Catherine T. MacArthur Foundation. Retrieved from http://digitallearning.macfound.org/site/c.enJLKQNlFiG/b.2029291/k.97E5/Occasional_Papers.htm

Jenkins, H. (2005). From YouTube® to youuniversity. *The Chronicle of Higher Education, 53*(24), B9.

Johnson-Eilola, J. (2005). The database and the essay: Understanding composition as articulation." In A. F. Wysocki, J. J. Johnson-Eilola, C. L. Selfe, & G. Sirc (Eds.), *Writing new media: Theory and applications for expanding the teaching of composition* (pp. 199-235). Logan, UT: Utah State University Press.

Jones, S., & Lea, M. R. (2008). Digital literacies in the lives of undergraduate students: Exploring personal and curricular spheres of practice. *The Electronic Journal of e-Learning, 6*(3), 207-216.

Lenhart, A., & Fox, F. (2006). Bloggers: A portrait of the Internet's new storytellers. *Pew Internet & American Life Project*. Retrieved from http://www.pewinternet.org/PPF/r/186/report_display.asp

Lenhart, A., Arafeh, S. , Smith, A., & Macgill, A. R. (2008). Writing, technology and teens. Pew Internet & American life project. Retrieved from http://www.pewinternet.org/PPF/r/247/report_display.asp

Lorenzo, G., & Ittelson, J. (2005). An overview of institutional e-portfolios. *EDUCAUSE Learning Initiative*, 2005. ELI Paper 1. Retrieved from http://www.educause.edu/ir/library/pdf/ELI3001.pdf

Maloney, E. J. (2007). What web 2.0 can teach us about learning. *The Chronicle of Higher Education, 53*(1), B26.

Martin-Kniep, G. (1999). *Capturing the wisdom of practice: Professional portfolios for educators.* Alexandria, VA: Association of Supervision and Curriculum Development.

The New Media Consortium and the EDUCAUSE Learning Initiative. (2008). *The Horizon Report.* Retrieved from http://connect.educause.edu/Library/ELI/2008HorizonReport/45926

Oblinger, D. G. (2003). Boomers, gen-xers, and millennials: Understanding the "new students." *EDUCAUSE Review, 38*(4), 37-47.

Penrod, D. (2007). *Using blogs to enhance literacy: The next powerful step in 21st-century learning.* Lanham, MD: Rowman & Littlefield Education.

Salaway, G., Caruso, J. B., & Nelson, M. R. (9/12/2007). *The ECAR study of undergraduates and information technology*. Research Study from the EDUCAUSE Center for Applied Research, *6*. Retrieved from http://www.educause.edu/library/resources/ecar-study-undergraduate-students-and-information-technology-2007

Schmidt, J. (2007). Blogging practices: An analytical framework. *Journal of Computer-Mediated Communication, 12*(4), 1409-1427.

Schnurr, S. (2013). *Exploring professional communication: Language in action*. London: Routledge.

Shepherd, R., & Goggin, P. (2012). Reclaiming "old" literacies in the new literacy information age: The functional literacies of the mediated workstation. *Composition Studies, 40*(2), 66-91.

Stefani, L., Mason, R., & Pegler, C. (Eds.), (2007). *The educational potential of e-Portfolios: Supporting personal development and reflective learning* (Connecting With E-Learning). New York: Routledge.

Stephens, B. R., & Moore, D. (2006). Psychology ePortfolios enhance learning, assessment, and career development. In A. Jafari, & C. Kaufman (Eds.), *Handbook of research on ePortfolios* (pp. 520-531). Hershey, PA: Idea Group Reference.

Tosh, D., Light, T. P., Flemming, K., & Haywood, J. (2005). Engagement with electronic portfolios: Challenges from the student perspective. *Canadian Journal of Learning and Technology/La revue canadienne de l'apprentissage et de la technologie, 31*(3). Retrieved from http://www.cjlt.ca/index.php/cjlt/article/view/97/91

Ward, C., & Moser, C. (2008). E-portfolios as a hiring tool: Do employers really care? *EDUCAUSE Quarterly, 31*(4), 13-14.

Warnick, B. (2004). Online *ethos*: Source credibility in an "authorless" environment. *American Behavioral Scientist, 48*(2), 256-265.

Waters, J. K. (2007, October 1). ePortfolios meet social software. *Campus Technology*, Retrieved from http://www.campustechnology.com/Articles/2007/10/ePortfolios-Meet-Social-Software.aspx

Wortham, J. (2009, August 30). More employers use social networks to check out applicants. *New York Times*, Retrieved from http://bits.blogs.nytimes.com/2009/08/20/more-employers-use-social-networks-to-check-out-applicants

Yancey, K. B., Cambridge, B., & Cambridge, D. (2009, January 7). Making common cause: Electronic portfolios, learning, and the power of community. *Academic Commons*, Retrieved from http://www.academiccommons.org/commons/essay/making-common-cause-electronic-portfolios

CHAPTER 8.

ACCESSIBLE EPORTFOLIOS FOR VISUALLY-IMPAIRED USERS: INTERFACES, DESIGNS, AND INFRASTRUCTURES

Sushil K. Oswal
University of Washington, Tacoma

This chapter conceptualizes the design and pedagogy of an accessible, online ePortfolio and the content it might house from the perspective of universal design for users with visual disabilities in particular and other disabilities generally. While enrolled disabled students are demanding universities meet their special learning needs, the U.S. Department of Justice and U.S. courts are pressuring these institutions to live up to their legal and ethical obligations under the Americans with Disabilities Act, Section 504 of the Rehabilitation Act as well as the Individuals with Disabilities Education Act. Likewise, the Department of Justice, the Access Board, and Congressional reports assert that institutions of higher learning need to be ready for students with disabilities at all times, and required accommodations for student success at school, whether in face-to-face, blended, or in online environments, is both their legal and ethical responsibility.

THE DISABILITY TECHNOLOGICAL LITERACY DIVIDE

Many academic researchers have expressed reservations about how well digital technologies live up to their promise for disabled populations. Seymour and Lupton (2004), for instance, warn that digital technologies might actually increase the divide between people with and people without disabilities because of the industry's tendency to design educational environments mainly for the able-bodied. They see an intrinsic tension between designers' efforts at forging interesting and engaging, media-rich e-learning environments for average students and addressing the usually more technologically-intensive functional needs of disabled students. An instance of such a divide is obvious in how universities employ electronic technologies in existing structures—libraries, classrooms, administrative systems—without carefully studying their impact on already underrepresented disabled members of educational communities. And the absence of research on such digitalization of campus learning spaces itself does not bode well for the disabled. Most of the research about multimodal digital spaces focuses on visual interfaces, for instance, although scattered references to sound can be found in the review of the literature. For example, abundant research has been published on concept map-based visual interfaces where other modalities are mentioned, but multimodal digital spaces for the disabled have not yet been sufficiently worked into these models (Alpert & Grueneberg, 2001; Cicognani, 2000; Kim, 2006; Kinchin, 1998; Novak, 1998).

Researchers like Stefani et al., however, claim that "e-portfolios could be an advantage for students who need to maintain a record of their learning over an interrupted programme of study, perhaps spanning several years and several institutions," even though they concede that such benefits can only be reaped if portfolio designers and facilitators invest in principles of inclusivity and accessibility (p. 107). While enrolled disabled students are demanding universities meet their special learning needs, the U.S. Department of Justice and U.S. courts are pressuring these institutions to live up to their legal and ethical obligations under the Americans with Disabilities Act, Section 504 of the Rehabilitation Act as well as the Individuals with Disabilities Education Act. Likewise, the Department of Justice, the Access Board, and Congressional reports assert that institutions of higher learning need to be ready for students with disabilities at all times, and required accommodations for student success at school, whether in face-to-face, blended, or in online environments, is both their legal and ethical responsibility. An accessible design for electronic portfolios is within our reach because accessible user interfaces, inclusive web design guidelines for building such systems, and adequate machine and human resources for testing these systems already exist. I argue for integration of accessibility features in the design and pedagogy of electronic portfolios so that disabled instructors, students, and workers could avail of the benefits of these portfolios as well.

Before I expand on the accessibility of ePortfolios for the visually disabled users, both inside and outside the academy, a few definitions of technical terms are in order for the sake of specificity and clarity. The Americans with Disabilities Act (ADA) defines disability as "a physical or mental impairment that substantially limits one or more of the major life activities of such individual" (U.S. Department of Justice, 2008). This definition of disability can be interpreted in many ways, but for the purposes of this chapter it delineates the legal parameters within which institutions of higher education must provide accommodations to students and offer equal learning opportunities to all. By visual impairment, I mean the limited ability to see which nevertheless restricts one's ability to function in print or digital environments without adaptive technologies such as magnifying lenses, screen readers, or Braille displays. By blindness, I imply total or near total loss of sight where the user must depend upon alternate means for accessing print or digital information.

An ADA-based legal definition of accessibility is also important in the context of higher education because nearly all colleges receive some Federal funding directly or indirectly and are held legally responsible for implementing all U.S. disability laws. Speaking in systemic terms, ADA states that "An accessible information technology system is one that can be operated in a variety of ways and does not rely on a single sense or ability of the user. For example, a system that provides output only in visual format may not be accessible to people with visual impairments and a system that provides output only in audio format may not be accessible to people who are deaf or hard of hearing" (U.S. Department of Justice, 2009). In *Maximum Accessibility*, Slatin and Rush (2003) also offer a formal definition of accessibility which is straightforward and represents the perspective of Disability Studies closely. They write, "web sites are accessible when individuals with disabilities can access and use them as effectively as people who don't have disabilities" (p. 3). Here, we need to note that Slatin and Rush expand the concept of accessibility to include usability. They argue that in certain contexts a website can be both accessible yet unusable. Such a phenomenon has become common with many commercial websites where owners are trying to meet Section 508 or Web Content Accessibility Guidelines primarily to fulfill requirements for obtaining government contracts.

In academia, this phenomenon is on display almost with every online academic space, and a few management systems are documenting both accessibility and usability well. For example, the popular course management system, Canvas, offers the copy of a completed accessibility checklist, known as the "Canvas Voluntary Product Accessibility Template," on its website which would suggest two things to a casual reader: 1) Canvas is voluntarily doing this accessibility work, and 2) it follows all guidelines included in this list and therefore it is an accessible system for people with disabilities. In the second half of this chapter I present a firsthand report on the state of accessibility of the Canvas ePortfolio tool to demonstrate the effectiveness and how Canvas can be a useful model for other ePortfolio performance support systems.

Inside and outside the academy, ePortfolios are becoming sites of power display while enhancing each creator's virtual caché in the digital space. For instance, the president of Westminster College in Utah maintains a complete ePortfolio of his life and his life work to attract not only visitors from his own campus but also web surfers from all over the world. As the editors of this collection state, ePortfolios are quite distinct from paper portfolios. They collect, develop, exhibit and enhance the cumulative work of the creator, but they also can easily spread their limbs to other spaces through social networking tools. A Twitter® hash tag, a link on a friend's Facebook® wall, a link in a blog or even a Word or PowerPoint document, or a casual illusion in a second life performance can move an ePortfolio from a narrowly framed space for collecting and displaying to a network of presences in multiple sites. Other chapters in these collections examine such models, in fact. And these networks go beyond expanding the reach of the creator's work because they recontextualize the original content and open it to new interpretation by transforming the meaning of what had been exhibited in the authorial frame. As Lauren F. Klein points out elsewhere in this collection, ePortfolios in association with social network sites can form additional bridges between the academic and the work world. However, the shifting nature of such networks and their very idiosyncratic choices for structuring and managing their spaces pose a virtual nightmare for those accessing the web through adaptive devices such as screen readers, magnifiers, and speech recognition systems. The free and self-regulating nature of the World Wide Web has so far rendered all attempts at enforcing any web accessibility standards across the board useless. While Web Accessibility Initiative (WAI), a voluntary organization consisting of members worldwide and one of the four domains of the World Wide Web Consortium (W3C), has released Web Content Accessibility Guidelines Version 2.0 (WCAG 2.0) just recently in fall 2012; however, a large majority of websites in the United States do not yet meet standards set by WCAG 1.0 in 1999.

Though technical communication scholars do not agree on whether specific tools and software ought to be taught to undergraduates, the application of these tools in developing ePortfolios raises other questions, particularly questions about access. Do universities have the responsibility to choose and teach only accessible tools and software? While supporters of workplace-centered curricula might object to such a suggestion because most of the digital infrastructure remains off-limits to blind workers, the idea of such a choice opens up a new space for negotiating access for people who are disabled. If our graduates have learned and achieved proficiency in tools and software for building accessible capstone projects and ePortfolios, they are more likely to advocate for the use of such accessible systems in the workplace. While their accessible projects themselves can serve as emblems of a shift toward integrated accessibility, in terms of technology transfer, these graduates can reformulate the functionality and purpose of these academic electronic portfolios to restructure and reform the circulation of ideas, information, and often closely held departmental intellectual capital in the workplace. Whereas working groups in business are utilizing bulletin boards, LISTSERVs, and social networks for exchange of ideas, these exchanges often have the qualities of transient communities. Because many of these discussion groups are formed around specific projects and problems, the end of such projects can also result in a sudden demise of these virtual communities (see Rice, 2013). Electronic portfolios can be organized around similar purposes, but if they are anchored in a particular unit of the organization and if the portfolio manager is permitted to retain a degree of autonomy and control, they can avoid the fate of a typical virtual community. Since ePortfolios are no longer static entities restricted to a solitary presence on a single E-server, they can become broader interactive spaces for construction of information, ideas, and knowledge networks.

Equipped with new tools for presenting, archiving, and transporting, ePortfolios now cultivate important technical skills, employ digital formats that allow sharing across institutions and platforms, and remain relevant technologies beyond school for graduated professionals in many fields (Gatlin & Jacob, 2002; Gibson & Barrett, 2002, 2004; Heath, 2002). Further, ePortfolios are effective means for proving certification requirements, exhibiting the pertinence of the candidate's skills for a specific job description, and demonstrating one's professional development in an existing career for advancement (Jafari & Greenberg, 2003).

The discrete skills of textual writing, graphic design and imaging, and video or audio composing are now being taught in Technical Communication courses as multimodal projects, and ePortfolios admirably lend to a holistic and seamless representation of such student work. Beyond the academy, such multimodal composing is finding a foothold in all sorts of organizations ranging from the ones who are in the business of producing digital consumer wares and are obviously a part of the emergent digital economy to the ones who were erstwhile considered manufacturers of consumer goods of the other kind but have now transformed themselves into an economy residing on the Internet and capable of transacting significant portions of its business in these digital spaces.

ePortfolio proponents are now creating bridges between the academic and workplace portfolios. This is a topic expounded on by many writers in this collection, and while educational ePortfolios are attributed to a three-phase cycle of independent learning—planning of goals, review of individual progress, and reflection for future improvement (Chau & Cheng, 2010; Mason, Pegler, & Weller, 2004; Stefani, Mason, & Pegler, 2007)—it is the additional fourth post-graduation phase where ePortfolios can best benefit the graduates with disabilities. With up to 70% unemployment rate among visually impaired working age adults (American Community Survey, 2009), a professionally produced ePortfolio can showcase a job candidate's competence better than any well-crafted résumé or a perfectly executed interview. In discussing recent trend toward lifelong and workplace portfolios, researchers in our field have not paid attention close enough to the extended benefits of electronic tools for disabled workers whose physical attributes can often act as barriers between their professional abilities and the employers (Cambridge, 2008; Willis & Wilkie, 2009).

Researchers in the United Kingdom have researched the accessibility of standardized assessment ePortfolios for disabled students (Ball, 2007; Heath & Giorgini, 2007). However, it is apparent that we need more research on workplace and lifelong ePortfolios (see Cambridge, 2010). It also needs to be stressed that we require pedagogical guidance on how to support disabled students in developing skills for managing and using ePortfolio tools and creating accessible content for themselves and others.

Workplace studies from other disciplines also indicate that employers often do not understand the nature of disabilities, are not familiar with disabled candidates' abilities, and fail to see how they can contribute to the workplace (Hendren & Sacher, 1992). For example, to counteract the deep-seated human prejudice toward blindness, a visually-impaired candidate can employ a multimodal ePortfolio to substantiate her capabilities, skills, and achievements not only at the time of hiring but also later to exhibit, clarify, and quantify her achievements to co-workers and supervisors. However, to construct such a work portfolio, the disabled college student today must fully participate in ePortfolio construction, presentation, and assessment work in their classes. They must acquire necessary technical and professional skills for accomplishing portfolio goals, learn to design spaces for presenting their work, create relevant content to attain their career goals, and develop strong presentational and design skills to showcase this content. These are all valuable rhetorical skills.

More than a decade ago, web accessibility scholar, John Slatin (2002), pointed out that "Accessibility is fundamentally a rhetorical issue, a matter of fleshing out (literally) our conception of audience to include an awareness that there are people with disabilities in that audience and developing effective skills and strategies for addressing the entire audience" (p. 37). What John Slatin wanted to stress by placing "accessibility" in the "rhetorical" category is that we can't place it in some additional or separate category; rather, it ought to be included in our original conception of audience and remain an integral fact throughout the development of the document, the project, or the website just the way disability is an essential fact of life. Slatin's discussion of accessibility is also more meaningful to the context of accessibility of ePortfolios because it applies both to the system and its content—the container and the contained. Likewise, Sean Zdenek (2009) reminds us that "Students with disabilities are in danger of being either excluded from the new media revolution or accommodated as after-thoughts of pedagogies that fail to anticipate their needs." At the breakneck pace new digital technologies have been adopted in higher education in this century, and if the various accessibility-related complaints against several universities during the past three years can be seen as indicative of the state of accessibility at other colleges, these dangers of being left out are certainly real (see the Pennsylvania State University Agreement with National Federation of the Blind or NFB; see also the ADA Settlement Agreement by the Arizona State University, 2010). Ellis and Kent (2011) further warn us that we must counter the "dangerous trend in digital design where socially constructed features from the analog world are migrated to the digital environment" (p. 39). Whereas visually impaired writers were largely dependent on others for putting together their paper portfolios in the past, digital tools today have the potential of endowing complete independence on them if these users could receive adequate instruction for designing accessible ePortfolios. Disabled users also have a unique opportunity to participate in electronic portfolios culture as readers, workers, and evaluators if the field of ePortfolio design follows principles of accessibility.

Universal Design for Learning (UDL) is an educational philosophy which pairs well with accessible and flexible ePortfolio construction. Developed by The Center for Applied Special Technology (2004), it has begun to gain traction in our schools and will most likely begin to receive serious consideration in higher education as we admit increasing numbers of disabled students to our programs (Burgstahler, 2008; Dolmage, 2009; Dunn & De Mers, 2002; Oswal & Hewett, 2013). Based on Principles of Universal Design in Architecture originally developed by Ronald Mace in the 1970s, the UDL framework promotes a process that works with flexible goals, adopts divergent teaching methods, and advocates for assessment tools which accommodate learner differences. Its tenets for designing curriculum and pedagogy ask for multiple means of representation, of action and expression, and for engagement. If ePortfolio infrastructure and pedagogy remain flexible and do not become what Kathleen Yancey warns as a system of "*two* composers, (1) a student and (2) the system, with the system's override capability exerting greater authority " (p. 745), they are a perfect example of progressive practical theory. While commercially-grown ePortfolio systems may or may not adhere to a set of accessibility standards, probably an open-source, nonprofit system like the kind of Open Source Portfolio Initiative (OSPI) in the long run has the potential of delivering a sustainable, accessible platform for constructing UDL-driven ePortfolios.

ACCESSIBLE EPORTFOLIO DESIGN AT PRESENT

The question remains: where do we presently stand with design and infrastructure of ePortfolios as far as their accessibility to the blind in particular and visually impaired in general is concerned? I will organize this discussion around a user experience report on the electronic portfolio space offered by Instructure, the company behind the learning management system called Canvas. I have elected to give a significant room in this chapter to one practical example of accessibility problems to provide relevant, detailed examples. The accessibility of campus technology has largely been left to those who need it for survival in academia. Even when disabled students assert their legal rights to access, the conversation about the accessibility problems experienced seldom goes beyond the instructor and the Disability Services office, in my experience. Corporations behind these learning management systems are equally evasive about accessibility unless a complaint is brought against their product through a lawsuit or through an inquiry by the Justice Department. For example, the much-cited accessible course management system, Blackboard, was made accessible after several years of complaints by blind students and faculty. To the dismay of blind faculty, only the student side of Blackboard Version 9.1 was made accessible and faculty still continue to experience many accessibility problems. Likewise, relative newcomers on the ePortfolio market like Canvas have not invested in accessibility of their system from as early as the design planning stage as much as is needed. Since new companies do not have the baggage of old, inaccessible developer tools, they can integrate accessibility in their products from the early stages of choosing a platform and designing interfaces for the new products. Further on, since ePortfolios are often viewed as electronic shells or containers for displaying and storing user-generated content, in most people's views, these course management and portfolio software companies do not have the responsibility of making the content accessible. Considering the easy employability of ready-made digital tools for Web pages, content creators with little knowledge of accessibility are populating the digital spaces with inaccessible content. No reliable filters or content checkers have yet been built into the electronic portfolio systems I have researched which would alert the composer about the accessibility issues in their work.

To attain the goals of an accessible system, emerging approaches to digital design of ePortfolios can be employed offering multiple user interfaces from a single-source using differing modalities. For instance, Parallel User Interface Rendering (PUIR) is based on a "single consistent conceptual model," which can render a user interface simultaneously in multiple modalities and thus be accessible to people with differing sensory and usability needs simultaneously (Van Hees & Engelen, 2012). These versatile interfaces and electronic performance support systems also have the potential for communicating more efficiently and efficaciously with specialized adaptive devices necessary for certain people with disabilities.

Cooper and Heath's (2009) approach to personalizing interfaces for users with disparate needs, an approach they label as "a standardized intermediate representation," works to develop interface work with popular consumer devices and educational software presently on the market. For example, they examine able-bodied users' abilities to individualize the look and feel of their cellular phones and tablets to accommodate greater accessibility needs. Just as students and instructors can subscribe or unsubscribe to services of their interest or disinterest in a course management system, disabled users should be able to add features and services which enhance their abilities to function in digital environments and remove features which distract or obstruct from effective interaction. This approach has been implemented in some Google and Microsoft and Apple products where users can turn on a built-in screen reader, magnifier, or speech recognition system without additional adaptive technology. Whereas such devices at this time only add extra modalities without paying close attention to usability, Cooper and Heath foresee a future where accessibility standards would be integrated as norm for digital usability. Thus, disabled users won't remain an after-thought for developers and designers. Instead, designers would have a vision for interfaces requiring no retrofitting—interface designs which would represent all users, would allow personalization of content, and would have the scope for individualized interfaces (Cooper & Heath, 2009; p. 1140). Some of the approaches within the Web Content Accessibility Guidelines 2.0 also aim at building such flexibility in initial digital environment design and can be implemented in ePortfolio building and pedagogy for users with a variety of sensory and learning disabilities to provide improved access to multimodal content as well as portfolio management systems themselves. An examination of one such ePortfolio system, Canvas, helps substantiate claims about accessibility and usability problems for visually impaired and blind users.

An ePortfolio can include any online multimodal document management tool with a set of specific display and management characteristics. Such systems collectively define the shared space between the creator and its imagined readers. Providing a complete survey of ePortfolio models or the tools various ePortfolios offer is beyond the scope of this discussion (see Kimball, 2006 for a fairly recent list). Rather, the primary goal here is to delineate some of the chronic accessibility issues these ePortfolio performance support systems presently suffer from in order to help illustrate how the lack of inclusivity in the design of these tools can adversely affect visually impaired students' abilities to effectively participate in portfolio development in academia and the workplace. The availability of an accessible ePortfolio tool can have subtle, hard-to-detect yet immensely significant implications for students in their educational and workplace careers. If the portfolio tool is inaccessible or unusable in any way in school, it is very likely that the user will also lack necessary expertise to use similar technologies in the workplace. Again, the following description of Canvas Portfolio tool is not aimed to analyze or evaluate all product features.

ACCESSIBLE USER EXPERIENCE WITH THE CANVAS PORTFOLIO TOOL

Let's examine the Canvas Portfolio tool from the point of entry into the portfolio page to the place where users can add and edit sections. There are user experience accessibility problems for users with screen readers. The blind tester is an expert JAWS-for-Windows screen reader user, Version 13. A sighted university technician in charge of the management of Canvas participated as an observer. We replicated our earlier test with Canvas Portfolio six months later. Our results were almost identical. This is what we found. And note that since blind users cannot point to a mouse target, they navigate the screen with the help of the tab and arrow keys while JAWS reads the information from the cursor location. JAWS also has many sophisticated commands to permit faster navigation by expert users but nothing works unless Web pages have been coded accurately in accordance with the screen reader accessibility standards.

Once the user enters Canvas Portfolio, the first item JAWS reads is the Organize/Manage Pages area in the right navigation menu as garbage code "36,941. Reorder entries." After being serenaded by these random numbers and phrases from the underlying Web code by my favorite JAWS voice, Reed, we decided to test first things first and launched the Getting Started wizard. The wizard started okay, but once "introduction" or "portfolio sections" were selected within the wizard, a pop-up box came up with instructions and "show me" links, and JAWS did not read anything to the user to indicate that the box was displaying information. Upon being prompted by the sighted observer, the blind user was able to get the content by employing the "find" command in JAWS. The point here is that without a prompt from a sighted observer, the blind user would not even know about the existence of the text box.

At this point, the tester decided to explore this page further to understand its actual layout in comparison with the order in which JAWS was reading the page. This is what JAWS saw and read; the sighted observer filled in the invisible items unread by JAWS:

> complementary landmark
> wizard link
> panic level 2 home
> organize pages
> heading for pages for this section
> ePortfolio
> 12,465 number garbage (all not visible)
> welcome
> times (all not visible)
> add another page (all not visible)
> 694- reoder entery garbage (all not visible)
> edit page

At this point, we tried to create a portfolio page using the "ADD" button. When we tried to save the page, JAWS provided no response. Again, you can see how this would be impossible for a blind user to navigate without much assistance.

The next test we tried was for adding sections within the portfolio. When clicked on, the "done editing" window popped up but the "add section" button was not read. Once we clicked on it, the cursor moved in the box to enter a section name, but it was not verbalized by JAWS. After adding a section with sighted help, the last step to get the new section to show in the list of sections again did not read, and there was no way for the blind user to know that it is the last step before this added section will show in the navigation.

Further on, once a section was created, the next text box for creating another section came up but was not read. Instead JAWS read garbage after informing the user about a Twitter® link at the bottom of the page. At this stage, we decided to perform the next logical action: to edit the page with the new section. Again, using the "find" function in JAWS, the blind user located the added sections, but just by using the arrows or tab keys JAWS could not read them. Similarly, when editing a section page, the tab key did not take the user to the "add content" menu on the right, where the user needed to go. Employing the arrow keys, the user eventually reached that section, but again the tab key did not land the user on the menu.

The last test we performed was on uploading files from the user's PC into this newly created portfolio section. Interesting enough, here we found that when browsing for a file to upload, the "BROWSE" button on the page is voiced if the user moved the cursor backwards. But the button was not voiced when the user read forward and down the page, which is the norm. Likewise, "uploading a file" gave no verbal indication initially that the software was uploading until the user moved the arrow up.

To summarize this user experience, most of the accessibility problems recorded during this session are solvable. They would fall under four categories: the user getting lost in information organization, confusing navigation menus, invisible information, and not providing enough control to users. A separate but common accessibility/usability issue repeatedly confronted during this testing pertained to the positioning of keyboard focus when a feature was opened or closed. The system often moved the screen reader cursor back to the start of the page requiring the blind user to track back to the place where he had initiated the earlier action.

Further, an overall page design which caters to visual users, employs repetitive navigation menus with inadequate labeling, and codes various page elements poorly cannot serve disabled users. If we view questions of accessibility and usability as two interrelated phenomena, as Petrie and Kheir (2007) in their study of blind and sighted Web users have shown, many of accessibility problems confronted by blind users overlapped with usability issues experienced by the nondisabled. Addressing one group's needs can benefit the other. Attention to Section 508 or Web Content Accessibility Guidelines could have taken care of all the technical issues in this case, although it would have been a monumental undertaking.

CONCLUSIONS

As it has been substantiated by this brief user experience report, in spite of major leaps in ePortfolio technologies, accessibility for disabled students and faculty rarely comes with these new digital tools. Campus administrators acquiring ePortfolios systems, and the instructors adopting them in their courses, must raise some difficult questions before selecting and implementing such systems for all users, both legally and ethically but also in order to adequately prepare students with functional technological literacies.

As Lawrence A. Scadden of the National Science Foundation writes, "[E]ducation professionals can be considered the gatekeepers to the future for many students with disabilities because education controls the boundaries of participation in our society. With a solid education (mediated by the essential adapted computer technology), multiple career options will be open to them, permitting them to flourish independently in the twenty-first century. (VIII) the colleges can hardly ignore the needs of their disabled students and faculty today in light of the U.S. Justice Department's recent interventions in the Kindle cases in Arizona, Wisconsin, and Pennsylvania to protect the rights of this population in the higher education institutions" (Dear Colleagues Letter from DOJ, 2011). By overlooking accessibility aspects of ePortfolios we might also end up squandering precious institutional resources in providing band aid solutions in the form of able-bodied assistants to disabled students and retrofitting these ePortfolios with accessibility if the tools are home grown.

The adoption of such inaccessible ePortfolio tools happens under an range of circumstances—lack of a clear accessibility clause in the school's purchasing policies, the senior technology executives' knowledge of accessible technologies and accessibility laws, these executives' general attitudes toward disability, the admission departments' success in keeping the percentage of disabled students on campus low, and often these students' own unawareness about their educational rights. As far as cost is concerned, accessible ePortfolios should not cost a single extra penny to colleges in most cases since they are third-party commercial products. As it is apparent from the Kindle eReader cases in Arizona, Pennsylvania, and Wisconsin, any institutions of higher education receiving direct or indirect funding from the U.S. Government are obligated to purchasing accessible technologies for all users. Besides adopting accessible an ePortfolio system, we also need to ask other accessibility-related questions before ePortfolios performance support system implementation:

- What are the teaching and learning goals associated with the technological aspects of ePortfolios? Are these goals also achievable by disabled students considering the current state of ePortfolios technology? Is it possible for us to deliver our portfolios curriculum equitably to all students?
- What are the pedagogical benefits of ePortfolios to students? Will disabled students also receive comparable benefits with or without accommodations? How are these benefits assessed for students? Is the same methodology applied in the case of disabled students?
- Since various multimodal technologies integrated in ePortfolios create both opportunities and barriers for students with sensory disabilities, what content standards should be applied across the board to provide a level playing ground to all students? How do we build institutional capacity for training faculty and students in the use of technologies so that all the portfolios content generated is accessible to all as a matter of routine?
- What are the technical issues with the accessibility of ePortfolios in higher education which go beyond the question of meeting general Web

standards? Which academic or professional organization should take a leadership role for sorting out these technical problems? What commitment for integrating accessibility should be expected from the third-party vendors of ePortfolios?

RECOMMENDATIONS

These recommendations provide some suggestions for instructors to bring accessibility to their ePortfolio pedagogy so that it could be inclusive of their disabled students. While automated accessibility testing tools such as WAVE for Internet Explorer and Fangs for Firefox can highlight some key accessibility problems disabled users will experience with an ePortfolio system, a hands-on accessibility testing session can provide a visceral view of how disabled users interact with electronic pages. WCAG 2.0 lists 38 success criteria or checkpoints for achieving Web accessibility. Twelve of these checkpoints can be verified manually and can make instructors aware of the state of accessibility of a particular Web page.

Perform a manual test on all Web pages/screens of your ePortfolio tool three times and learn firsthand how your students with disabilities will interact with the system and will or will not experience accessibility problems with the various menus, links, buttons, mouse-overs, and other navigation. Conduct one test for learning about visually impaired users with a screen reader such as JAWS-for-Windows (see http://www.freedomscientific.com) or NonVisual Desktop Access (NVDA) (see http://www.nvda-project.org) for speech output and a keyboard for input but no mouse; another for speech and hearing impaired users without a speaker or microphone; and yet another without a keyboard and mouse but through a speech input software such as Dragon NaturallySpeaking (see http://www.nuance.com/dragon) for users unable to operate other input devices. When the ePortfolio homepage one tests fails to make links visible to the user using a screen reader, one realizes that access to this information is not really that easy. Similarly, when one's screen reader informs that the page has several links but they cannot be clicked without a mouse, a problem is clearly identified. Very suddenly the wonderful World Wide Web begins to appear not so wonderful.

Here are some disability-centered general guidelines to improve accessibility and usability performance of ePortfolios through an accessible pedagogy. Because manufacturers of ePortfolio tools primarily test their systems with nondisabled users, disabled users always face more technical problems. Consequently, they require strong technical support on campus for troubleshooting. Another central accessibility issue relates to the need for a smooth interfacing of the electronic portfolio tools with other learning management system tools used by the instructor. Equally crucial is a functional interface with other university digital systems such as library Web pages, campus storage drives where instructors and students park materials, and any other university websites housing materials related to portfolio work.

EMPHASIS ON ACCESSIBLE CONTENT GENERATION

Besides ensuring the accessibility of the ePortfolio system, making use of only accessible tools for content development is central to disabled students' success with their portfolio projects. We often forget to check whether our own Web pages follow WCAG 2.0 guidelines. We may not remember that our videos often lack descriptive transcripts of visual elements for the blind and text transcripts of audio elements for the deaf and other users with audio processing disorders. The same rules apply to plug-ins and other third-party links. Last, information overload, or general confusion, is a major issue in multimodal presentations for users with a range of disabilities.

MULTIMODAL ASSIGNMENTS

We can develop assignments that utilize disabled students' differing capabilities and skills just the way we design assignments for able-bodied students' diverse capabilities and skills. We also cannot expect all students to accomplish the same level of competency in each area/goal of the assignment when we take into account how no two human bodies are alike. By no means do I suggest that we should not expect our disabled students to employ more than one modality or learning approaches. For example, blind students might be interested in exploring the possibilities of video whereas deaf students might be interested in soundscapes. Stefani et al. (2007) emphasize that for optimal accessibility an ePortfolio's content must be useable in more than one medium. They suggest that students create multimodal portfolios that could be experienced with "audio turned off, with screen-readable text to supplement or replace graphics, with captioning of digital video, with descriptions to accompany flash animations" (p. 114). This is a post-process pedagogy of divergency. As workplaces happen to be collaborative, and this mode of learning has become acceptable in higher education, use of collaborative assignments can permit students to apply their diverse capabilities and skills without instituting new power hierarchies.

ACTIVITIES SURROUNDING ePORTFOLIO CONTENT DEVELOPMENT

Again, when developing content for ePortfolios, at least the instructor-directed activities must draw on different abilities and skill-levels of disabled and non-disabled students. The rule of thumb for inclusive pedagogy is that we incorporate a range of activities in ePortfolio design, content development, and eventual portfolio management so that every student has an opportunity to shine in some of them rather than getting penalized for failing to perform an overwhelming number of activities beyond their bodily ability. In the same vein, involvement of disabled students in evaluating the effectiveness of assignments and activities from their vantage point as disabled designers and learners is crucial. Last, making the purpose of such activities and interactions obvious to all students is important, and presenting this information in more than one modality is even more important. In our own assessment and feedback, we must become introspective in choosing our methods for evaluating student work. We must devise methods that do not favor student work in a certain modality and penalize another. Further, experiments in providing feedback in diverse modalities can be constructive in specific student circumstances and disabilities; however, instructors ought to remember to offer more than one option for receiving this feedback because "not one size fits all" adage can be true even within a single disability category (Thompson & Lee, 2012). Last, spreading grade distribution broadly and keeping the weight of individual assignments low enough that failing one assignment does not affect final grade adversely is fair and helpful to all students.

REFERENCES

Alpert, S., & Grueneberg, K. (2001). Multimedia in concept maps: A design rationale and web-based application. In C. Montgomerie, & J. Viteli (Eds.), *Proceedings of world conference on educational multimedia, hypermedia and telecommunications 2001*, (pp. 31-36). Chesapeake, VA: AACE.

Ball, S. (2009). Accessibility in e-assessment. *Assessment & Evaluation in Higher Education, 34*(3), 293-303.

Burgstahler, S. A. (2008). Universal design in higher education. In S. R. Burgstahler & R. Cory (Eds.), *Universal design in higher education from principles to practice* (pp. 3-20). Cambridge, MA: Harvard Education Press.

Cambridge, D. (2008). Audience, integrity, and the living document: eFolio Minnesota and lifelong and lifewide learning with ePortfolios. *Computers & Education, 51*(3), 1227-1246.

Cambridge, D. (2010). *Eportfolios for lifelong learning and deliberative assessment*. San Francisco: Jossey-Bass.

Canvas voluntary product accessibility template. *Canvas by instructure*. Retrieved from http://www.instructure.com/canvas_vpat

Center for Applied Special Technology. (2004). Universal design for learning. Retrieved from http://www.cast.org.

Chau, J., & Cheng, G. (2010). Towards understanding the potential of e-portfolios for independent learning: A qualitative study. *Australasian Journal of Educational Technology, 26*(7), 932-950.

Cicognani, A. (2000). Concept mapping as a collaborative tool for enhanced online learning. *Educational Technology & Society, 3*(3), 150-158.

Cooper, M., & Heath, A. (2009). Access for all to eLearning. In A. Méndez-Vilas, M. Solano, J. A. Mesa Gonzalez, & J. Mesa Gonzalez. (Eds.), *Integrating ICT in education* (pp. 1139-1143). Retrieved from http://oro.open.ac.uk/24796

Dolmage, J. (2009). Disability, usability, universal design. In S. K. Miller-Cochran & R. L. Rodrigo (Eds.), *Rhetorically rethinking usability: Theories, practices, and methodologies* (pp. 167-190). New York: Hampton.

Dunn, P. A., & De Mers, K. D. (2002). Reversing notions of disability and accommodation: Embracing universal design in writing pedagogy and web space. *Kairos: A Journal of Rhetoric, Technology, and Pedagogy, 7*(1). Retrieved from http://www.technorhetoric.net/7.1/coverweb/dunn_demers

Ellis, K., & Kent, M. (2011). *Disability and new media*. New York: Routledge.

Gatlin, L., & Jacob, S. (2002). Standards-based digital portfolios: A component of authentic assessment for preservice teachers. *Action in Teacher Education, 23*(4), 35-42.

Gibson, D., & Barrett, H. (2002). Directions in electronic portfolio development [Paper presented in an online forum of ITForum]. ITFORUM Paper #66. Retrieved from http://it.coe.uga.edu/itforum/paper66.htm

Gibson, D., & Barrett, H. (2004). Directions in electronic portfolio development. *Contemporary Issues in Technology and Teacher Education, 2*(4), 556-573.

Hendren, G., & Sacher, J. (1992). Employer agreement with the Americans with Disabilities Act of 1990: Implication for rehabilitation counseling. *The Journal of Rehabilitation, 58*, 481-408.

Jafari, A., & Greenberg, G. (Eds.) (2003, November 3). Electronic portfolio white paper: Version 1.0. Retrieved from http://www.immagic.com/eLibrary/ARCHIVES/GENERAL/EPORT/E031103J.pdf

Kim, P. (2006). Perspectives on a visual map-based electronic portfolio system. In A. Jafari & C. Kaufman (Eds.), *Handbook of research on ePortfolios* (pp. 44-53). Hershey, PA: IDEA Group Reference.

Kimball, M. (2006). Database e-portfolio systems: A critical appraisal. *Computers and Composition, 22,* 434-458.

Kinchin, I. M. (1998, August). *Constructivism in the classroom: Mapping your way through.* Paper presented at the Annual Student conference of the British Educational Research Association Annual Student Conference in The Queen's University, Belfast.

Mason, R., Pegler, C., & Weller, M. (2004). E-portfolios: An assessment tool for online courses. *British Journal of Educational Technology, 35*(6), 717-727. doi:10.1111/j.1467-8535.2004.00429.x

Novak, J. D. (1998). Creating, and using knowledge: Concept maps as facilitative tools in schools and corporations. Mahwah, NJ: Lawrence Erlbaum.

Oswal, S. & Hewett, B. (2013). Accessibility challenges for visually impaired students and their online writing instructors. In L. Meloncon (Ed.), *Rhetorical accessibility: At the intersection of technical communication and disability studies.* Amityville, NY: Baywood.

Petrie, H., & Kheir, O. (2007, April-May). The relationship between accessibility and usability of websites. Paper presented at the Conference on Human Factors in Computing Systems, San Jose, CA.

Reese, M., & Levy, R. (2009). Assessing the future: E-portfolio trends, uses, and options in higher education. *Research Bulletin, 4.* Boulder, CO: EDUCAUSE Center for Applied Research. Retrieved from https://jscholarship.library.jhu.edu/bitstream/handle/1774.2/33329/ECAR-RB_Eportfolios.pdf

Rice, R. (2013). Constructing new mediated knowledge in the process of writing for life. In G. Desai (Ed.), *The virtual transformation of the public sphere: Knowledge, politics, identity* (pp. 246-257). New Delhi, India: Routledge.

Scadden, L. A. (1997). In C. Cunningham & N. Coombs, *Information access and adaptive technology* (Foreword). Phoenix, AZ: Oryx.

Seymour, W., & Lupton, D. (2004). Holding the line online: Exploring wired relationships for people with disabilities. *Disability & Society, 19*(4), 291-305.

Slatin, J. M. (2002). The imagination gap: Making web-based instructional resources accessible to students and colleagues with disabilities. *Currents in Electronic Literacy,* (Spring 6). Retrieved from http://currents.cwrl.utexas.edu/spring02/slatin.html

Slatin, J. M., & Rush, S. (2003). *Maximum accessibility: Making your web site more usable for everyone.* Boston: Addison-Wesley.

Stefani, L., Mason, R., & Pegler, C. (Eds.), (2007). *The educational potential of e-Portfolios: Supporting personal development and reflective learning* (Connecting With E-Learning). New York: Routledge.

Thompson, R., & Lee, M. J. (2012). Talking with students through screencasting: Experimentations with video feedback to improve student learning. *The Journal of Interactive Technology and Pedagogy*, *1*(1). Retrieved from http://jitp.commons.gc.cuny.edu/talking-with-students-through-screencasting-experimentations-with-video-feedback-to-improve-student-learning

U.S. Census Bureau. (2009). American Community Survey. U.S. Census Bureau. Retrieved from http://factfinder2.census.gov/faces/nav/jsf/pages/index.xhtml

U.S. Department of Education and U.S. Department of Justice (2010). Electronic book reader dear colleague letter: Questions and answers about the law, the technology, and the population affected. Retrieved from http://www2.ed.gov/about/offices/list/ocr/docs/504-qa-20100629.html

U.S. Department of Justice. (2009). A Guide to disability rights laws: Section 508. U.S. Department of Justice. Retrieved from http://www.ada.gov/cguide.htm#anchor65610

Walters, S. (2010). Toward an accessible pedagogy: Dis/ability, multimodality, and universal design in the Technical Communication classroom. *Technical Communication Quarterly*, *19*(4), 427-454.

Van Hees, K., & Engelen, J. (2012). Equivalent representations of multimodal user interfaces. *Universal access in the information society*, 1-30. doi:10.1007/s10209-012-0282-z

Web Content Accessibility Guidelines (WCAG 2.0). Retrieved from http://www.w3.org/TR/WCAG20

Willis, L. & Wilkie, L. (2009). Digital career portfolios: Expanding institutional opportunities. *Journal of Employment Counseling*, *46*(2), 73.

Yancey, K. B. (2004). Postmodernism, palimpsest, and portfolios: Theoretical issues in the representation of student work. *College Composition and Communication*, *55*(4), 738-761.

Zdenek, S. (2009). Accessible podcasting: College students on the margins in the new media classroom. *Computers and Composition Online*, 1-21.

CHAPTER 9

FROM METAPHOR TO ANALOGY: HOW THE NATIONAL MUSEUM OF THE AMERICAN INDIAN CAN INFORM THE AUGUSTA COMMUNITY PORTFOLIO

Darren Cambridge
American Institutes for Research

The museum metaphor captures some of the more obvious affordances of the digital, networked environment in which ePortfolios are composed and used. Museums feature multiple media working in concert and offer their visitors a choice of multiple ways of navigating their collections. Many ePortfolio scholars emphasize the importance of individual, rather than institutional, ownership of ePortfolios and the capability of the ePortfolio genre to create a highly personalized representation of individual learning and identity. The chapter proposes an extended analogy between the National Museum of the American Indian (NMAI) and the Augusta Community Portfolio to map to key debates about ePortfolio practice.

MUSEUM AS METAPHOR

Metaphor has long been a powerful tool for thinking about portfolios (see Barrett, 2009). Metaphors help teachers and learners envision purposes for portfolios, most famously through the three offered by Mary Dietz (1996): the mirror (portfolio as reflection of the past and the self), the map (portfolio as plan for the future), and the sonnet (portfolio as form that helps identify what is most significant). Metaphors have also been used to think critically about issues of ownership and motivation, such as through Helen Barrett and Joanna Carney's (2005) juxtaposition of ePortfolio as test and ePortfolio as story. Metaphor has played a central role in the design of portfolios as well. Students are often encouraged to choose personal metaphors for their ePortfolios to guide their visual design (Kimball, 2002). At the institutional level, metaphors can also provide scaffolding for reflection, such as the metaphor of a journey of an outrigger canoe used at Kapi'olani Community College (Kirkpatrick, Renner, Kanae, & Goya, 2009). ePortfolio metaphors proliferate: a page on Barrett's website lists at least 25, and I can think of dozens more that have been employed in conversations about ePortfolio practice in which I've participated over the last ten years (Barrett, 2009).

Of the many possibilities, the ePortfolio as museum has proven powerful for my own thinking. While I do not know who was first to suggest it, Kathleen Yancey (2004) often refers in her work to items within a portfolio, most commonly called artifacts, as "exhibits," implicitly evoking the museum. Both museums and portfolios work by taking artifacts out of their original contexts and recontextualizing them within new and purposeful interpretive structures. The museum metaphor captures some of the more obvious affordances of the digital, networked environment in which ePortfolios are composed and used. Museums feature multiple media working in concert and offer their visitors a choice of multiple ways of navigating their collections. Up and beyond these features, a museum is fundamentally a space, not just a text. Populated by both objects and people, it is made more powerful through the interactions that happen within, and are elicited by, that space. Adding to the affordances of interlinked Web pages, the interactivity offered by ePortfolio systems and social software, ePortfolios are becoming simultaneously text and space. Authors who design their ePortfolios to capitalize on this dual character are likely to reflect more deeply and connect more fruitfully to the audiences they value.

Many ePortfolio scholars emphasize the importance of individual, rather than institutional, ownership of ePortfolios and the capability of the ePortfolio genre to create a highly personalized representation of individual learning and identity. The museum metaphor also appeals to me because it complicates those orthodoxies. Through the sponsorship of institutions with cultural capital and high production values made possible through that sponsorship, museums' messages are socially validated. Similarly, although ePortfolios are traditionally highly individualized, the additional persuasiveness offered to authors by institutional endorsement and the mediation of technology that viewers perceive as professional and cutting edge should not be discounted. Museums are also fundamentally collaborative creations, the product and site of the work of teams of experts with a range of areas of expertise. Because they reflect not only their primary author's ideas and achievements but also the design decisions of technology developers, the feedback of peers and instructors, the responses of other audiences, and, often, shared conceptual frameworks for understanding learning and performance, all contemporary ePortfolios are in some sense collaborative efforts.

For several years, I have been interested in the possibility of the ePortfolio genre as more explicitly collaborative, representing the achievement, reflections, goals, and plans of groups and organizations as well as individuals. The Urban Universities Portfolio Project, sponsored by the American Association for Higher Education in the late 1990s, demonstrated the power of electronic portfolios to represent the work of an entire higher education institution to multiple audiences, both on campus and in the larger community the institution serves (Kahn, 2001, 2002). Some of these institutional portfolios, such as those of Indiana University Purdue University Indianapolis and Portland State University, have played a key role in presenting evidence of institutional performance to regional accreditors, and the Western Association of Colleges and Schools now encourages such portfolios as part of their review process (Western Association of Schools & Colleges, 2002). A growing number of regional ePortfolio projects, in the US and particularly in Canada, the UK, and Europe, seek to link individual ePortfolios to collaborative portals to services offered to citizens to support their learning and civic participation by a range of organizations (le Carpentier, Groot, & Wasko, 2008; Hartnell-Young, Smallwood, Kingston, & Harley, 2006; Slade, 2008). Synthesizing the collective representation function of the university institutional portfolios and the portal to services focus of the regional initiatives, Serge Ravet (2005) has proposed an "ePortfolio city" in which a single ePortfolio represents and helps to enact the capabilities, activities, aspirations, and plans of an entire community. This call echoes the vision of a community ePortfolio with which individuals and their individual self-representations can interact as envisioned by Barbara Cambridge and me (2003).

AUGUSTA COMMUNITY PORTFOLIO

It was with this vision in mind that Barbara, Kathleen Yancey, and I, in our roles as leaders of the Inter/National Coalition for Electronic Portfolio Research, jumped at the opportunity to work with David Joliffe, of the University of Arkansas, and community leaders in Augusta, Arkansas to build and study the Augusta Community Portfolio (ACP). Still in its early stages, we intend the ACP to represent the capabilities, history, and desired future directions of the town as a whole through exhibits featuring the products of residents' literate activity and their individual and collective reflections upon them.

The ACP builds on two years of the work of the Augusta Community Literacy Advocacy Initiative. The Initiative has achieved impressive results in a relatively short time. Based out of the White River Rural Health clinic, with which many of the potential literacy activity participants already have a valued relationship, the Initiative has worked extensively with local schools, the county library, and several churches, work coordinated by Joy Lynn Bowen, a retired teacher with seemingly limitless energy and deep roots in the community. Through the partnerships the Initiative has engaged students in oral history work that has produced plays and poems, improved the reading skills of new mothers alongside their children, paired younger members with elders to write about the meaning of church life, help community members compose stories and gather documentation of the experiences of WWII-era veterans, and raised awareness of the centrality of reading and writing in community life through distributing books and information in doctor's and dentists' office and in many other businesses throughout Augusta. Public celebrations of achievement feature prominently into many of these initiatives, reflecting such events' central role in building community identity in rural communities (Procter, 2005). In choosing this distributed approach, the Initiative builds on recent research that shows that multiple sponsors, not just schools and families but a wide range of institutions and cultural traditions, shape the development of literacy over the course of a lifetime (Brandt, 2001). Engaging multiple sponsors of literacy has led to measurable results. In two years, the number of graduating seniors at Augusta High School admitted into college rose from three to 33.

To date, most of the Initiative's work has focused on print-based literacies. An eventual goal of the ACP project is engaging residents of Augusta in cultivating their digital literacies as well, combining audio, video, hyperlinks, and interactivity with text to effectively communicate with their audiences. An exhibit within the ACP, Augusta@College, is a first step in this direction. Students from Augusta in their first year of college are blogging about their experiences, including posting videos they have made using cameras provided by the project. By reading and commenting on their peers' posts, the students support each other as they transition into college life. The blog provides residents of Augusta, particularly high school students, with the opportunity to learn about the realities of college life, perhaps making the prospect of enrolling after graduation less intimidating. It is one thing to get more students admitted into college and universities; it is another to get them to go and then to graduate. While helping students and residents work with multiple media and interact online and develop important digital literacy skills, we hope Augusta@College also helps address this larger challenge.

Primarily because I was the person involved in the project with the most appropriate media and coding skills, I designed the first version of the ACP in consultation with leaders of the various existing literacy projects, drawing on artifacts produced by participants. In addition to Augusta@College, three additional exhibits focus, respectively, on the Delta Oral History Project, through which advanced high school students researched local history and produced creative works based on their research; the Soundtracks of My Life project, which asked younger students to create and annotate selections of music that expressed their identities; and the Augusta Veterans' Stories project, which involved a diverse group of residents in composing stories and gathering artifacts to represent the experiences of veterans from Woodruff County. Each exhibit is an interactive Flash movie in which selected documents, such as the veterans' stories, and complementary images, such as the cover artwork of the Soundtracks, are combined with video clips. In the videos project participants reflect on the processes of composing the texts, their meaning, and what they have to say about the present and future of Augusta. The ACP also links to pieces of writing contributed by individual Augusta residents to the National Council of Teachers of English's National Gallery of Writing. Rather than being natively digital creations, most of the initial exhibits remediate the print based activity and artifacts into an attractive and usable digital form (Bolter & Grusin, 1999).

The video sections of the exhibits are one form of reflection within the portfolio, focusing on the interpretations of participants in the literacy projects. Readers can join the site, adding their photos to those of other members on the ePortfolio's main page, comment on exhibits, respond to the comments of other members, and link to other websites that provide additional perspectives. The connections between the physical space that defines the community and the new virtual space created by the ePortfolio is emphasized through having the primary entry point to the exhibits be an interactive map that displays the geographical locations of the literacy work across the county. This map-based interface was suggested and enthusiastically received by Initiative participants.

The expert-produced exhibit media and visual interface, the tightly integrated and customized interactive social software functionality, and the map combine to give the ACP a professional, technically sophisticated feel. To a reasonable extent, it seems to be on par with what many Web sites residents see as high profile and cutting edge, particularly when compared with other representations of Augusta found online. In the contemporary culture of the US, representation in media is a powerful means of validating knowledge and identity (Miller & Shepherd, 2004). See also Shepherd and Goggin (2012). Towns like Augusta—indeed, much of rural and lower class America—are almost invisible on the Web. In its design, the ACP makes the implicit argument that the experiences and achievements of all Augusta residents are on par with those of communities and individuals with greater access to the Internet, which shapes what many see as real and valuable.

A DIFFERENT KIND OF MUSEUM

The use of "exhibits" throughout this brief description of the initial iteration of the ACP points to the importance the museum metaphor has played in our thinking so far. David Joliffe first suggested it on our first trip to Augusta to introduce the concept of a community ePortfolio to participants in the literacy initiative. As discussed in the opening section, making public, validating, and enabling reflection about the products of activity is also at the heart of ePortfolio practice, so the conceptual jump from museum to ePortfolio appears straightforward.

However, one of the challenges of employing the museum metaphor to help residents of Augusta understand the idea of a community ePortfolio is the problem of ownership. Traditionally, historical and anthropological museums have been designed and curated by academic experts from outside of the culture being represented (Archuleta, 2008; Griffin, 2007; Isaac, 2008). In contrast, portfolios have traditionally been designed and composed primarily by the people who are also their subjects, and the author's ownership of the portfolio is generally considered a central principle of good practice, both from ethical and pragmatic standpoints (Joint Information Systems Committee, 2009; Yancey, 2004). While a museum is designed about you, you design an ePortfolio about yourself. Although the initial version of the ACP was largely expert-designed, we want it to become increasingly the product of community members' reflection, deliberation, and composition, for the residents to feel that they themselves are the designers and owners of the ePortfolio.

In order to encourage residents to begin making this conceptual shift, at the launch of the ACP at the Woodruff County Educational Forum in August 2009, I used an analogy to the National Museum of the American Indian to suggest that a different kind "museum" was possible for Augusta. The National Museum of the American Indian (NMAI) opened in September 2004, occupying the last remaining spot on the National Mall in Washington, DC. The mission and design of the museum was the product of extensive consultations with Native leaders and community members from throughout the Americas. Rather than presenting primarily what expert anthropologists or art historians believe is important about American Indian culture and notable in the museum's extensive collection of artifacts, the NMAI seeks to offer a genuinely indigenous perspective (Archuleta, 2008; C. Smith, 2005). Beyond just consultations in the planning stages, the NMAI embraced a community curation model in which groups of community members from the nations profiled in the museum's exhibits collaborated with NMAI staff throughout the design process, choosing the stories and objects to be featured, deciding how they are arranged, and offering their interpretations through written labels and video commentary (Lamar, 2008; P. C. Smith, 2008). In addition, members of the native communities serve as cultural interpreters at the museum itself, interacting with visitors through guiding tours and conducting other programming. While certainly not the first museum to adopt the community curation model, the NMAI is unique in its scale and international visibility (Lonetree, 2008).

Analogously, we hope that future exhibits within the ACP will be curated by teams of participants in the Augusta Community Literacy Initiative's projects. While experts on portfolios, media production, and Web development will certainly continue to play a role in building the portfolio, we hope that our job will be to facilitate reflection that catalyzes the groups' visions for their contributions to the portfolio and to provide technical assistance as needed to translate those visions into compelling digital texts.

ANALOGOUS TENSIONS

In the five years since its opening, the NMAI has produced an outpouring of popular and scholarly commentary, including numerous newspaper and magazine reviews, scholarly articles in multiple disciplines, special issues of several journals, and an edited collection. These critical perspectives run the gamut from highly celebratory to flatly dismissive. The tensions scholars have identified in their analyses of the NMAI also warrant consideration as we continue the development of the ACP. In fact, these tensions map to key debates about ePortfolio practice more generally. While the analogy to the NMAI cannot offer resolutions, it can help to identify key questions we must consider as we move forward.

HERITAGE VERSUS HISTORY

Much of the critical commentary on the NMAI focuses on the respective roles and responsibilities of the American Indian curators representing their communities and the professional curators employed by the Smithsonian with whom they collaborated. While sections of each exhibit are curated by professionals, most exhibits include sections that are curated by groups of members of the communities on which they focus. For example, the Our People exhibit, which presents a historical perspective on American Indian culture, includes a central display that frames the exhibit as a whole, surrounded by installations focusing on eight different native Nations. These installations were designed in close collaboration between the staff and the community curators, and the community members made the final decisions about what to include and what to foreground. Many critics, particularly in the popular press, saw the exhibits as "unscholarly" or even "random," failing to provide a single, authoritative curatorial voice that would enable viewers to "judge" the perspectives offered by community members and as neglecting items from the collection that they deemed more objectively important than those chosen by community members (Fisher, 2004; Richard, 2004; Rothstein, 2004). The exhibits do indeed differ from the conventions of traditional museums in presenting multiple voices and styles of presentation, many unfamiliar, and in choosing not to judge which are more truthful or significant.

In addition, critics saw most of the community-curated exhibits not as honest reflections about the history and current cultural state of the native nations but as purely celebratory "sales booths" within a museum-wide "trade show" that failed to represent the very real problems facing the communities and glossing over the conflicts within them to present a falsely unified voice (Fisher, 2004). To some extent, the reflections of NMAI staff curators working on the exhibits support this interpretation. For example, Cynthia Chavez Lamar (2008, pp. 147-148) reports that the design process of a number of the nations' contributions led to candid discussions about restrictive gender roles and concerns about youth engagement, but "these frank, difficult representations of the communities proved prohibitive to include in the exhibit for various reasons. Considered sensitive topics by some of the co-currators, they felt the inclusion might be perceived as 'airing dirty laundry.'" Because of the hard-won trust she had established, she did not feel it was "within [her] authority or conscience to include sensitive information" the community curators did not wish to become public, even if it would have made for a more engaging exhibit.

Views on the appropriate balance of power of making decisions about the museum's content and design reflect different understandings of the purpose of a museum and the source interpretive authority. Stephen Conn (2006, p. 72) quotes the historian David Lowenthal to distinguish between history and heritage: "History tells all who will listen what has happened and how things came to be as they are. Heritage passes on exclusive myths of origin and continuance, endowing a select group with prestige and common purpose." Conn argues that what the NMAI is really doing is cultivating American Indian heritage while trying to pass that off as history. In foregrounding Native voices, Conn is certainly right that part of the NMAI's mission is to support a sense of pride and agency on the part of American Indians.

However, his assumptions that doing so is necessarily at odds with history and that heritage is intended only for insiders and not an appropriate focus of a museum are problematic. Like many of the other critics, Conn does not see the non-academic community members who co-curated the exhibits as true authorities on their own history and culture. Exhibits produced through community consensus are presumed to lack objectivity. However, many supporters of the museum see its message as an important corrective to how the Americas' indigenous people have been represented in Western history and anthropology, particularly through museums that have often cast them as frozen in their ancient culture and passive victims of inevitable historical forces of colonization. Much of the museum is centered on Gerald Vizenor's concept of "survivance," highlighting the ways in which Indians have embraced change and continued to develop their cultural heritage within the settler society while also resisting their displacement, assimilation, and extermination. While this narrative theme does indeed celebrate continuance and cultivate a sense of common identity and purpose, it is also an important corrective to an inaccurate Western historical tradition (Atalay, 2008; Lonetree, 2008). The NMAI is hardly unique in advancing both heritage and history through a museum. Although more commonly local on focus, many of the numerous "heritage museums" throughout the United States attempt to present historical narratives both grounded in evidence and foregrounding the achievements and shared identity of a community (Katriel, 1993; Procter, 2005).

Conn objects not only on behalf of his understanding of historical accuracy but also on aesthetic grounds. The absence of accounts of controversy within communities is particularly troublesome to him because this "is the only thing that is interesting in the first place" to a non-native audience (Conn, 2006, p. 72). A museum needs to tell a good, as well as truthful, story, and doing so requires the narrative skill of a professional curator. Supporters of the museum, in contrast, explain its distinctively indigenous style of storytelling. Invoking Leslie Marmon Silko's account of Pueblo storytelling, Elizabeth Archuletta (2008, p. 190) suggests that, rather than offering a single, linear path, "museum curators structured their displays like 'many little threads' of a spider's web, each strand adding to the larger picture, radiating out from the center that is the NMAI." Properly understood, this alternative narrative structure can be powerful for both native and non-native audiences. However, it does ask more from the viewer than a traditional museum, an issue to which I will return.

FAILURE, AUTHENTICITY, AND MULTIPLICITY IN EPORTFOLIOS

In charting the future directions of the ACP, we are faced with analogous issues. Like many of the community curators of the NMAI, residents and leaders of Augusta are likely to be reluctant to foreground conflicts and controversies within the community in the ePortfolio, to "air dirty laundry." Some of those already investing their energy in its development see it primarily as a celebration of the successes of the literacy work and as a means to demonstrate that Augusta has an educated workforce to businesses that might choose to set up shop there. At present, the ACP focuses overwhelmingly on the most compelling outputs of the Augusta Community Literacy Advocacy Initiative, and the reflections of participants are almost uniformly positive. As in some parts of the NMAI, failures and setbacks—such as the difficulty in locating funding for the planned Woodruff County Veteran's Memorial, with which the unveiling of the Veteran's Stories project's publication was originally conceived to coincide—are glossed over if they are mentioned at all.

Should a community portfolio be primarily a showcase of achievements, or should it try to offer a broader perspective on community activity, including conflict, controversies, and deficits? In order for the ACP to be successful, all of us engaging in developing it—academic experts, community leaders, residents, and, perhaps, even visitors to the portfolio from beyond the community—will need to deliberate about what is most desirable and appropriate in the local context. Participants in the Urban University Portfolio Project developing institutional portfolios for colleges and universities faced a similar dilemma to the one we face with ACP. A common topic of discussions during early meetings was the degree to which the portfolios should include evidence of and reflections on things the institutions were not currently doing well. Numerous potential audience members, such as accreditors, members of the media, and policy makers, advised the project participants that their ePortfolios were unlikely to be taken seriously unless they included accounts of deficits as well as strengths. In the end, some institutions chose to present only their successes, while others used their portfolios to also reflect on areas in which they saw the potential for improvement. The institutional portfolios of two of the schools that chose the latter, Indiana University Purdue University Indianapolis and Portland State University, have proved the most successful of those coming out of the project, their development having been sustained over a decade and playing an important role in accreditation (Hamilton, 2002; Kahn, 2001, 2002; Ketcheson, 2001, 2009).

Barbara Cambridge (2001, p. 8) argues that the portfolio genre, whether individually or collectively authored, has the potential to help individuals and institutions develop a more productive relationship to failure. When used well, portfolios can help turn perceived deficiencies into catalysts for innovation, challenging the systems within the academy that punish failure rather than productively address it:

> We all fail sometimes. Even with carefully established goals
> and conscientiously executed work, we do not meet the
> goals because of any number of circumstances. Yet we set
> up systems that condemn students, faculty members, and
> institutions for not meeting goals. Portfolios can be part
> of such systems if we choose to include in them only those
> pieces of evidence that bear good news .... Although we know
> that learning can and often does occur at times of dissonance
> or moments of difficulty, we look there not for the learning
> but for the problems.

Cambridge goes on to suggest that portfolios that do incorporate evidence of lack of success can do so in ways that promote individual and institutional learning through providing context. First, in portfolios, it is possible to provide explanations that help authors and audiences to understand what factors are responsible and to imagine ways in which they might transform them to prepare for future success. Second, because good portfolios include multiple and heterogeneous sources of evidence collected over time, less successful performances can be presented in relationship to more successful ones. By acknowledging the reality of imperfection and contextualizing failure within a structure that celebrates success, that affirmative message becomes both more useful and more convincing.

Some of the work featured in the initial version of the ACP does begin to employ these strategies. While a number of Augusta students allude to hardships they have experienced in the "liner notes" that accompany their Soundtracks, such as difficult relationships with multiple foster parents and the challenges of living in poverty, these are framed in terms of their success in overcoming them. These are stories of a kind of survivance that are powerful in large part because they provide the context to understand what the students have survived. In planning future activities focused on such texts, we should consider ways to help students reflect critically about how the stories they wish to tell for public consumption match the concrete reality of their current situations and future prospects. Whether such reflections should become part of the portfolio itself is another question that I return to below.

A second, related issue that the ACP shares with NMAI is the degree to which the artifacts chosen by community members curating exhibits within the portfolios and the reflective narratives they compose about them are authoritative accounts of the literate activity the exhibits are intended to represent. Do the community members' self-representations need to be validated by some external authority to be credible? Will their self-assessments bear weight? In what sense can we expect their writing and reflecting to speak for itself without the need for expert commentary? Many of the answers may hinge on whether the purpose of the portfolio is to celebrate the heritage and contemporary achievements of the community or present a more academic account of the community's history and level of literacy.

The scholarship on the NMAI surveyed above suggests that we may not need to pick one over the other. While the primary purpose of the portfolio may be to highlight accomplishments, showcase notable texts, and give voice to community experiences, making such evidence of literate activity in Augusta visible online in a compelling fashion may also contribute to providing a more accurate assessment of the town's fortunes and potential than is currently available to the audiences the community hopes to reach, such as potential new business owners, political leaders, philanthropic foundation officers, and residents themselves.

The tradition of ePortfolios in education also supports the validity of community members' own selections and interpretations. Yancey (1998) suggests that portfolio pedagogy and assessment is fundamentally grounded in the premise that "students are authoritative informants about their own learning." Some of the most important aspects of learning and identity development can only be made visible to the learners themselves. As Ross' (2006) review demonstrates, that self-assessment can be both accurate and contribute to strengthening learning, engagement, and motivation has been shown in numerous studies. As Barbara Cambridge (2001) argues, portfolios can be more convincing and more accurate because they allow for context, providing reflective explanations and juxtaposing multiple, heterogeneous evidence of differing levels of quality to present an account of progress that does not discount challenges and missteps along the way.

In my own work, I show that much of contemporary ePortfolio practice is grounded in the cultural ideal of authenticity—the idea that each person, and perhaps each community, may have distinctive ways of knowing and taking action that are most appropriate to themselves and that knowledge making and decision making ought to be shaped by that distinctiveness (D. Cambridge,

2010). While this ideal, prominent in Western culture since Romanticism, has been criticized for its apparent solipsism, I argue, following contemporary philosophers such as Charles Taylor, Bernard Williams, and Charles Guignon, that authenticity can be reconceived as firmly grounded in social relationships and commitments (Guignon, 2004; Taylor, 1989, 1991; Williams, 2002). When the ideal of authenticity is extended from individual to collective identity and action, this social dimension becomes inescapable. Procter (2005, p. 147) suggests that one key form of community building in rural communities is "the rhetoric of grace," which appeals to the distinctiveness of community identity and the opportunities that present themselves at the moment of collective reflection. The development of the ACP presents a powerful opportunity to capitalize on and further develop a social understanding of authenticity's power to chart the course of a community.

The ACP also shares with the NMAI the lack of a master narrative. Even more so than in the museum, portfolio visitors face the choice of what to view, in what order, and are not offered an expert voice that tells them how to interpret what they are experiencing. As is often the case of with personalized individual ePortfolios, and more so than in other self-representations such as résumé or transcripts, the audience needs to play an active role in making meaning from the exhibits (Hartnell-Young et al., 2006). While in individual ePortfolios, coherence is often achieved through the consistency of the author's voice throughout, a community portfolio such as the ACP includes a multiplicity of voices. Like the NMAI, the ACP does not judge which of these multiple perspectives is most truthful or authoritative. Unlike in the NMAI, this multivocal structure does not originate in the indigenous ways of knowing of the community; rather, it is a characteristic of the ePortfolio genre introduced by the experts working with community members on the design.

While the hypertextual organization of ePortfolios, and the corresponding role of audience choice in reading, is a central characteristic of the genre, many ePortfolios do include a central narrative that helps the reader make sense of its contents (Yancey, 2001). For example, many ePortfolios created for writing assessment include a "cover letter" that reflects on and explains the relationships between the different samples of writing incorporated (Hamp-Lyons & Condon, 2000). Many institutional portfolios, such as those discussed above, include text that summarizes the portfolio's content and purpose and guides the reader through it (Kahn, 2001).

Therefore, another question for the future of the ACP is whether we need a guiding narrative and to what extent it should make judgments about the multiple texts and perspectives the ePortfolio encompasses. If such a master narrative is necessary, how can it be composed in a way that honors the community's ownership of the ePortfolio? What kind of deliberative process is needed to determine which voices and artifacts are privileged and which are questioned? The answers may depend on what we decide is the most appropriate relationship to the ACP's audiences, an issue discussed below.

CELEBRATION VERSUS CRITICAL REFLECTION

In contrast to the popular critiques of the NMAI, many scholars of American Indian history and culture are sympathetic to some of the alterative processes and formats embraced by the museum, seeing their roots in native ways of knowing. However, some these more appreciative researchers criticize the NMAI for what they see as a significant failure of those processes and formats to deliver on the goal of representing American Indian survivance. The museum fails to present a clear account of the history and contemporary consequences of colonialism (Atalay, 2008; Carpio, 2008; Lonetree, 2006, 2008). Without such an account, there is insufficient historical context for visitors to truly appreciate the fierce American Indian resistance to colonialism.

For example, while the Our Peoples exhibit seeks to frame the historical narratives of the native nations it profiles in terms of an overarching story of the impacts of contact, visually it does so primarily through abstraction (Lonetree, 2008). It offers display cases of numerous guns, gold artifacts, bibles, and treaties, representing the impact of violence on native communities, the immense transfer for wealth to Europeans, the influence of Christianity on the education and spiritual lives of American Indians, and the role of legal agreements in curtailing but also to some extent protecting Indian rights. Unlike the National Holocaust Museum, which one of the exhibit's curators cites as an inspiration, there are no literal displays of this impact, such as photographs of slaughtered Indians or blankets laced with smallpox (P. C. Smith, 2008). While some of the labels that accompany the cases of artifacts do cite dramatic decreases in native population, the damage to Native religious traditions wrought by enforced Christianity, and specific instances of violence and broken treaties, they are unlikely to make clear to visitors that these negative consequences stemmed from explicit policies of the governments of Western nations, particularly the United States, to displace, disinherit, and either assimilate or annihilate the Native peoples of the Americas. Outright resistance, as opposed to negotiation, is marginalized. For example, the American Indian Movement, a powerful adversarial force for change through much of the 1960s and 1970s, receives only a single, passing reference.

In other words, according to the critics, while the NMAI to some extent represents the negative impacts of colonization, it treats it as disembodied and inevitable, something that must be dealt with rather than rejected. In trying to portray American Indians as active shapers of their history, rather than victims of oppression, it actually renders them subjects of fate (Brady, 2008). This is an empty sort of agency, one that does little to help empower visitors to challenge the legacies of colonialism at the root of many of the problems facing Native people today. Some fear that the museum offers a shallow kind of reconciliation between settler society and indigenous people, pushing for historical closure through official recognition of the value of contemporary Native culture without assuming responsibility for substantively addressing the negative legacies of colonialism (Wakeham, 2008).

The ACP faces a similar dilemma. The ePortfolio makes visible and celebrates the creative responses of the Augusta community to low levels of literacy of many residents. Rather than simply accepting the lack of an educated workforce or their state as underdeveloped readers and writers, residents and community leaders have made impressive strides toward increasing the quantity and sophistication of literate activity throughout the town. In many cases, evidence of this reading and writing is accompanied in the portfolio by moving reflections on the experience of participating in this collective act of cultivating learning. However, there is little as yet in the ACP that explores the root causes of the situation that drove the Augustans into action. That situation arguably is the result, for example, of several decades of neo-liberal policies of globalization and corporate welfare that led to the decline of the Arkansas Delta's agricultural economy and the current focus on attracting non-unionized factories, for which an "educated workforce" is presumably necessary. The state of the educational system also likely reflects the legacy of segregation. Portfolio contributors testify to their impressive efforts to cope with change, but they do not yet question the inevitability of that change. That the ACP does not take a critical stance is typical of events and spaces in rural America intended to cultivate community. Because of their institutional sponsorship, they are generally conservative in nature, reifying existing power structures (Procter, 2005, p. 144). Whether or not residents reflecting on their community in the ACP should be questioning the sources of the structural inequalities with which they are coping, and, if so, how to encourage them do so while also honoring their ownership of the portfolio, remain open questions for me.

The distinction between the largely celebratory reflection currently evident in the ACP and the kind it, and the NMAI, currently lack is similar to the distinction between reflection in general and critical reflection made by prominent scholars of adult education (Brookfield, 1986, 1995; Freire, 1970; Mezirow, 1990). While learners are often encouraged to reflect on how well their performance matches measures of quality established by institutional authority or traditional practice within a discipline or domain, or to make connections between concepts they are asked to learn and their personal experience, critical reflection goes further to question the assumptions underlying the choice of measures and concepts. Through critical reflection learners question the justifications of the power relationships they uncover, and ask whether and how they could be transformed.

Many experts see critical reflection as the ideal for reflection within ePortfolios, albeit an ideal that often gets left behind in actual practice (Delandshere & Arens, 2003). Particularly in professional education and in relationship to learning beyond the classroom, projects at institutions such as the University of Wolverhampton, Virginia Tech, and the University of Michigan have developed pedagogies that are proving successful in moving learners toward genuinely critical reflection (Hughes, 2009; Peet, 2005; Young, 2009). For example, at Michigan, students learn "generative interviewing," a technique for helping them make their tacit knowledge of how social systems work explicit through dialog in order to envision avenues for change their abilities position them to take.

However, some research on reflection also suggests that the ability to effectively reflect critically may be a developmental, requiring preexisting skill at other, simpler forms of reflection (Broadbank & McGill, 2007). It may be that critical reflection should indeed be a goal of the ACP, but one that requires a level of readiness that the community needs to develop through reflective practice over time (Pitts & Ruggierillo, 2012). Expecting ePortfolio contributors to immediately jump into critical reflection may be a mistake. At the same time, any postponement must be planned carefully so as to not offer at ACP, or even the Literacy Advocacy Initiative more generally, as a celebratory false reconciliation, as a substitute for government policy reforms to address the problems of the town and the region. The ideal goals of the work should be transformative rather than therapeutic.

TEXT, ACTIVITY, AND AUDIENCE

The success of the ACP in reaching its goals will in large part be determined by how effectively the portfolio engages its audience. Issues of audience engagement constitute a final theme in the critical conversation about the NMAI. Defenders of the museum accuse its detractors of failing to appreciate the ways in which the museum is designed to facilitate audience experiences differently than traditional museums.

A first difference is that activities beyond simply viewing the exhibits are central to the museum's intended function. Douglas Evelyn (2006, p. 54), past associate director of the NMAI, points to the activities that the museum mediates as equal in importance to the static content of its exhibits. The museum maintains an intensive, ongoing relationship with numerous indigenous nations, hosts large-scale events attended by both Indians and non-Indians, and features numerous educational activities led by indigenous cultural interpreters, as well as frequent guest artists and speakers from throughout the Americas. Evelyn rightly objects to critics evaluating the museum solely on the basis of the content of its exhibits, discounting the activities the museum mediates. When my own students wrote about their visit to the NMAI on a course fieldtrip this fall, they pointed to their dialog with tour guides and artists offering demonstrations as among the most powerful learning experiences of the day.

I have already touched upon the second difference between the NMAI and a traditional museum. Audience members are challenged to be active meaning makers rather than passive receivers of expert-authorized truth. In contrast to the approach of reviewers who singled out artifacts or texts in isolation from the larger contexts into which they were incorporated, for audience members to take full advantage of the exhibits, they need to consider them holistically, examining the elements that make them up in relationship to all the others within the exhibit and to the museum as a whole (C. Smith, 2005). As previously noted, many scholars connect this style of museum design to indigenous ways of knowing and to Native narrative traditions, as a challenge to museums' role as instiller of the conventions of Western historical and anthropological discourse. Some also see it as a critique of the modernist conception of a single historical truth, offering an alternative version of historical interpretation that foregrounds the role of the audience member in making situated meaning (Isaac, 2008).

On the other hand, some scholars who do understand the transformative intentions and indigenous cultural grounding of the exhibits nevertheless question whether this design is likely to be successful in reaching non-Native audiences, or, indeed, even Native audience members without an academic understanding of American Indian storytelling and poststructuralist critiques of historical knowledge. Given that addressing a broad audience of visitors to the National Mall, including both American Indians and non-natives from numerous countries around the world is central to the NMAI's mission, it may not be wise to demand so much work from visitors. As Amy Lonetree (2008, p. 311) puts it:

> Is this really an effective way to present Native American history and culture to a nation and world with a willed ignorance of this history of [genocide and colonialism]? Or a

society that carries with them so many stereotypes about who we are as Indigenous people and to a nation that has defined itself by "playing Indian"?

By leaving so much of the interpretive work to visitors, the NMAI runs the risk of having its objects and narratives "hijacked" in service of ethnocentric stereotypes of _Indianess_ and an ideology of manifest destiny. These scholars point out that museum research shows that visitors vary considerably in the amount of time and energy they are willing to invest in taking in exhibits and that they choose different styles of engagement (Atalay, 2008). The more casual visitors, like the initial newspaper reviewers, may either dismiss the NMAI in its current form as unscholarly and incoherent, or, worse, ascribe to it ideas that work against its mission.

These debates can inform the design the ACP. First, the issue of interpreting the NMAI by its content versus also taking into account the activity it mediates raises several important questions: How much of the reflective and self-representational activity that the ACP project produces ought to be incorporated into, or occur within, the portfolio itself? In what sense might the activities that the ACP mediates count as part of the portfolio, even if ephemeral and producing no tangible record?

Like the NMAI, a goal of the ACP is not just to showcase artifacts and stories but also to be a forum through which community and audience members can engage in reflective dialog. When records of that dialog are preserved and incorporated into the content of the ACP itself, the portfolio will arguably become a more transparent—and so, perhaps, more credible—representation of the process of community deliberation and identity building. Both live and archived, the presence of community members' voices within the portfolio made possible through its social software functionality becomes central to its message. The full meaning of the portfolio comes not just from the content of the exhibits but also from the conversations that surround them.

Research on ePortfolios has shown that the conversations and events they mediate can be as important to understanding and learning from them as their content. Perhaps the most important contribution of the ePortfolio systems that have been developed and implemented over the last decade is the ability for multiple audiences to provide feedback within the portfolio space and to have that feedback become available to be used as part of the author's self-representation (Lane, 2009). Offline, institutions and programs have successfully used individual conferences with students and public presentations of their portfolios to engage audiences in dialog (Yancey, Cambridge, & Cambridge, 2009). These conversations are sometimes recorded in order to become part of the students' ePortfolios. Some institutions, such as LaGuardia Community College, have even established physical spaces, ePortfolio studios, within which such dialog can be supported (Eynon, 2009).

At the same time, stressing the often highly personal nature of reflection, many ePortfolio teachers and learners value the ability to share portfolio content selectively offered by ePortfolio systems and similar database-driven technology for managing and sharing content. The principle of ownership suggests that portfolio authors need to decide for themselves how public to make their reflections and self-representations. While some ePortfolios are published on the open Web, others are shared only with a select group of peers, mentors, or potential employers. Portfolio authors often benefit from bouncing ideas off of each other, sharing work in progress, and receiving encouragement from a group with which they have established a trusting relationship (D. Cambridge, 2008).

Research on supporting groups in developing capacity to pursue collaborative inquiries into their own practice and to participate in public deliberations points to the importance of what the rhetorician Rosa Eberly (2000) terms "protopublic spaces," in which individuals can share their private experiences and ideas with trusted others and develop the skills they need to present them effectively in more fully public forums. In their analysis of faculty communities in the scholarship of teaching and learning, Randy Bass and Dan Bernstein (2008) call such interstices between the privacy of the classroom and the publicity of scholarly publication "middle spaces" and stress their essential role.

A question for the ACP going forward is how to create such trusted spaces for dialog. One option is to create spaces for social interaction within the social software functions of the portfolio only accessible to certain groups, such as verified residents of Augusta or members of the community teams developing exhibits. Face-to-face events provide another opportunity. We plan to host a series of community reflection events in which members of the community come together to view and talk about the contents of the portfolio and what it says about the history, identity, and future of the community. While it may make sense to record some such events for integration into the ACP, others might remain ephemeral, limiting how widely what was said is shared. We will have to think carefully about how to balance the need for a safe space for open discussion and the desire to make community process visible.

The second challenge the NMAI controversy about audience and activity raises for the ACP is how to balance fidelity to the conventions of the ePortfolio genre with the expectations and motivations of the audiences the portfolio is intended to address. My own recent scholarship has focused on demonstrating how the ePortfolio genre powerfully addresses needs for lifelong learning and identity development that individuals and institutions face in contemporary Western society (D. Cambridge, 2010). My collaborators and I chose to develop the collective representation of literacy in Augusta as an ePortfolio, rather than some other digital genre, because we believe the genre also has the potential to address similar needs of communities. However, it may need to adjust to the new context in order to have the desired impact.

My empirical research on the eFolio Minnesota project shows that one of the two most important factors predicting a self-reported high level of impact of composing an ePortfolio in learning and identity is what I term integrity (D. Cambridge, 2008). An ePortfolio has integrity when it helps its author show coherence across multiple life contexts and roles, such as career, family life, and civic engagements. An ePortfolio with integrity helps its author demonstrate how his or her core commitments are consistently evidenced by his or her activity across these boundaries and to reflect on conflicts and inconsistencies when they do occur, helping him or her plan for future action that is true to those commitments. Through its ability both to incorporate diverse artifacts from multiple contexts and to draw interpretive connections between them, the ePortfolio genre appears to be well suited to helping individuals articulate integrity to their own satisfaction.

Achieving integrity to one's own satisfaction through the process of composition does not necessarily mean that the resulting portfolio will prove effective in communicating that integrity to an audience. Even some of the most compellingly integral ePortfolios require significant work on the part of the audience to grasp how the whole is more than the sum of the parts. For example, Samantha Slade, an instructional designer in Montreal, composed an ePortfolio to "find the thread in [her] life," to articulate integrity. At first look, the portfolio appears to consist of arbitrarily ordered lists of competencies, skills, activities, work products, and assorted videos about Slade's experiences and beliefs. However, when these elements are considered not in isolation but as part of an integral whole, the portfolio presents a powerful story of how Slade's commitment to creating resource-rich social environments for learning not only informs her diverse professional engagements but also shapes the way she interacts with her family and participates in her community (D. Cambridge, 2010). Like the NMAI, portfolios such as Slade's require a level of engagement that many casual visitors may not be motivated to invest.

For the ACP, another compelling characteristic of the ePortfolio genre is its ability to link up diverse types of artifacts and reflection. Like NMAI, we hope that the ACP will speak with many voices that represent the range of experiences and values of the people of Augusta. Yet this very multivocality can work at cross-purposes with the goals of representing integrity and connecting with multiple audiences. Finding consistency and coherence across a single life is difficult enough. As the ePortfolio genre moves from individual to collective, this challenge intensifies. Again we face the question of how to maintain multiple voices without imposing an unrepresentative master narrative while still providing enough orientation for the audience to appreciate the whole.

While the best ePortfolios have traditionally asked a lot of readers, in practice they have also been adapted in order to meet successfully the needs of the audiences to which they are addressed. This often entails compromises about the depth of reflection, range of artifacts, and distinctiveness of design (Hartnell-Young et al., 2006; Kimball, 2006). It may be possible to better accommodate audiences through providing explicit guidance on how to read the ePortfolio for readers unfamiliar with its purposes and structure, such as through the "readers guide" that is sometimes suggested by faculty as a useful component of student portfolios. Scholars have suggested that the NMAI could become more accessible by making it clear to visitors as they enter exhibits the logic behind the choice and arrangement of artifacts and the context of indigenous ways of knowing that informs those choices (Atalay, 2008). Similarly, the ACP might include on its homepage an account of how it differs from other community websites, why the design serves the goals of literacy project participants, and why it might prove worthwhile for readers to engage with it despite its unfamiliar form.

I hope we can achieve a balanced relationship between community ePortfolio authors and readers, developing design and content that both provides audiences with immediate value and convinces them to stretch a bit beyond their comfort zone to create a more powerful experience. I hope that we will both take advantage of the potential of the ePortfolio genre for literacy learning and community building but also not be afraid to depart from it when it doesn't serve our purposes. The same balance of fidelity and flexibility would be welcome in the process of composing individual portfolios and in the design of museums.

UNITY AND DIFFERENCE

The metaphor of portfolio as museum was powerful for envisioning and launching the Augusta Community Portfolio project. The analogy to the National Museum of the American Indian has the potential to help guide it into maturity. Through evoking unity between the familiar and novel, metaphors provide an active, immediate entry point into a new domain. Analogies, in contrast, acknowledge difference alongside similarity. They honor the complexity of situated identity and practice. As the ePortfolio field matures, transforming from a marginal innovation into a pervasive practice, it may also want to shift its focus from metaphors for ePortfolios in general to analogies that capture the complexity of specific contexts and purposes.

REFERENCES

Archuleta, E. (2008). Gym shoes, maps, and passports, oh my!: Creating community or creating chaos at the National Museum of the American Indian? In A. Lonetree, & A. J. Cobb (Eds.), *The National Museum of the American Indian: Critical conversations* (pp. 181-207). Lincoln, NE: University of Nebraska Press.

Atalay, S. (2008). No sense of struggle: Creating a context for survivance at the National Museum of the American Indian. In A. Lonetree, & A. J. Cobb (Eds.), *The National Museum of the American Indian: Critical conversations* (pp. 267-290). Lincoln, NE: University of Nebraska Press.

Barrett, H. (2009). Metaphors for portfolios. Retrieved from http://electronic-portfolios.com/metaphors.html

Barrett, H., & Carney, J. (2005). Conflicting paradigms and competing purposes in electronic portfolio development. Retrieved from http://electronic-portfolios.com/portfolios/LEAJournal-BarrettCarney.pdf

Bass, R., & Eynon, B. (2009, March 18). Electronic portfolios: A path to the future of learning. *The Chronicle of Higher Education.* Retrieved from http://chronicle.com/blogPost/Electronic-Portfolios-a-Path/4582

Bolter, J. D., & Grusin, R. (1999). *Remediation: Understanding new media.* Cambridge, MA: MIT Press.

Brady, M. J. (2008). Governmentality and the National Museum of the American Indian: Understanding the indigenous museum in a settler society. *Social Identities, 14*(6), 763-773.

Brandt, D. (2001). *Literacy in American lives.* New York: Cambridge University Press.

Broadbank, A., & McGill, I. (2007). *Facilitating reflective learning in higher education* (2nd ed.). Milton Keynes, England: Open University Press.

Brookfield, S. (1995). *Becoming a critically reflective teacher.* San Francisco: Jossey-Bass.

Brookfield, S. (1986). *Understanding and facilitating adult learning.* San Francisco: Jossey-Bass.

Cambridge, B. (Ed.). (2001). *Electronic portfolios: Emerging practices in student, faculty, and institutional learning.* Washington, DC: American Association for Higher Education.

Cambridge, D. (2008). Audience, integrity, and the living document: Efolio Minnesota and lifelong and lifewide learning with ePortfolios. *Computers & Education, 51*(3), 1227-1246.

Cambridge, D. (2010). *Eportfolios for lifelong learning and deliberative assessment.* San Francisco: Jossey-Bass.

Cambridge, D., & Cambridge, B. (2003, October). *The future of ePortfolio technology: Supporting what we know about learning.* Paper presented at the ePortfolio Conference, Portiers, France.

Carpio, M. V. (2008). (Un)disturbing exhibitions: Indigenous historical memory at the National Museum of the American Indian. In A. Lonetree, & A. J. Cobb (Eds.), *The National Museum of the American Indian: Critical conversations* (pp. 305-327). Lincoln, NE: University of Nebraska Press.

Conn, S. (2006). Heritage vs. history at the National Museum of the American Indian. *Public Historian, 28*(2), 69-73.

Delandshere, G., & Arens, S. A. (2003). Examining the quality of the evidence in preservice teacher portfolios. *Journal of Teaching Education, 54*(1), 57-73.

Dietz, M. (1996). The portfolio: Sonnet, mirror, and map. In K. Burke (Ed.), *Professional portfolios* (pp. 17-26). Arlington Heights, IL: IRI Skylight.

Eberly, R. (2000). *Citizen critics.* Urbana, IL: University of Illinois.

Evelyn, D. E. (2006). The Smithsonian's National Museum of the American Indian: An international institution of living cultures. *Public Historian, 28*(2), 51-55.

Eynon, B. (2009). Making connections: The LaGuardia eportfolio. In D. Cambridge, B. Cambridge, & K. Yancey (Eds.), *Electronic portfolios 2.0: Emergent research on implementation and impact* (pp. 59-68). Sterling, VA: Stylus.

Fisher, M. (2004, September 21). Indian museum's appeal, sadly, only skin deep. *The Washington Post*, p. B01.

Freire, P. (1970). *Pedagogy of the oppressed* (15th ed.). New York: Seebury.

Griffin, R. E. G. (2007). The art of native life: Exhibiting culture and identity at the National Museum of the American Indian. *American Indian Culture and Research Journal, 32*(5), 167-180.

Guignon, C. (2004). *On being authentic.* New York: Routledge.

Hamilton, S. (2002). Red light districts, washing machines, and everything in-between: Creating iport (the IUPUI electronic institutional portfolio). *Metropolitan Universities, 13*(3), 11-21.

Hamp-Lyons, L., & Condon, W. (2000). *Assessing the portfolio: Principles for practice, theory & research.* Cresskill, NJ: Hampton.

Hartnell-Young, E., Smallwood, A., Kingston, S., & Harley, P. (2006). Joining up the episodes of lifelong learning: A regional transition project. *British Journal of Educational Technology, 37*(6), 853-866.

Hughes, J. (2009). Becoming ePortfolio learners and teachers. In D. Cambridge, B. Cambridge, & K. Yancey (Eds.), *Electronic portfolios 2.0: Emergent research on implementation and impact* (pp. 51-58). Sterling, VA: Stylus.

Isaac, G. (2008). What are our expectations telling us? Encounters with the National Museum of the American Indian. In A. Lonetree, & A. J. Cobb (Eds.), *The National Museum of the American Indian: Critical conversations* (pp. 241-266). Lincoln, NE: University of Nebraska Press.

Joint information systems committee. (2009). E-portfolios infokit. Retrieved from http://www.jiscinfonet.ac.uk/e-portfolios

Kahn, S. (2001). Linking learning, improvement, and accountability: An introduction to electronic institutional portfolios. In B. Cambridge (Ed.), *Electronic portfolios: Emerging practices in student, faculty, and institutional learning* (pp. 135-158). Washington, DC: American Association for Higher Education.

Kahn, S. (2002). The urban universities portfolio project: Overview essay. *Metropolitan Universities, 13*(3), 7-10.

Katriel, T. (1993). Our future is where our past is. Studying heritage museums as ideological and performative arenas. *Communication Monographs, 60*(1), 69-75.

Ketcheson, K. A. (2001). Portland state university's electronic institutional portfolio: Strategy, planning, and assessment. In B. Cambridge (Ed.), *Electronic portfolios: Emerging practices in student, faculty, and institutional learning* (pp. 178-191). Washington, DC: American Association for Higher Education.

Ketcheson, K. A. (2009). Sustaining change through student, departmental, and institutional portfolios. In D. Cambridge, B. Cambridge, & K. B. Yancey (Eds.), in *Electronic portfolios 2.0: Emergent research on implementation and impact* (pp.137-144). Sterling, VA: Stylus.

Kimball, M. (2006). Database e-portfolio systems: A critical appraisal. *Computers and Composition, 22*, 434-458.

Kimball, M. (2002). *The web portfolio guide: Creating electronic portfolios for the web*. New York: Longman.

Kirkpatrick, J., Renner, T., Kanae, L., & Goya, K. (2009). A values-driven ePortfolio journey: Nā wa'a. In D. Cambridge, B. Cambridge, & K. Yancey (Eds.), *Electronic portfolios 2.0: Emergent finding and shared questions* (pp. 97-102). Sterling, VA: Stylus.

Lamar, C. C. (2008). Collaborative exhibit development at the Smithsonian's National Museum of the American Indian. In A. Lonetree, & A. J. Cobb (Eds.), *The National Museum of the American Indian: Critical conversations* (pp. 144-164). Lincoln, NE: University of Nebraska Press.

Lane, C. (2009). Technology and change. In D. Cambridge, B. Cambridge, & K. B. Yancey (Eds.), *Electronic portfolios 2.0: Emergent research on implementation and impact* (pp. 149-154). Sterling, VA: Stylus.

le Carpentier, J. L., Groot, R. D., & Wasko, P. (2008, October). *EPortfolio for regions and territories*. Paper presented at the ePortfolio Conference, Maastricht, The Netherlands.

Lonetree, A. (2006). Continuing dialogs: Evolving views of the National Museum of the American Indian. *Public Historian, 28*(2), 57-61.

Lonetree, A. (2008). Acknowledging the truth of history: Missed opportunities at the National Museum of the American Indian. In A. Lonetree, & A. J. Cobb (Eds.), *The National Museum of the American Indian: Critical conversations* (pp. 305-327). Lincoln, NE: University of Nebraska Press.

Mezirow, J. (Ed.). (1990). *Fostering critical reflection in adulthood: A guide to transformative and emancipatory learning*. San Francisco: Jossey-Bass.

Miller, C. R., & Shepherd, D. (2004). Blogging as social action: A genre analysis of the weblog. In L. Gurak, S. Antonijevic, L. Johnson, C. Ratliff, & J. Reyman (Eds.), *Into the blogosphere: Rhetoric, community, and culture of weblogs*. Minneapolis: University of Minnesota Press. Retrieved from http://blog.lib.umn.edu/blogosphere/bloggin_as_social_action.html

Peet, M. (2005). *We make it the road by walking it: Critical consciousness, structuration, and social change school*. Ann Arbor, MI: University of Michigan Press.

Pitts, W. & Ruggierillo, R. 2012). Using the e-portfolio to document and evaluate growth in reflective practice: The development and application of a conceptual framework. *International Journal of ePortfolio. 1*(1). 49-74.

Procter, D. E. (2005). *Civic communion: The rhetoric of community building*. Lanham, MD: Rowan & Littlefield Education.

Ravet, S. (2005, May). ePortfolio for a learning society. Paper presented at the 2005 eLearning Conference, Brussels, Belgium.

Richard, P. (2004, September 21). Shards of many untold stories: In place of unity, a mélange of unconnected objects. *The Washington Post*. Retrieved from http://www.washingtonpost.com/wp-dyn/articles/A36886-2004Sep20.html. p. C01.

Ross, J. A. (2006). The reliability, validity, and utility of self-assessment. *Practical Assessment, Research & Evaluation, 11*(10), 1-13.

Rothstein, E. (2004, December 21). Who should tell history, the tribes or the museums? *The New York Times*. Retrieved from http://www.nytimes.com/2004/12/21/arts/design/21muse.html

Shepherd, R., & Goggin, P. (2012). Reclaiming "old" literacies in the new literacy information age: The functional literacies of the mediated workstation. *Composition Studies, 40*(2), 66-91.

Slade, S. (2008, October). ePortfolio for immigrants: Modular personal portal supporting lifelong learning,. Paper presented at the ePortfolio and Digital Identity Conference, Maastricht, Netherlands.

Smith, C. (2005). Decolonising the museum: The National Museum of the American Indian in Washington, DC. *Antiquity, 79*, 424-439.

Smith, P. C. (2008). Critical reflections on the Our Peoples exhibit: A curator's perspective. In A. Lonetree, & A. J. Cobb (Eds.), *The National Museum of the American Indian: Critical conversations* (pp. 131-143). Lincoln, NE: University of Nebraska Press.

Taylor, C. (1991). *The ethics of authenticity.* Cambridge, MA: Harvard University Press.

Taylor, C. (1989). *Sources of the self: The making of modern identity.* Cambridge, MA: Harvard University Press.

Wakeham, P. (2008). Performing reconciliation at the National Museum of the American Indian: Postcolonial rapproachement and the politics of historical closure. In A. Lonetree, & A. J. Cobb (Eds.), *The National Museum of the American Indian: Critical conversations* (pp. 353-383). Lincoln, NE: University of Nebraska Press.

Western Association of Schools & Colleges (2002). *Evidence guide.* Oakland, CA: Western Association of Schools & Colleges.

Williams, B. (2002). *Truth and truthfulness: An essay in genealogy.* Princeton, NJ: Princeton University Press.

Yancey, K. B., Cambridge, B., & Cambridge, D. (2009, January 7). Making common cause: Electronic portfolios, learning, and the power of community. *Academic Commons.* Retrieved from http://www.academiccommons.org/commons/essay/making-common-cause-electronic-portfolios

Yancey, K. B. (1998). *Reflection in the writing classroom.* Logan, UT: Utah State University Press.

Yancey, K. B. (2001). Introduction: Digitized student portfolios. In B. Cambridge (Ed.), *Electronic portfolios: Emerging practices in student, faculty, and institutional learning* (pp. 15-30). Washington, DC: American Association for Higher Education.

Yancey, K. B. (2004). Postmodernism, palimpsest, and portfolios: Theoretical issues in the representation of student work. *College Composition and Communication, 55*(4), 738-762.

Young, C. The MAEd English education electronic portfolio experience: What preservice English teachers have to teach us about EPs and reflection. In D. Cambridge, B. Cambridge, & K. B. Yancey (Eds.), *Electronic portfolios 2.0: Emergent research on implementation and impact* (pp. 181-192). Sterling, VA: Stylus.

SECTION 4: AUTHENTIC ASSESSMENT TOOLS AND KNOWLEDGE TRANSFER

Improving productivity in our complex business environments through technology means improving *human* performance—enabling *people* to do more with less, and to do it better, faster, cheaper. Technology can be an enabler, but not the panacea predicted with each new wave. Each technology must be targeted at the correct problem, and people must become the masters of the technology in order for benefits to be realized. The formula for improving productivity is about striking a balance between people and technology, but the people must take center stage in this production enhancement process.

—Bielawski & Boyle, *Electronic Document Management Systems: A User Centered Approach for Creating, Distributing and Managing Online Publications* (1996), p. 3

Paulos, "Interaction Design Studio" (Spring 2012), http://www.chloefan.com/design/ happystance/process.html

CHAPTER 10.

MAPPING, RE-MEDIATING, AND REFLECTING ON WRITING PROCESS REALITIES: TRANSITIONING FROM PRINT TO ELECTRONIC PORTFOLIOS IN FIRST-YEAR COMPOSITION

Steven J. Corbett
Southern Connecticut State University

Michelle LaFrance
The University of Massachusetts, Dartmouth

Cara Giacomini
University of Washington

Janice Fournier
University of Washington

New technologies are often introduced to teachers and administrators in terms of their ideal use, and they are often disconnected from issues of context. Accounts of "best practices" in implementing technology can be similarly misleading. While such accounts might provide a sense of what can be done with the technology and the kinds of outcomes that can be achieved, best practices often fail to specify the conditions that contributed to success in a particular context, or to discuss what was involved in learning to use the technology successfully. We trace initial steps in the journey toward best practices, describing the "implementation path" for ePortfolios in first-year composition (FYC) courses at the University of Washington (UW).

Portfolios do more than move a writer's work from paper to screen. In "Postmodernism, Palimpsest, and Portfolios: Theoretical Issues in the Representation of Student Work," reprinted in this collection, Kathleen Blake Yancey claims that ePortfolios substantially "re-mediate" traditionally linear paper portfolio models. She suggests that, with collections like *Situating Portfolios* (1997) and *New Directions in Portfolio Assessment* (1994), compositionists have done a fair job of mapping the value of paper portfolios: their ability to highlight writing as a process and showcase student learning (Elbow, 1994; White, 1994; Yancey & Weiser, 1997, "Introduction") and their usefulness in encouraging teacher formative versus summative evaluation (Belanoff & Dickson, 1991; Perry, 1997; Weiser, 1994). Indeed, leading authorities in composition have done much to chart the theoretical and practical terrain of paper portfolios. But, as Yancey asserts, "we are only beginning to chart the potential of the digital" (p. 757).

Composition scholars have begun to further link reflective practice to writing assessment, especially portfolio assessment (Peters & Robertson, 2007; Pitts & Ruggierillo, 2012; White, 1994, 2005; Yancey, 2004a, 2004b; Yancey & Weiser, 1997). In *Teaching Literature as Reflective Practice*, Yancey (2004b) highlights the insights she gained while transitioning from paper portfolios to ePortfolios. On a practical level, she found that grading ePortfolios took less time, for example; it was easier for her to click between links than scramble through printed pages (p. 81). Yancey's biggest insight, however, from moving to ePortfolios involves student reflection. Drawing on John Dewey, Lev Vygotsky, and Donald Schön, Yancey maintains that reflection requires both scientific and spontaneous thinking, technical and nontechnical knowing, and is goal-directed, habitual, and learned (pp. 12-15). In "The Scoring of Writing Portfolios: Phase 2," writing assessment expert Edward White believes the reflective letter is so important (and consequently so difficult for students to prepare) because "few of them are accustomed to thinking of their own written work as evidence of learning, or to taking responsibility for their own learning" (p. 591). Portfolios offer students exactly this opportunity for deeply purposeful and guided reflection. White argues further that reflection is also an important element in assessing student written work and their performances as evolving writers. White contends that two documents must accompany portfolio assessment of student work: first, a set of goals that outline the purposes of the particular course, program, or purpose of the collected works; and second, a reflective letter written by the student arguing how those goals may or may not have been met, using evidence from the portfolio (p. 586).

For proponents of portfolios, paper portfolios are indeed exercises in "deeply reflective activity," but activity that can be "more singular than plural" (Yancey, 2004a, p. 91). ePortfolios, on the other hand, require students to reflect on their work from various angles, for multiple readers, and in multiple contexts. Students can use links and images like a gallery to link internally to their own work and externally to outside sources. In our two-year study of ePortfolio implementation at UW, our observations of the differences between paper portfolios and ePortfolios were similar to Yancey's. We found that beginning to unlock the educational potential of these aspects of ePortfolios is reliant on incremental and interconnected changes in attitudes and practices among instructors and students.

Unfortunately, new technologies, such as ePortfolios, do not come with directions for how to create the environment that will support their most effective use (Lunsford, 2006). As suggested by Yancey, traditional conceptions of "composition" imply a linear organization of ideas presented on printed pages; ePortfolios, however, challenge instructors to expand on this notion and consider how visual rhetoric and design, and multiple navigational paths (afforded by hypertext) may also figure in the work of composing. Katerine Bielaczyc uses the term "implementation path" to describe the sequence of phases teachers move through as they progress from initial trials with a new technology to more sophisticated and effective use. Advancing along this trajectory, Bielaczyc argues, involves more than gaining familiarity with the functionality of a tool; it may also require shifting the mindset of students and teachers, engaging students and teachers in new types of learning activities, and moving toward new types of interactions among students and others outside of the classroom (p. 321). As research in the learning sciences has demonstrated, classrooms are complex learning environments where variables such as curriculum and instructional practices, cultural beliefs, social and physical infrastructure, and experience with technology all interact and influence how effectively technology is used (Brown & Campione, 1996; Collins, Joseph, & Bielaczyc, 2004). As Shepherd and Goggin (2012) suggest, reclaiming literacies in terms of new media infrastructures is critical. In the sections that follow, we highlight changes in the learning environment and classroom practice that emerged from our study as critical for advancing along the trajectory toward an effective implementation of ePortfolios.

OUR PARTNERSHIP

Supporting the use of instructional-technology on the UW campus, Learning & Scholarly Technologies (LST) develops and maintains the Catalyst Tool Kit, a suite of Web tools for use by faculty members, students, and staff, and conducts research on the use of technology for teaching and learning. Catalyst tools include *Portfolio* and *Portfolio Project Builder*; the former allows individuals to create portfolios and the latter allows instructors to create portfolio templates to help direct their students' portfolios. As participants in the Inter/National Coalition for Electronic Portfolio Research (I/NCEPR), LST researchers have been collaborating with representatives from nine other colleges and universities since 2003 to study ePortfolio adoption. Our ongoing research on ePortfolios seeks to understand how students learn to compose in this medium—to select and reflect on artifacts, combine words and images in a coherent whole, effectively employ hypertext, and demonstrate awareness of audience and purpose. In autumn 2005, LST had the opportunity to enter a partnership with the Expository Writing Program (EWP) in the UW Department of English to better understand the effects of using ePortfolios in a specific context. During the 2005/06 academic year, LST researchers partnered with EWP to pilot the use of ePortfolios in nine sections of FYC. Participants in the pilot also agreed to take part in a study on the opportunities and challenges involved in ePortfolio adoption. The following academic year, 2006/07, EWP administrators gave all FYC TAs the choice of teaching with electronic or paper portfolios. In this essay, we share findings from our joint study of the ePortfolio pilot and second year of implementation. In the conclusion, we share observations on the current status of ePortfolio use within EWP.

THE SETTING

Several characteristics of EWP made it an ideal setting for adoption of ePortfolios. For one, the program had in place clearly articulated course outcomes and a well-developed paper portfolio assignment; administrators and instructors easily saw a fit between the *Portfolio* tool and the established curriculum. Although individual instructors determine the exact texts and assignments for each section of FYC, all students complete assignments designed to target four course learning outcomes. For the final portfolio, students are required to select 5-7 papers and develop a statement about how these works demonstrate achievement of the outcomes. In the traditional paper portfolio, students are asked to write their statement in the form of a cover letter to their instructor.

Other aspects of the program and classroom practice, however, posed challenges for our pilot. The first was how we could successfully train instructors on the functionality of the tool. Upwards of 30 sections of English 131 are offered each quarter, all of which are taught by teaching assistants. Nearly all of these TAs are in their first year of appointment; many have no prior teaching experience. Use of Catalyst *Portfolio* needed to be made as easy as possible for TAs already burdened with learning to teach, never mind teach with technology. More daunting challenges were posed by the department's physical and social infrastructure. The majority of classrooms assigned to EWP courses, and many other courses in English, do not have technology available that would make the demonstration or discussion of ePortfolios easy. Exceptions to this pattern were courses in the department's Computer-Integrated Courses (CIC) program, which has two computer classrooms dedicated to instructional use. Teaching in CIC is not an option for the majority of graduate students teaching FYC, however, since the program's facilities serve a large population and have limited availability. Traditional practices and beliefs, as well as the physical infrastructure of English department classrooms, were challenges we anticipated might require a longer time frame to address.

STUDY DESIGN

PARTICIPANTS

During the ePortfolio pilot in 2005/06, six TAs assigned to teach sections of FYC in fall, winter, and spring volunteered to participate in the study. Two of the six TAs were instructors in CIC. While all TAs expressed interest in implementing ePortfolios in their classes, they ranged widely in their knowledge of and comfort with educational technology. Two administrators from the English department also participated in the study, as did 48 students from the 12 sections of composition taught by TAs participating in the pilot study.

During the 2006/07 academic year, the EWP's approach to implementing ePortfolios was two-fold: it gave all TAs teaching English 131 the option of teaching with ePortfolios and also began using ePortfolios in English 567, a required course on composition theory for TAs of 131. During the second year of our study (2006/07), 16 TAs, two instructors of 567, two program administrators, and 90 students participated in the study.

STUDY PROCEDURES

In autumn 2005, Catalyst researchers worked with the director and assistant director of EWP to create a project template, *Portfolio Project Builder*, which TAs could easily modify. The design closely matched the traditional paper portfolio in asking students to demonstrate achievement of the course outcomes, but distributed portions of the cover letter over several Web pages and enabled direct links to student documents. We created two ePortfolio templates—one in which pages were organized by outcomes, the other by papers—to match the organizational structure students most often used in their cover letters. Figure 1 shows a sample template page. The instructions and prompts disappear when students publish their portfolios, leaving only the students' writing visible.

We also made two sample ePortfolios using these project templates; materials for these portfolios came from students who had taken FYC in the fall. Figure 2 shows a page from one of these sample portfolios initially created for the project. Figures 3 and 4 show pages from FYC students' actual portfolios.

At the start of winter 2006, we used the sample templates and ePortfolios as resources for participating TAs in a one-hour training session. We encouraged TAs to modify the project templates as they saw fit and to share the ePortfolio models with their students. They were also encouraged to make a model portfolio of their own, if possible. To control for effects of teaching the course a second time, 3 TAs taught with paper portfolios during winter quarter and 3 taught with ePortfolios; all 6 used ePortfolios in spring.

DATA COLLECTION

At the start of winter quarter 2006, all participating TAs in the pilot study completed a questionnaire about what challenges and opportunities they anticipated, for themselves and for their students, in the transition from paper to ePortfolios. At the end of winter and spring quarters, we interviewed TAs and asked them about their experiences using paper or ePortfolios and what they discovered (positive and negative) in this process. We also collected copies of each TA's portfolio assignment and any support materials they distributed to their students. During the interviews, TAs shared three sample portfolios that represented a range of responses to their assignment.

Students in participating sections also completed a brief survey at the end of winter and spring quarters for the pilot study. The surveys asked students about their overall experience completing the paper portfolio (three sections in winter) or ePortfolio (three sections winter, six in Spring). At the start of winter quarter and again at the completion of the pilot, we interviewed two administrators from English about the challenges and opportunities they anticipated in a transition from paper to ePortfolios, and later what they had experienced or learned as a result of the study.

The following academic year, 2006-07, our data collection built upon the pilot and expanded to include more TAs and an additional class. The EWP gave the ePortfolio option to all of its TAs and included the design of an ePortfolio in the required composition theory class, English 567, so that all TAs teaching English 131 would have the experience of developing their own portfolios. At the end of autumn quarter, we interviewed two instructors of 567 about their experiences using ePortfolios and distributed an online survey to all TAs, inquiring into their experiences using ePortfolios, their teaching practices, and their plans and rationales for integrating or not integrating various technologies into classes. From this initial group of respondents, we selected seven TAs to for follow-up interviews later in the academic year. Consenting students in participating sections of English 131 received online surveys at the end of each quarter. These surveys asked students to comment on their overall experience completing electronic or paper-based portfolios. In all, 46 students in ePortfolio based courses and 44 students in paper-based portfolio courses responded to the online survey.

FINDINGS

EWP administrators and TAs participating in the pilot study both considered the initial introduction of ePortfolios to be a success. Students in the nine sections (three in Winter, six in Spring) where ePortfolios were used completed their ePortfolios with only a few minor technical difficulties. In addition, all TAs reported that the quality of students' ePortfolios equaled, and at times surpassed, the quality of paper portfolios that students had created during previous quarters. Several

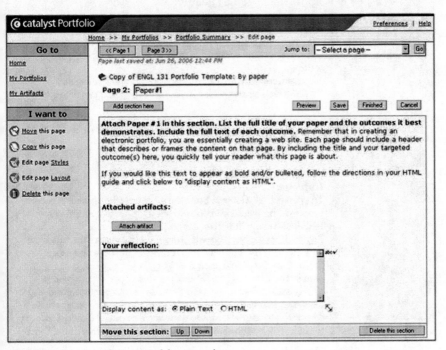

Figure 1: Section of an ePortfolio Template.

TAs observed that students who completed ePortfolios were better able to connect their writing with the course outcomes than students who completed paper portfolios. At the end of the pilot, administrators saw the potential for expanding this technology in EWP and eventually to other writing programs at the UW.

In the second year of our study, LST stepped back from its support role and the CIC program became the central technological support service for ePortfolio adoption in the classroom. The CIC program included resources such as templates and instructions on their website and provided assistance, at times on-to-one, to TAs who wanted to use ePortfolios and/or other technology in their classes. With the CIC program primed to provide technical support, the EWP took on the role of supporting the pedagogical applications of ePortfolios for new TAs. Despite greater departmental uptake and technological support within the department during the second year of our study, however, the num-

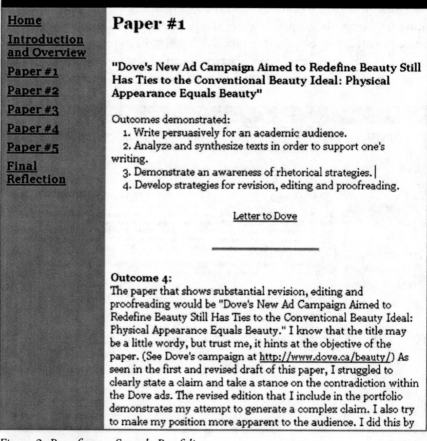

Figure 2: Page from a Sample Portfolio.

ber of TAs who adopted ePortfolios over paper-based portfolios was minimal. Overall, TAs in 2006/07 demonstrated a greater use of technology beyond ePortfolios compared with TAs in the 2005/06 pilot, but this trend was most apparent in CIC classes, where TAs attribute their usage of technology to the support and information they received from the CIC program. While, in general terms, the first leg of the journey toward the implementation of ePortfolios was traversed with ease, our research on the ePortfolio pilot identified four critical variables within the instructional context that affected, positively and/or negatively, the implementation of ePortfolios within particular course sections and had implications for long-term success of the project within the EWP. These include: portfolio assignment function, instructional practice, access to technology, and audience engagement. In the following section we discuss each

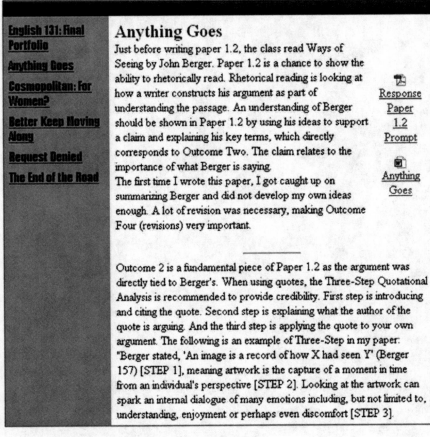

Figure 3: Excerpt from a FYC student's ePortfolio.

variable in detail, providing insights from TAs and administrators and sharing our observations on various aspects of the research data.

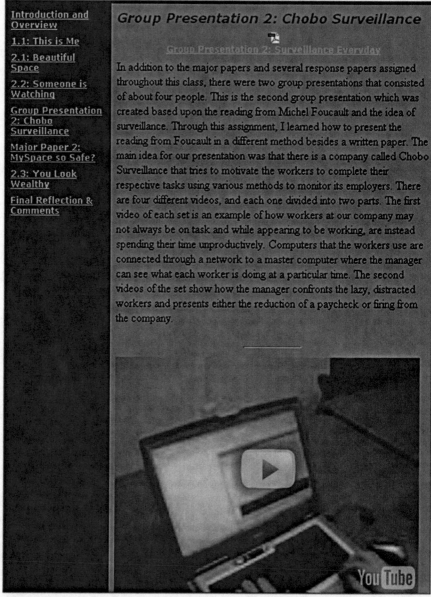

Figure 4: Excerpt from a FYC Student's ePortfolio, with Multimedia Elements.

PORTFOLIO ASSIGNMENT FUNCTION

Portfolio assignment function has two inter-related aspects: TAs' understanding of the function of the portfolio assignment, paper or electronic, in the curriculum and their understanding of how the functionality of the Catalyst *Portfolio* tool reconfigures ("re-mediates" in Yancey's terms) the standard paper portfolio. In our review of TAs' portfolio assignments, we observed that TAs described a portfolio, whether paper or electronic, in the following ways: as a comprehensive collection of all course writing, as a vehicle for students to describe their journey as writers, and as a forum for persuasive argument.

The traditional paper portfolio used in EWP begins with a "cover letter" addressed to the instructor, in which the student introduces the contents of the portfolio and discusses them in relation to the course outcomes, followed by a comprehensive collection of all writing assignments, from revised papers to early paper drafts with instructors' comments. The ePortfolio is not simply an electronic version of the cover letter. Instead, it takes the reflective writing traditionally done in the cover letter and distributes it across several pages of the portfolio. This distributed form of reflection allows students to discuss artifacts (papers, segments of papers, images, or other materials) at the point at which they are introduced. It also emphasizes the selection and organization of artifacts over the comprehensiveness of the collection. As Glenda Conway suggests, instructors should consider encouraging reflection throughout the quarter, rather than only at the end of a course with an all-inclusive cover letter. ePortfolios hold the potential for the realization of this sort of ongoing course reflection.

In general, during the 2005/06 pilot, we found that TAs who emphasized the portfolio as a comprehensive collection of all course work had the most difficulty transitioning from the paper to the electronic format. For instance, one TA, Amanda, felt strongly that the ePortfolio would not be complete without a distinct cover letter, in addition to the distributed reflections. Thus, she had students begin their ePortfolio with a page (or screen) containing the complete cover letter. They then copied various sections from this cover letter and distributed them throughout the pages where they introduced artifacts (papers, etc). Another TA, Ivy, felt strongly that all of her handwritten comments on early drafts of papers should be a part of the ePortfolio, so she asked her students to scan all comments. In both cases, the TAs' desire for a comprehensive ePortfolio directly translated into more work for their students than would have occurred with the traditional paper portfolio model or using the ePortfolio templates without the addition of a separate cover letter or scanned comments. In interviews, both TAs indicated that their students expressed some resentment over the workload, although they were able to complete the assignment successfully. In contrast, TAs that emphasized students' journeys as writers or students' abilities to write persuasively about course outcomes adjusted more easily to the electronic format. Jenna was pleased that the ePortfolio allowed students to talk about individual artifacts more directly than the paper portfolio did:

> The traditional portfolio (the paper one) is set up so it is all in the cover letter and you have got to make the matching yourself, which defeats the purpose for me, because it doesn't highlight each artifact the way the ePortfolio does.

Cole described the difference between the paper and ePortfolio as follows: "Paper is a little more holistic and I think ePortfolios get specific." Both Jenna and Cole felt students presented more compelling and detailed accounts of their progress with the ePortfolio than they had with paper portfolios. Adjusting assignments to play to the strengths of the ePortfolio represents a tangible step in the journey toward best practices, and one that can be taken with relative ease. Even TAs that initially struggled with this adjustment were able to identify the changes that would lead them to better practice in the future.

INSTRUCTIONAL PRACTICE

Achieving seamless integration between the ePortfolio and other course elements required flexibility in TAs' instructional practice. In the final interview for the pilot study, Ivy, the TA who asked her students to scan all comments, observed, "I think it is impossible to just pretend [the ePortfolio] can be taught the same way as the paper portfolio." Indeed, in year one all 6 TAs described various aspects of their instruction where they had made adjustments, or felt that they should have made adjustments, to integrate the ePortfolio into the curriculum. For instance, several TAs felt that the ePortfolio needed to be introduced early in the course, rather than at the end, so that any technical difficulties could be diagnosed and overcome with less time pressure. In addition, they acknowledged that this would allow students to have more opportunities to share their ePortfolios and learn from each other and the transition between the earlier paper assignments and the ePortfolio would be less abrupt. TAs also observed that the ePortfolio influenced the other assignments they designed for the course. Amanda explained: "I don't think the ePortfolio should be the kind of thing that dominates the course, but the way you think about it can help shape the kind of assignments you create." One TA intentionally designed a paper assignment with a visual component so students would have more visual elements to include in their ePortfolios.

TAs expressed that ePortfolios had a long-term potential to become vehicles for teaching students how to integrate text and images and for introducing multimedia elements into the course. In our review of students' work we encountered a handful of visually sophisticated portfolios and a couple that experimented with multimedia, but these skills were not widely evident. In the final interview, one TA, Rob, shared his vision for the future of ePortfolios: "It becomes less of 'this is an English paper' and more of 'this is an interdisciplinary project' where students can bring in various media and bring in various resources." Like portfolio assignment function, instructional practice is an area where individual initiative leads to a readily attainable course of action for the future.

ACCESS TO TECHNOLOGY

The six TAs participating in the pilot study had widely divergent access to technology in their classrooms. Two TAs were a part of CIC, where they alternated their class sessions between a computer lab and a traditional classroom. Consistent access to tech-ready classrooms and basic hardware also continued to be problematic for TAs in the 2006/07 academic year. Other than CIC, the EWP does not have dedicated instructional space, so the classrooms assigned to TAs varied each quarter. As graduate student instructors, teaching small classes (20-22 students), in a department that does not have a strong reputation for technology use, most TAs typically were assigned small classrooms with very limited technology—no computer station, no data projector, and limited or non-existent Internet access. Regular access to a computer station and Internet in classrooms influences how fully ePortfolios can be integrated into all aspects of the course. While it is possible to use ePortfolios in non-technological classrooms, the lack of access limits the full realization of their potential, since TAs are not able to display ePortfolios for discussion or to walk students through the aspects of the ePortfolio creation process and students are not able to easily share their work during class sessions.

During the pilot and follow-up studies it was relatively simple for participating TAs, due to the small number of courses involved, to reserve a campus computer lab for one day during the quarter to show students ePortfolio models and orient them to Catalyst *Portfolio*. However, this solution loses viability as more sections of beginning composition use ePortfolios, since lab reservations are limited. While the CIC program does provide technology facilities, it does not have the capacity to accommodate all FYC TAs. Expanding the use of ePortfolios to a larger number of course sections will require taking steps to ensure TAs have adequate access to technology in classrooms. Making progress in this area will likely require action at the programmatic level, since instructor initiative will only overcome part of this challenge.

AUDIENCE ENGAGEMENT

At the outset of the pilot study, both TAs and administrators felt that ePortfolios presented the opportunity for students to compose for a public audience. By the end of the pilot we observed that some progress had been made in this area; students' writing in ePortfolios tended to address an audience beyond the instructor, unlike the cover letter in the traditional paper portfolio. Mary Perry maintains the importance of having students involved in the negotiation of audience with portfolios (also see Conway; Yancey *Teaching Literature*, "Postmodernism"). ePortfolios magnify this exigency. Some TAs, however, questioned the extent of audience engagement that was possible with the current use of ePortfolios. They observed that opportunities for students in their sections to share their ePortfolios with each other were limited. Introducing ePortfolios earlier in the quarter and access to better-equipped classrooms would facilitate the sharing of student work within a course section. Engaging an audience beyond an individual course section represents a larger challenge. As Amanda observed, "The writing might look really different if it were not being evaluated by their composition instructor." By the end of the pilot, she felt an ideal ePortfolio would use less formal language that explained its contents in a manner that would engage an outside audience: "I mean it's bizarre for the instructor to be requesting less formal language, but that is what I had to do with a few of my students."

Publishing an ePortfolio online does not make it automatically "public." Building an authentic external audience requires a substantial effort from TAs, program administrators, and LST or other technology support units. Facilitating the sharing of ePortfolios between students in the EWP program would be a useful next step toward expanding audience engagement. Enabling such an exchange would likely require a technical solution for collecting, sharing, and sorting students' ePortfolios, along with changes in program curriculum to encourage interaction between courses. At the end of the second year of the study, we observed that building an audience beyond the program constitutes an even larger challenge. This leg of the ePortfolio implementation path covers difficult terrain, since making this journey requires a cultural shift toward increased connection between EWP and other individuals and units at the UW and beyond the institution.

IMPLICATIONS FOR EWP

The work of Bielaczyc, Yancey, and others foreground the idea that the implementation of new pedagogical technologies requires students and teachers to adjust their attitudes and practices. These sorts of adjustments of mind and action were clearly seen during the first-year pilot among participating instructors. A year later, additional adjustments are evident on a wider scale as EWP continues its implementation of ePortfolios. All TAs who taught with ePortfolios reported that they improved each quarter in understanding their own expectations for the ePortfolio and communicating these to their students (particularly in terms of visual design), and all found that showing examples of other ePortfolios to their students was critical to their student's success.

In year two, the EWP and the English department as a whole took greater role in promoting ePortfolios in the program. Although use of ePortfolios was not yet a requirement, all FYC instructors new in 2006-07 were offered the option of teaching with ePortfolios or the standard paper model in their sections. In addition, all new TAs in EWP gained personal experience with Catalyst *Portfolio* during their first quarter. The director of EWP and a fellow professor agreed to teach with ePortfolios in the required composition theory course, asking each TA to construct a teaching portfolio using the Catalyst portfolio tools. TAs and professors underwent the same negotiations of attitude and practice that students and TAs experienced in the classroom during the pilot study. In this context, however, professors were able to expand on the "lifelong learning" benefits of portfolios (see Chen, 2009 and the conclusion below), emphasizing to TAs their value as tools for reflection and for self-promotion on the job market (Heinrich, Bhattacharya, & Rayudu, 2007). Both professors confessed minimal experience teaching with technology at the start. One commented: "Like most faculty in the department, I haven't used much technology. I never developed expertise with it. Until I taught with ePortfolios in 567, I never used ePortfolios, listservs, or Web sites for my courses." Both professors came away at the end of the quarter delighted with the results of their experiment and enthusiastic about promoting more systematic ePortfolio use next year.

Additional structures within the department—formal and informal—also helped to advance best practices with ePortfolios. LST and EWP together conducted only one information session early in the year to discuss technical and pedagogical strategies associated with successful integration of the technology. Later discussion of "best practices" happened informally, as TAs in shared offices talked about their experiences and innovative assignments using ePortfolios. Extending beyond the program, the implementation of ePortfolios in the curriculum was also a topic of Practical Pedagogy roundtables hosted by the Department of English.

Further change was evident in the department's computer classrooms. The CIC program became directly involved in the implementation of ePortfolios in all 100- and 200-level English courses, housing the easily navigable ePortfolio guidelines and templates on their Web page and providing substantial support to any instructors wishing to use ePortfolios (http://depts.washington.edu/engl/cic/portfolio_final.php). In CIC's quarterly training seminars, the CIC director and assistants introduced instructors who are often new to teaching with technology to the potential educational benefits of multiple tools, including ePortfolios. The close connection between ePortfolios and other Catalyst tools (i.e., online discussion, homework collection, and file sharing) becomes clear to new instructors as they witness the compatibility between various computer technologies that may be used inside or outside of the classroom to enhance student learning. TAs teaching with ePortfolios felt that EWP and the larger English department should embrace multiple educational technologies, because students were already using them or would need to learn them. One TA even expressed the belief that use of technology should be incorporated into the outcomes for English 131 more broadly. With CIC promoting their use, ePortfolios are extending to courses beyond FYC and being more tightly integrated with other technologies; several CIC instructors over this last year have expressed enthusiasm about "going paperless" in their classes. More sophisticated uses of ePortfolios (for example, students creating their own portfolios without the help of a template) may also be possible and appropriate in intermediate or advanced writing classes.

Some TAs in the study did report that "TA resistance" was the main obstacle to more widespread adoption of ePortfolios—a moniker that described a number of affective responses, including discomfort with technology, a sense that workload might increase, and uncertainty about the pedagogical ends of the electronic format. At the end of our two-year study we anticipated that the English department would continue to advance on a trajectory of more effective and sophisticated use of ePortfolios, with teaching assistants and CIC playing a major role in their implementation.

MAPPING STUDENT AND TA EXPERIENCE

We turn now to discussing in more depth the experience of students and TAs who used ePortfolios in their classes. In the second year of this study, we collected paper and electronic portfolios from consenting students in participating sections of English 131. From these portfolios we chose a random sample of 12 paper portfolios and 12 ePortfolios to analyze on several dimensions: the intended audience for the portfolio, degree and type of evidence used to support claims, visual organization of information, total word count for commentary, and use of multimedia artifacts. We also asked TAs to share with us student portfolios that represented a range of responses to their assignments.

Our initial findings demonstrate differences between the ways students approach paper versus electronic portfolios. When using paper portfolios, students tended to address the instructor as the primary audience for their work. In general, however, those students who created ePortfolios addressed an audience beyond the classroom, while at the same time assuming that audience had knowledge of the EWP and the UW. Portfolio format seemed to have little effect on students' abilities to use evidence in support of a claim, but those who created ePortfolios tended to include direct references to or excerpts from their work more often than those who created paper portfolios. Students who used paper portfolios used the cover letter to organize and present information about the work that followed, but students who created electronic portfolios used visual cues to organize their work via headings, fonts, colors and bullets. Students using ePortfolios did vary widely in the extent to which they used particular visual cues to make their portfolios more readable. Although the electronic environment allows for inclusion of a greater array of artifacts than the paper portfolio, only five of 12 ePortfolios reviewed included linked or embedded multi-media artifacts. Images were included in each portfolio, but they were not explicitly referenced or discussed. Finally, our data shows that students who completed ePortfolios wrote almost twice as much in their reflections overall than for students who completed paper portfolios (see Table 1).

Table 1: Total Word Count for Two Portions of Electronic and Paper Portfolios

	Overall Reflection	
	Average	Range
ePortfolio	3341	1458-5226
Paper Portfolio	1714	1139-2652

Overall, the student ePortfolios shared in the second year of the study were not just longer, but clearly more sophisticated than those shared by TAs during the pilot year. Several students, on their own initiative, chose to use a theme to connect the various elements of their ePortfolios (i.e. one student compared her growth as a writer to musical composition and used language and images connected to music throughout her ePortfolio). By Spring quarter, some TAs reported that they encouraged students to use themes. The range in design strategies and total words in both portfolio formats are likely the result of different instructions and/or templates provided by TAs.

Online survey responses demonstrated further differences of perception among students creating paper portfolios and those using ePortfolios. Students who completed the paper portfolios tended to interpret the survey as asking about the effects of the portfolio process on their learning. Those who completed ePortfolios interpreted the survey as asking them about the technology. Students who created paper portfolios indicated at higher rates that they had "benefited" from the portfolio process, attributing all positive experiences to the acts of reflection, receiving feedback, and working on a revision cycle in and of themselves, while students who created ePortfolios frequently wrote about the benefits or drawbacks of the portfolio software.

At the same time, students overwhelmingly recommended the ePortfolio format that they had used for future courses, with 65.2% of students endorsing the ePortfolio format and only 50% endorsing the paper format. TAs teaching with ePortfolios also tended to express high levels of enthusiasm for the ePortfolios their students created. However, these TAs also expressed confusion over the relationship of some elements of the ePortfolios to students' grades. For instance, TAs reported telling students that the visual elements of the ePortfolio would have little or no effect on grades, unless students made poor design choices that made the portfolio difficult to read. TAs expressed some further uncertainty about whether or not this was the correct choice, since in the end they preferred the ePortfolios that incorporated visual elements. Interestingly, the most visually sophisticated assignment encountered during the study—a project that asked students to integrate visual and textual materials—was created by a TA using the paper portfolio format.

CONCLUSION

While recognizing the pedagogical implications of tools that enable student reflection, Ed White also advises practitioners to provide explicit instruction to students in how to negotiate the reflective letter as a rhetorical, persuasive document or argument. He writes: "without instruction, students are likely to give a hasty overview of the portfolio contents, including much personal experience about the difficulty of writing and revising—along with some fulsome praise of the teacher—without attending to the goals of the program at all" (p.

591). White urges direct, focused instruction in how and why to compose the portfolio cover letter so that students will be more likely to see how *they* met the goals and expectations of the course and how *they* did or not apply themselves with full effort and engagement in their learning. Our findings demonstrate that new instructors need similar support for understanding the applications of portfolio tools and their usefulness in encouraging student reflection in their classrooms. Simply having an electronic portfolio tool available to instructors does not mean that tool will be widely adopted or used efficaciously. Like students, new instructors benefit from being shown and supported in the effective use of tools that enable non-traditional forms of student learning, reflection, and movement toward course learning objectives.

In the years following our data collection, progress continues to be made toward more closely integrating the support and services available to TAs teaching portfolio-based classes in the EWP. Working closely with the CIC, the EWP has set out to introduce TAs to the ePortfolio option earlier in their orientation process and has worked to increase the availability of sample assignments and examples of student-designed projects for TAs to adopt and adapt. To alleviate the techno-anxieties of new TAs, the CIC program has not only continued to provide one-to-one support services for TAs using ePortfolios in their classrooms, but also increased its availability for classroom visits to all TAs using the ePortfolio option. CIC program staff have also developed a website specifically tailored to answering student questions and can be available in person when necessary. The result of these efforts is that TAs now no longer bear sole or full responsibility for teaching their students how to use or design with the tool. Most importantly, practices within the EWP are changing: the ePortfolio has been made the default mode for new TAs in the program and the ePortfolio is no longer described as an optional alternative to paper portfolios in program documents or support materials. In fact, the online version of the portfolio tool is no longer differentiated as an "ePortfolio" at all, but is referred to as simply the "portfolio." These recent moves on the programmatic level encourage all involved in planning and support for new TAs—as time advances, ePortfolios are becoming a more familiar pedagogical fixture of teaching in the EWP.

On a final note, during the academic year 2008/09, LST informed the EWP that Catalyst *Portfolio* and *Portfolio Project Builder*, the current tools available for ePortfolios, were going to be phased out of use at the UW by the end of the 2009/10 academic year, due to the advanced age of the software. Discussion is currently underway on whether LST will build a new portfolio tool or will encourage adoption of a commercial or open-source solution. This change initially created anxiety among administrators of the EWP and CIC, as much time and energy had been devoted to developing resources for TAs who chose to use ePortfolios in their classrooms. A new tool will require that all resources available to TAs (directions and guidelines for classroom use, troubleshooting tips, and examples of students' portfolios) be redesigned. At the time of submission of this article, an EWP/CIC working group (in coordination with LST) has been set up to investigate options for moving forward. This reaction is heartening. Instead of simply abandoning ePortfolios, the EWP has committed to having electronic options available to those TAs who would chose to include technological tools for reflection in their classes. This change in the educational software and technology availability, however, has prevented EWP/CIC from making ePortfolios mandatory at this time. But even without required use, ePortfolio implementation is continuing to advance in the program.

While visualizing ideal use provides inspiration and commitment to the development of support for new technologies, analyzing the journey of technology implementation increases our practical understanding of educational change. On the one hand, our study reveals the early stages of a journey that may eventually lead to more extensive and well-supported ePortfolio use within the institution. On the other hand, it emphasizes the everyday challenges of ePortfolio adoption, rather than the ideal outcome. Our research highlights subtle shifts in practice and culture that could over time—with further on-going support and more purposeful recruitment and training of new instructors—culminate in dramatic transformations.

Other individuals and/or institutions that are embarking on the implementation journey need to remember that true transformation takes time. Unlocking the full potential of new technology, such as ePortfolios, requires a series of changes, many of which will not be obvious until the technology has been introduced. For EWP, our study of the ePortfolio pilot made visible early changes in practice and identified areas where shifts will need to be made as the journey continues. One valuable aspect of our research study was that it provided an opportunity for those participating in the ePortfolio pilot to reflect on their experiences and partnerships. More importantly, we provided a means of communicating the lessons from that reflection. Brad Peters and Julie Robertson, reflecting on their analyses of WAC portfolio partnerships, believe that portfolio learning can be "a social force that also gives rise to a faculty "culture of assessment,' where reflection becomes the dominant mode of uniting faculty practice and theory" (p. 208). Venues for reflection and communication are important components of any technology implementation, since the experiences and ideas of early participants can help shape and unify future steps in the process. Other individuals or institutions may not follow the same path that we traced in this paper, but this case identifies variables, both pros and cons, to consider as they chart their own progress with ePortfolios.

Within the ePortfolio community it is important to recognize the incremental stages of transformation, in addition to focusing on the long-term goals for this technology. While ePortfolios do have the potential to promote lifelong learning and reflection, making this future viable will require an extended series of subtle transformations in instructional practice and departmental and institutional culture, as well as expanding awareness and collaboration within social and professional spheres.

REFERENCES

Belanoff, P., & Dickson, M. (Eds.). (1991). *Portfolios: Process and product.* Portsmouth, NH: Boynton/Cook.

Bielaczyc, K. (2006). Designing social infrastructure: Critical issues in creating learning environments with technology. *The Journal of the Learning Sciences, 15*(1), 301-329.

Black, L., Daiker, D. A., Stygall, G., & Sommers, J. (Eds.). (1994). *New directions in portfolio assessment: Reflective practice, critical theory, and large-scale scoring.* Portsmouth, NH: Boynton/Cook.

Brown, A. L., & Campione, J. C. (1996). Psychological theory and the design of innovative learning environments: On procedures, principles, and systems. In L. Schauble, & R. Glaser (Eds.), *Innovations in learning: New environments for education* (pp. 289-325). Hillsdale, NJ: Lawrence Erlbaum.

Chen, H. L. (2009). Using eportfolios to support lifelong and lifewide learning. In D. Cambridge, B. Cambridge, & K. B. Yancey (Eds.), *Electronic portfolios 2.0: Emergent research on implementation and impact* (pp. 29-35). Sterling, VA: Stylus.

Collins, A., Joseph, D., & Bielaczyc, K. (2004). Design research: Theoretical and methodological issues. *The Journal of the Learning Sciences, 13*(1), 15-42.

Conway, G. (1994). Portfolio cover letters, students' self-presentation, and teachers' ethics. In L. Black et al. *New directions in portfolio assessment: Reflective practice, critical theory, and large-scale scoring* (pp. 83-92). Portsmouth, NH: Boynton/Cook.

Elbow, P. (1994). Will the virtues of portfolios blind us to their potential dangers? In L. Black et al. (Eds.), *New directions in portfolio assessment: Reflective practice, critical theory, and large-scale scoring* (pp. 40-55). Portsmouth, NH: Boynton/Cook.

Greenberg, G. (2004). The digital convergence: Extending the portfolio model. *Educause Review, 39*(4), 28-37.

Heinrich, E., Bhattacharya, M., & Rayudu, R. (2007). Preparation for lifelong learning using ePortfolios. *European Journal of Engineering Education, 32*(6), 653-663.

LaCour, S. (2005). The future of integration, personalization, and ePortfolio technologies. *Innovate Online, 1*(4). Retrieved from http://www.innovateonline.info/pdf/vol1_issue4/The_Future_of_Integration,_Personalization,_and_ePortfolio_Technologies.pdf

Lunsford, A. (2006). Writing, technologies, and the fifth canon. *Computers and composition, 23*(2), 169-177.

Perry, M. (1997). Producing purposeful portfolios. In K. B. Yancey, & I. Weiser (Eds.), *Situating portfolios: Four perspectives* (pp. 182-195). Logan, UT: Utah State University Press.

Peters, B., & Robertson, J. F. (2007). Portfolio partnerships between faculty and WAC:

Lessons from disciplinary practice, reflection, and transformation. *College Composition and Communication, 59*(2), 206-236.

Pitts, W. & Ruggierillo, R. (2012). Using the e-portfolio to document and evaluate growth in reflective practice: The development and application of a conceptual framework. *International Journal of ePortfolio. 1*(1), 49-74.

Schofield, J. (1997). Computers and social processes: A review of the literature. *Social Science Computer Review, 15*, 27-39.

Shepherd, R., & Goggin, P. (2012). Reclaiming "old" literacies in the new literacy information age: The functional literacies of the mediated workstation. *Composition Studies, 40*(2), 66-91.

Weiser, I. (1994). Portfolios and the new teacher of writing. In L. Black et al. (Eds.), *New directions in portfolio assessment: Reflective practice, critical theory, and large-scale scoring* (pp. 219-229). Portsmouth, NH: Boynton/Cook.

Wheeler, B. (2004). The open source parade. *Educause Review, 39*(5), 68-69.

White, E. M. (1994). Portfolios as an assessment concept. In L. Black et al. (Eds.), *New directions in portfolio assessment: Reflective practice, critical theory, and large-scale scoring* (pp. 25-39). Portsmouth, NH: Boynton/Cook.

White, E. M. (2005). The scoring of writing portfolios: Phase 2. *College Composition and Communication, 56*(4), 581-600.

Yancey, K. B. (1997). *Situating portfolios: Four perspectives* (pp. 1-17). Logan, UT: Utah State University Press.

Yancey, K. B. (2004a). Postmodernism, palimpsest, and portfolios: Theoretical issues in the representation of student work. *College Composition and Communication, 55*(4), 738-762.

Yancey, K. B. (2004b). *Teaching literature as reflective practice.* Urbana, IL: NCTE.

Yancey, K. B., & Weiser, I. (1997). Situating portfolios: An introduction. In K. B. Yancey, & I. Weiser (Eds.), *Situating portfolios: Four perspectives* (pp. 1-20). Logan, UT: Utah State University Press.

CHAPTER 11.

EPORTFOLIOS AS TOOLS FOR FACILITATING AND ASSESSING KNOWLEDGE TRANSFER FROM LOWER DIVISION, GENERAL EDUCATION COURSES TO UPPER DIVISION, DISCIPLINE-SPECIFIC COURSES

Carl Whithaus
University of California, Davis

ePortfolios can both facilitate and assess knowledge transfer from lower division, general education courses to upper division, discipline-specific courses. The chapter opens with a discussion of Teaching/Writing in Thirdspaces (Grego & Thompson, 2008) and argues that the notion of thirdspace can apply to the distance between general education courses and the information skills required within students' majors. By tracking student learning in general education courses, ePortfolios provide a tool for faculty and administrators to make visible the connections and disjunctures between the delivered curriculum in lower division courses and the expectations for students' competencies expressed by faculty teaching upper division courses for majors.

In *Teaching/Writing in Thirdspaces: The Studio Approach*, Rhoda Grego and Nancy S. Thompson (2008) develop the concept of "thirdspaces" as a means to account for how work with student writing "was influenced by institutional politics, preferences, and power relations" (p. 5). Drawing on the cultural geography work of Edward Soja (1996) and Doreen Massey (1994; 2005) as well as Nedra Reynolds' (2004) analysis of writing as "spatial, material, and visual" (p. 3), Grego and Thompson account for how local institutional pressures can influence writing instruction as much as the national-level discussions about basic writing and composition pedagogies (Bartholomae & Petrosky, 1986; Shaughnessy, 1977; Shor, 1987, 1996). Grego and Thompson develop the Writing Studio as a systematic method of helping student writers, but their pedagogical practices also allow an understanding of composition's meaningful work as contingent upon localized needs. As a method, Grego and Thompson clarify that their model of the Writing Studio:

> is not limited to a course per se but is a configuration of
> relationships that can emerge from different contexts.
> Writing Studio has what might be a fourth credit-hour (or
> otherwise-configured small group meeting) attached to an
> existing course. These Studios can appear anywhere across the
> curriculum. ... A Studio organizes small groups of students
> to meet frequently and regularly (typically once a week) to
> bring to the table the assignments they are working on for
> a writing course, another English course, or a disciplinary
> course or undergraduate research experience that requires
> communication products. (p. 7)

Their development of the Writing Studio not as "a pedagogy so much as an institutionally aware methodology" (p. 21) to improve writing instruction in both general education and disciplinary courses parallels Soja's concept of "thirdspace" (1996). For Grego and Thompson "thirdspaces" are institutional openings or locations where writing faculty engage what Jonathan Mauk (2003) has called "the spatial and material conditions that constitute the everyday lives of students" (p. 370). For Grego and Thompson, the Studio approach is not only what happens within an individual instructor's classroom but rather is the product of compositionists and writing program administrators using their knowledge about writing, student learning, and their local institutional environments to enact systemic changes that impact students (see also Thompson, 2005).

In "Integrating Undergraduate Research into Engineering," (Thompson, Alford, Liao, Johnson, & Matthews, 2005) describe how teaching writing in the "thirdspace" of a Studio connected with undergraduate engineering research makes explicit the connections between the "general education skill" of writing and the particular disciplinary moves that more experienced engineering students, graduate students, and faculty make in their own writing and communication processes. By focusing on communications, the Research Communications Studio (RCS) aims to "develop the cognitive abilities of undergraduate researchers" (p. 300). These cognitive abilities have been shaped by the students' experiences in their previous general education courses; however, the RCS approach engages participants in intensive communication practice for making sense of their engineering research experiences. The explicit focus on the communication of discipline-specific research improves both students' communication skills as well as their engineering abilities (pp. 300-304). The Studio method used in the RCS is a product of a thirdspace approach to postsecondary institutions' treatment of writing as a generalizable cognitive skill, that is, something that can be taught with what post-process theorists (Kent, 1999; Petraglia, 1998) have derisively called General Writing Skills Instruction (GWSI). The Studio approach recognizes the different forms of expertise that undergraduate engineering students, engineering faculty members, engineering graduate student mentors, communication/writing graduate students, and writing/communications faculty bring to the RCS. Combining these different forms of expertise to focus on students' developing cognitive abilities as effective engineers and writers cuts across disciplinary boundaries and, at the same time, requires a bringing together of those disciplinary knowledge.

The work of a highly situated Studio approach to teaching engineering writing is localized within the institutional politics, preferences, and power relations of the University of South Carolina. As such, the RCS is a thirdspace technique, in that it is not a stand-alone course offered through either an English department or an engineering department, but rather, like other incarnations of the Studio, a simultaneous "outside-but-alongside/inside" approach to the institutional location of (supplemental) instruction through writing (Grego & Thompson, 2008). The Studio approach and the notion of thirdspaces for understanding explicit instruction in writing are valuable because they highlight the disconnections that can occur between the articulated learning outcomes for general education courses and the articulated learning outcomes valued within disciplinary communities such as engineering. What students learn in their general education courses may not always transfer as effectively as intended to their disciplinary modes of inquiry. Researchers interested in understanding how students' knowledge and skills transfer from one learning environment to another could use the concept of thirdspaces as a way of articulating why and how these disconnections occur. To fully use the concept of thirdspaces, researchers and teachers need a tool to help measure learning outcomes. ePortfolios appear to be promising tools to use for measuring learning outcomes (Acker & Halasek, 2008; Desmet, Church Miller, Griffin, Balthazor, & Cummings, 2008; Lopez-Fernandez, 2009; Mauk, 2003; Van Aalst & Chan, 2007).

EPORTFOLIOS AS TOOLS FOR OUTCOMES-BASED ASSESSMENTS IN GENERAL EDUCATION

Measuring the learning outcomes of general education courses has become an increasingly important issue for postsecondary institutions (Humphreys, 2009; Schneider, 2008; "What General Education Courses Contribute to Essential Learning Outcomes," 2009). Within this larger push for accountability and the measurement of learning outcomes, Desmet et al. (2008) have shown that ePortfolios can effectively be used as tools for assessments of the types of learning that take place in lower-divisions writing courses. They argue that electronic portfolios, "creat[e] a large centralized database of documents" and thereby make "it possible to articulate classroom and program concerns with larger institutional imperatives for measurable outcomes in assessment" (p. 16). In particular, they point out the ways in which electronic portfolios can be used to support and study revision (p. 16) and enhance student reflection (pp. 16-19).

Students' abilities to reflect upon their own work are not only important in terms of improving writing, but are vital skills to develop as they move into professional environments (Argyris & Schön, 1974; Schön, 1983, 1987, 1991). Since reflection further develops professionals and their abilities to perform complex tasks, it is no surprise that as students progress from lower division courses into their major course work and pre-professional studies, they are asked to engage in more reflective activities (Butcher, 2009; Ostorga, 2009; Xiao, 2008). The increase in reflection is seen in fields as various as education (Butcher, 2009), design (Ostorga, 2009), and nursing (Xiao, 2008).

The development of student writing abilities underscores reflection as an important skill area transferable across various courses and writing situations (Yancey, 1998). Writing provides a means for developing students' abilities to reflect on their practices, whether that reflection is explicitly about their writing or about the development of skills they will need in their professional practices. As Dawn (Swartzendruber-Putnam, 2000) has written, "Able writers can think critically about their writing" (p. 88). This ability to reflect on writing practices—and really on communication practices and rhetorical situations—appears to be heightened when using ePortfolios. Desmet et al. (2008) found "the articulation of learning as a product, is what separates formal reflection in ePortfolios from the more dispersed processes of revision involved in the various exhibits of a [traditional print-based] writing portfolio" (p. 20). The large corpus of texts that Desmet et al. were able to analyze from the University of Georgia led them to find statistically significant evidence that "revision, at least within the context of ePortfolio assessment, improves student writing" (p. 25).

Not only does the ePortfolio system at the University of Georgia demonstrate connections between students working explicitly on revision and improvement in their writing, but this extensive database also allows for tracking student learning in general education courses. A system such as the EMMA-based ePortfolios provides a tool for faculty and administrators to make visible the connections, as well as the possible ruptures, between the delivered curriculum in lower division courses and the skills needed to succeed in upper-division, disciplinary courses.

ePortfolios then provide a way to operationalize Soja's (1996) concept of thirdspace within a university's writing curriculum that complements Grego and Thompson's Writing Studio model. ePortfolios may serve as an institutionally aware methodology that draws in the everyday conditions and concerns of students' lives and emphasizes building connections between general education courses and course work that prepares students for work in their professions. Understanding how knowledge about writing transfers from one educational environment or course to another is a key way in which a well-constructed ePortfolio program can help administrators, faculty, and students.

USING EPORTFOLIOS TO PROMOTE AS WELL AS ASSESS KNOWLEDGE TRANSFER

Acker and Halasek (2008) have examined the question of ePortfolios' abilities to facilitate knowledge transfer by looking at how ePortfolios can increase connections between secondary English courses and general education college writing courses. Working with faculty from Ohio State University and two high schools, Acker and Halasek designed and studied an ePortfolio program "through which high school and university personnel conducted joint research to address K-16 English language arts (ELA) alignment and student success in the postsecondary environment" (p. 2). High school students wrote essays and used an Open Source Portfolio (OSP) system to receive feedback from both university and high school writing faculty. The goal was to improve alignment between K-12 and postsecondary writing instruction and help students better understand what constitutes "good" writing in high school and the university. In addition, Acker and Halasek believed that an ePortfolio system would provide the "richer, innovative, and 'more authentic' measure of student writing" (p. 2) called for by the Center for Educational Policy Research's (CEPR) *Mixed Messages* study (Conley, 2003). The two key aspects of the knowledge transfer in Acker and Halasek's project turned out to be the benefits that students received from having feedback from differently situated readers (i.e., high school teachers and college instructors) and the discussions among high school and college faculty about the aspects of writing they valued.

While Acker and Halasek hypothesized that "methods of responding to student writing differ between high school language arts teachers and college composition teachers" and that "different response patterns ... have adverse effects on the quality of student writing and revision" (p. 4), they found that having different forms of comments actually benefitted students. Their study indicates that high school and college teachers' different types of responses "did not negatively affect the students' revisions" (p. 7). In fact, students may have benefitted from the "*two kinds of readers*—one who focused on local and a second who focused on global issues" (p. 7). Because ePortfolios easily allow the sharing of student documents among multiple readers, they encourage distributive assessment (Whithaus, 2005, pp. xxix-xxxii, 49-66; Warnock, 2009)—multiple readers reading, responding, and evaluating a document or an entire portfolio based on their own situation-specific criteria rather than using a rubric that strips away the authentic perspectives of different readers and different contexts.

In addition to increasing the amount and types of feedback students received, Acker and Halasek's ePortfolio system encouraged collaboration and community among high school and college faculty. By sharing curricula and discussing their evaluations of student writing, the participants talked across institutional boundaries about issues such as the value of "voice" in student writing. As an evaluation concept, "voice" is particularly difficult to quantify, but the differences between high school and college teachers were not solely focused on identifying students' use of personal voice, but on the appropriate context in which personal voice should be used. Acker and Halasek note that in their study "high school teachers typically encouraged students to create a voice in personal essays (e.g., personal narratives or opinion pieces) but discouraged them from using that same 'voice' in more academic pieces (e.g., research papers). The distinction was not one generally made by college teachers, who encouraged students to create voice in all of their academic writing" (p. 9). Although the study and the discussion among the high school and college faculty revealed a difference about the way that voice was defined and when personal voice was considered appropriate, the very act of having the discussion about ePortfolios across the institutional divide of high schools and colleges created a thirdspace where knowledge transfer could occur not only for students but also between faculty members.

While Acker and Halasek's study shows how ePortfolios can be used to both promote and assess knowledge transfer about writing, ePortfolios can also facilitate the transfer of multimodal composing abilities and information skills. Pinto and Sales (2008) have defined information literacy skills or INFOLIT as the ability to locate, evaluate, and manage information; these information literacy skills "are basic to the process of 'learning to learn' [and play] a key role in promoting the autonomy of the graduate and future professional" (p. 54). The concept of information literacy (INFOLIT) was introduced by Paul Zurkowski (1974). The American Library Association defines information literacy as "an understanding and set of abilities enabling individuals to recognize when information is needed" and "a capacity to locate, evaluate, and use effectively the needed information" (p. 58). Pinto and Sales' work on INFOLIT in Spanish universities helps address the question of how building information literacy competencies can enable knowledge transfer. It also addresses the question of how to transfer knowledge about information literacies from one context to another. Like the tensions between teaching writing as a general skill and teaching writing within the disciplines, Pinto and Sales point to the tensions between generic information literacy and the specific knowledge of any disciplinary or professional community. They claim that "despite the generic need for information literacy, it is also part of the specific competencies of any community of practice; and, in this sense, we believe that much effort still needs to be made in order to help to promote real user-centered information literacy instruction" (p. 72). ePortfolios as tools and the concept of a thirdspace between general education courses and discipline-specific competencies may help promote the "real user-centered information literacy instruction" that Pinto and Sales call

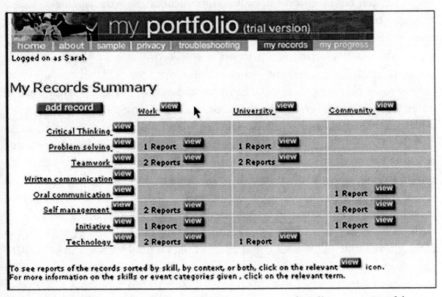

Figure 1: Attributes and Outcomes for the University of Wollongong ePortfolio (Lambert & Corrin, 2007).

for in Spanish universities. The increasing emphasis on information literacy in Spanish universities parallels the new focus on multimodal composing found in many North American postsecondary writing programs. Researchers (Gee, 2003; Kress, 2003; Whithaus, 2005) have found that effective writers in the early 21st-century are not only engaged in text-based literacy practices, but need to be able to use multimodal information and communication technologies (ICTs).

Lambert and Corrin (2007) have traced the development of an ePortfolio system that includes vigorous reflection for the development of text-based literacy practices as well as competence in the use of multimodal forms of composition. While this ePortfolio system at the University of Wollongong in Australia was designed to be customizable "for all students across all faculties," the pilot projects were run with 300 students in Performance and Journalism. Working with these disciplines foregrounds the need for ePortfolios to represent students' developing competence as writers and as composers able to work in multiple media. Like Pinto and Sales (2008) and many North American proponents of writing in the disciplines, Lambert and Corrin are aware of the tensions between developing generic skills and the more nuanced set of competencies required within disciplinary and professional contexts. Their ePortfolio system addresses these issues by having eight skills develop across three different contexts (see Figure 1). Notice how the eight skills (critical thinking, problem solving, teamwork, written communication, oral communication, self-management, initiative, and technology) cut across three different contexts (work, university, and community).

Lambert and Corrin's study shows that ePortfolios have the potential to represent students' movement from developing general skills when they enter college to developing professional competencies as they prepare to graduate and enter the workforce, graduate school, or professional schools. Taken together with Acker and Halasek's (2008) and Pinto and Sales' (2008) studies, Lambert and Corrin's work shows how ePortfolios may be used to promote as well as assess knowledge transfer across institutional and social divisions (i.e., high school to college, general education to disciplinary courses, college to professional training). Understanding these institutional and social divisions as liminal thirdspaces challenges ePortfolio developers to link outcomes assessments with the students' next learning environments. Acker and Halasek's (2008) examination of how ePortfolios could connect high school students in Ohio with the writing curriculum at Ohio State offers one illustration of using ePortfolios as a way of negotiating these thirdspaces. Lambert and Corrin's (2007) work with Performance and Journalism students at Wollongong suggests another. The question now is whether it would be possible to build an assessment of knowledge transfer onto a large-scale learning outcomes study such as Desmet et al. (2008), who measure the importance of revision within the required general education writing course at the University of Georgia. Using a multiyear, institution-wide ePortfolio (similar to the ones from Ohio and Australia discussed in this essay), it would be possible to expand their study to account for how students used revision in their upper division, disciplinary courses. This expansion of a learning outcomes assessment from within general education writing courses to the impact of general education writing courses on students' use of particular writing skills (such as revision) within upper-division, disciplinary courses, highlights the potentials of ePortfolios as systems. These systems can be used not only for the assessment of individual students' growth, but also for the assessment of the knowledge transfer that occurs when students take particular writing skills developed in general education courses into discipline-specific upper division courses.

USING THE OPEN SOURCE PORTFOLIO (OSP) TOOL WITHIN SAKAI TO MEASURE KNOWLEDGE TRANSFER FROM LOWER DIVISION WRITING COURSES TO UPPER DIVISION WRITING COURSES

What would an ePortfolio system for measuring knowledge transfer from lower division, general education courses to upper division, discipline-specific courses look like in practice? At the University of California, Davis, we are developing an ePortfolio system that would allow us to assess how students' knowledge about the writing skills stressed in their lower division writing courses transfer to their upper division writing experiences. This ePortfolio system works within UC Davis' build-out of the Sakai course management system and incorporates the Open Source Portfolio (OSP) tool that is integrated into Sakai. By collecting student writing samples from our first-year composition courses (University Writing Program, 1), we are assembling a corpus of texts that will allow us to replicate and extend the University of Georgia study (Desmet et al., 2008). In replicating the University of Georgia study, we will use ePortfolios to focus on revision and measure the impact that revision has on the quality of student writing within a given course. Extending the University of Georgia study, we will track the development of students' abilities:

1. To use evidence effectively,
2. To shape an essay for a particular audience and purpose, and
3. To use a variety of appropriate prose styles and to master accepted grammar, syntax, and usage.

Each of these areas relates to a set of explicitly articulated course goals for our first-year writing courses (see Table 1).

Table 1. Course Goals for UWP 1 and Areas to be Measured via Data Collected through a Sakai/OSP ePortfolio System

Areas to be Measured	UWP 1 Course Goals
Revision	• Not an explicit course goals of UWP 1
Evidence	• To explore the nature of evidence in academic and expository writing (and to synthesize multiple texts, formulate an original argument, and support it with appropriate evidence) • To provide students with instruction and practice in synthesizing multiple texts, formulating an original argument, and supporting it with appropriate evidence
Audience and Purpose	• To introduce students to the concepts of audience, purpose, persona, voice, authority, and tone as they relate to expository writing
Style and Usage	• To review the requirements of standard written English and to help students master accepted grammar, syntax, and usage • To develop students' ability to recognize the stylistic aspects of expository texts, and to develop a clear, reasonably sophisticated, and appropriately varied prose style in their own writing • To develop their awareness of language, including such concepts as diction, word choice, connotation/denotation, and figurative language
[Course Goals Excluded from ePortfolio Study]	• To develop the close reading skills necessary for analysis and interpretation of academic and scholarly writing • To introduce the forms and conventions of non-fiction prose • To explore, through readings, how assumptions, key questions, and fundamental concepts lead to the construction of knowledge in different disciplines • To introduce students to effective ways to structure and organize texts • To help students learn how to analyze individual arguments

The use of ePortfolios in upper division writing courses (including writing in the disciplines courses, writing in the professions courses, writing experience courses, and senior-level, discipline-based seminars with significant writing requirements) allows the creation of a text corpora where we can analyze the ways in which students revise texts, use evidence, adapt their writing for specific audiences and purposes, and effectively employ different writing styles and correct usage conventions. Comparing students' performances in lower division, general education writing environments and upper division, discipline-specific writing experiences allows us to map how knowledge about particular areas of writing moves with students as they advance in their academic careers. The Ohio State (Acker & Halasek, 2008) and Wollongong (Lambert & Corrin, 2007) studies suggest that knowledge transfer can not only be measured but also be encouraged by using an ePortfolio system; using the OSP tool within Sakia at UC Davis will allow us to test these findings about knowledge transfer.

While our proposed system focuses on writing skills, ePortfolios offer the potential to track other forms of knowledge transfer. By collecting a series of learning artifacts, ePortfolios can be used to measure how students' skills in areas such as critical thinking, problem solving, or teamwork develop in their general education coursework. The learning artifacts could include multimodal compositions, more traditional forms of assessments such as exams, and writing samples. If used on a university-wide level, ePortfolios could be used to compare how student growth and achievement in these areas in lower division courses transferred to discipline-specific competencies in their upper division, discipline-specific course work.

KNOWLEDGE TRANSFER, INVOLVED STUDENTS, AND COLLABORATIVE LEARNING

Tracking the knowledge transferred from lower division writing courses to upper division writing courses on a university-wide level is not about the assessment of individual students' abilities, but rather a systemic and programmatic assessment. Measuring how knowledge about revision, use of evidence, audience/purpose and style/usage moves (or does not move) with students is a question of the aggregate. Studies of Computer Supported Collaborative Learning (CSCL) (Dillenbourg, Eurelings, & Hakkarainen, 2001; Koschmann, Hall, & Miyake, 2002; Stahl, 2002; Van Aalst & Chan, 2007) provide models for ePortfolio developers and researchers interested in explicitly involving students in their own knowledge building activities. However, this research tends to emphasize collaborative processes and overlook learning outcomes. Van Aalst and

Chan's (2007) work aims to incorporate learning outcomes within a CSCL model where student designed ePortfolios play a significant role; drawing on three classroom studies they examine the evolution and roles of that student knowledge building plays in the ePortfolios.

In most ePortfolio systems, the framework for the portfolio is created by the classroom teacher or by the institution setting up the portfolio system and not by the students participating in the project. In Van Aalst and Chan's (2007) studies of ePortfolio and CLCS systems in Canada and Hong Kong, the students engage in knowledge building within frameworks that they have defined for themselves:

> The goal is to enable the class to articulate questions and ideas they have about the topic and to delineate the general scope of what they attempt to accomplish. Students may contribute their ideas to the database and talk to each other about them. With some assistance from the teacher, the class may settle on a general plan for what it hopes to accomplish in the unit. (pp. 178-179)

The idea of constructing an ePortfolio system where the participants are active builders of the ePortfolio's framework returns to early debates in writing studies ePortfolios about the differences between student-designed (webfolios) and database-driven, institutionally-designed (ePortfolios) (Batson, 2002; Whithaus, 2005). Van Aalst and Chan's (2007) model demonstrates the possibilities for integrating these models of ePortfolios into systems that incorporate databases, but allow students significant influence on the shape of their portfolios and the assessment of the learning taking place in them. These shifts not only affected the ePortfolios, but also the way that inquiry proceeded in the courses. In the classes, "instead of focusing on readings and topics, sustained inquiry and progressive problem solving could be facilitated by providing authentic problems and encouraging questions to emerge from student-directed inquiry" (p. 209).

For ePortfolio developers concerned with improving the alignment of lower division courses that focus on information skills and writing with the competencies required of students for work within their majors, this model implies the potential of incorporating student input into a programmatic assessment. How would students define the successful transfer of writing skills developed in lower division courses into their upper level, discipline specific writing experiences? In some studies, this question might be approached through student surveys. Within an ePortfolio system—especially one that would incorporate

Van Aalst and Chan's (2007) work on active student participation in knowledge building—the students would be invited to address these connections with the courses and the ePortfolio system themselves. Operationalizing a vision of students as active agents in the measuring of knowledge transfer is a difficult task. A large-scale ePortfolio system could be designed to measure how well discrete writing skills (such as revision, use of evidence, awareness of audiences and purposes, and the ability to use different writing styles and correct usage conventions) aligned in writing samples drawn from lower division courses and upper division courses. Having such a system incorporate the potential knowledge building functions of ePortfolios would require that the reflective element(s) used in the upper division courses associated with the ePortfolios explicitly asked students to consider how their earlier college writing experiences impacted their later work. In this way, data could be gathered that would include student perspectives on the knowledge about writing that transferred from their earlier college writing experiences to their later experiences. This data would be associated with writing samples, so that researchers could verify and investigate further the student perceptions. This follow up activity would create data with a greater depth and a greater validity than data gathered through a more traditional student survey. Light, Chen, and Ittelson (2012) describe qualitative and quantitative triangulation techniques through ePortfolio pedagogy in their recent book, *Documenting Learning with ePortfolios* (pp. 7-24).

CLOSING: USING EPORTFOLIOS TO MEASURE KNOWLEDGE TRANSFER

When applied to learning about writing in secondary and postsecondary contexts, the concept of thirdspaces (Grego & Thompson, 2008; Soja, 1996) suggests that students not only learn about writing in official "sanctioned," for-credit, writing-focused courses, but also have the potential to learn even more effectively through a variety of opportunities connected with research activities in their own disciplines. The concept of thirdspaces then is useful if we want to rethink traditional modes of delivering writing instruction. When ePortfolios operate on an institution-wide level, they can become a vehicle of measuring the learning about writing that occurs in these thirdspaces. They can also measure how specific writing skills acquired in one context (lower division writing courses) do, or do not, transfer into other contexts (e.g., upper division, disciplinary courses where there is a significant amount of writing required). These measures of knowledge transfer should include how students are using information literacies and multimodal composing skills as part of the developing abilities as writers. Finally, ePortfolios may even be designed in ways that incorporate the latest developments in computer supported collaborative learning (CSCL). By incorporating reflective cover letters or other reflective pieces of writing that ask students about how earlier course work informed the choices they made about their writing in later courses, a set of data can be collected that incorporates students' knowledge about their learning and their emerging knowledge base about writing (Goodwin-Jones, 2008). Combining the students' reflections with outcomes-based assessment tied to multiple samples of student writing from different course levels creates a rich matrix of data-driven assessments that can work as a feedback loop and help inform curriculum development and the faculty's pedagogical choices.

REFERENCES

Acker, S. R., & Halasek, K. (2008). Preparing high school students for college-level writing: Using ePortfolio to support a successful transition. *The Journal of General Education, 57*(1), 14.

Argyris, C., & Schön, D. A. (1974). *Theory in practice: Increasing professional effectiveness* (1st ed.). San Francisco: Jossey-Bass.

Bartholomae, D., & Petrosky, T. (1986). *Facts, artifacts, and counterfacts: Theory and method for a reading and writing course.* Portsmouth, NH: Boynton/Cook.

Batson, T. (2002, November 26). The electronic portfolio boom: What's it all about? *Campus Technology.* Retrieved from http://campustechnology.com/articles/2002/11/the-electronic-portfolio-boom-whats-it-all-about.aspx

Butcher, J. (2009). Off-campus learning and employability in undergraduate design: The "Sorrell Young Design Project" as an innovative partnership. *Art, Design and Communication in Higher Education, 7*(3), 13.

Desmet, C., Church Miller, D., Griffin, J., Balthazor, R., & Cummings, R. E. (2008). Reflection, revision, and assessment in first-year composition ePortfolios. *The Journal of General Education, 57*(1), 15.

Dillenbourg, P., Eurelings, A., & Hakkarainen, K. (Eds.). (2001). European perspectives on computer-supported collaborative learning: *Proceedings of the first European conference on computer-supported collaborative learning.* The Netherlands: University of Maastricht.

Goodwin-Jones, R. (2008). Emerging technologies web-writing 2.0: Enabling, document, and assessing writing online. *Language and Technology, 12*(2), 7-13.

Grego, R., & Thompson, N. S. (2007). *Teaching/Writing in thirdspaces: The studio approach.* Carbondale, IL: Southern Illinois University Press.

Humphreys, D. (2009). College outcomes for work, life, and citizenship. *Liberal Education*, *95*(1), 7.

Kent, T. (1999). *Post-process theory: Beyond the writing-process paradigm.* Carbondale, IL: Southern Illinois University Press.

Light, T. P., Chen, H. L., & Ittelson, J. C. (2012). *Documenting learning with eportfolios: A guide for college instructors.* San Francisco: Jossey-Bass.

Koschmann, T. D., Hall, R., & Miyake, N. (Eds.). (2002). CSCL 2: *Carrying forward the conversation.* Mahwah, NJ: Lawrence Erlbaum.

Lambert, S., & Corrin, L. (2007). Moving towards a university wide implementation of an ePortfolio tool. Australasian *Journal of Educational Technology*, *23*(1), 16.

Lopez-Fernandez, O., & Rodriguez-Illera, J. (2009). Investigating university students' adaption to a digital learner course portfolio. *Computers and Education*, *52*, 608-616.

Massey, D. B. (2005). *For space.* London/Thousand Oaks, CA: SAGE.

Massey, D. B. (1994). *Space, place, and gender.* Minneapolis: University of Minnesota Press.

Mauk, J. (2003). The "Real" (e)states of being, writing, and thinking in composition. *College English*, *65*(4), 21.

Ostorga, A., & Estrada, V. (2009). Impact of an action research instructional model: Student teachers as reflective thinkers. *Action in Teacher Education*, *30*(4), 9.

Petraglia, J. (1998). *Reality by design: The rhetoric and technology of authenticity in education.* Mahwah, NJ: Lawrence Erlbaum.

Pinto, M., & Sales, D. (2008). Knowledge transfer and information skills for student-centered learning in spain. Portal: *Libraries and the Academy*, *8*(1).

Reynolds, N. (2004). *Geographies of writing: Inhabiting places and encountering difference.* Carbondale, IL: Southern Illinois University Press.

Schneider, C. G. (2008). A different take on excellence. *Liberal Education*, *94*(1), 2.

Schön, D. A. (1987). *Educating the reflective practitioner* (1st ed.). San Francisco: Jossey-Bass.

Schön, D. A. (1983). *The reflective practitioner: How professionals think in action.* New York: Basic Books.

Schön, D. A. (1991). *The reflective turn: Case studies in and on educational practice.* New York: Teachers College.

Shaughnessy, M. P. (1977). *Errors and expectations: A guide for the teacher of basic writing.* New York: Oxford University Press.

Shor, I. (1987). *Freire for the classroom: A sourcebook for liberatory teaching* (1st ed.). Portsmouth, NH: Boynton/Cook.

Shor, I. (1996). *When students have power: Negotiating authority in a critical pedagogy.* Chicago: University of Chicago Press.

Soja, E. W. (1996). *Thirdspace: Journeys to Los Angeles and other real-and-imagined places.* Cambridge, MA: Blackwell.

Stahl, G. (Ed.). (2002). *CompUPter support for collaborative learning: Foundation for a CSCL community.* Mahwah, NJ: Lawrence Erlbaum.

Swartzendruber-Putnam, D. (2000). Written reflection: Creating better thinkers, better writers. *The English Journal, 90*(1), 6.

Thompson, N. S., Alford, E. M., Liao, C., Johnson, R., Matthews, M. A. (2005). Integrating undergraduate research into engineering: A communications approach to holistic education. *Journal of Engineering Education, 94*(3), 10.

Van Aalst, J., & Chan, C. K. K. (2007). Student-directed assessment of knowledge building using electronic portfolios. *Journal of the Learning Sciences, 16*(2), 175-220.

Warnock, S. (2009). Methods and results of an accreditation-driven writing assessment in a business college. *Journal of Business and Technical Communication, 23*(1), 24.

What general education courses contribute to essential learning outcomes (2009). *The Journal of General Education, 58*(2), 19.

Whithaus, C. (2005). *Teaching and evaluating writing in the age of computers and high-stakes testing.* Mahwah, N.J.: Lawrence Erlbaum.

Xiao, L. et al. (2008). Gerontological education in undergraduate nursing programs: An Australian perspective. *Educational Gerontology, 34*(9), 18.

Yancey, K. B. (1998). *Reflection in the writing classroom.* Logan, UT: Utah State University Press.

CHAPTER 12.

BALANCING LEARNING AND ASSESSMENT: A STUDY OF VIRGINIA TECH'S USE OF EPORTFOLIOS

Marc Zaldivar
Virginia Tech University

Teggin Summers
Virginia Tech University

C. Edward Watson
Virginia Tech University

This chapter explores the case of ePortfolio adoption at Virginia Tech. The idea that ePortfolios are useful reflective devices is a well-explored concept. The impact of ePortfolios on assessment of student learning is becoming an important ground for new research in ePortfolio usage. At Virginia Tech, we are finding ways to work on ePortfolios, both as a reflective medium for learning and as a tool for improving assessment of that learning, in order to deploy this learning technology across a large and varied student and faculty population.

Portfolios in educational settings are certainly not a new concept. Many disciplines, including English, art, and education, have made portfolios integral to their pedagogical process for years (Devanney & Walsh, 2002, Greenberg, 2004, Weimer, 2002); however, a number of technological innovations, as well as specific trends in academic and programmatic assessment, have brought ePortfolios to the forefront of recent discussion in higher education.

Like traditional portfolios, ePortfolios contain students' work collected over time (Hutchins, 1990). They foster dialogue and "interaction with teachers, mentors, peers, colleagues, friends, and family" (Greenberg, 2004, p. 30). This process and resulting product of co-working provide a context and opportunity for student reflection and revision and results in behaviors that are related to deep learning. The key difference between traditional and electronic portfolios, then, is the use of technology to collect, organize, manage, store, retrieve, and share a variety of information, including artifacts of learning, audio/visual files, and student reflections. In an ePortfolio, "all artifacts have been transformed into computer-readable form. An electronic portfolio is not a haphazard collection of artifacts (i.e., a digital scrapbook or multimedia presentation) but rather a reflective tool that demonstrates growth over time" (Barrett, 2000). Because of this archival nature, however, a new interest in ePortfolios has emerged from a variety of institutional stakeholders (Batson, 2009, Lorenzo & Ittleson, 2005).

In addition to encouraging students' reflection and learning, ePortfolios are currently celebrated as a way to facilitate and document more authentic forms of assessment. With increased calls for accountability at the state, regional and national workplaces, the collection and management of student learning outcomes has emerged as a complex and immediate challenge for colleges and universities. As a result, many programs see ePortfolios solely as an archival tool to document student learning which can then be mined for assessment purposes to respond to the aforementioned assessment pressures. The question then becomes how programs or institutions can structure their activities to take advantage of the learning benefits of the ePortfolio process yet meet the assessment needs best met by a product approach to ePortfolios. This chapter describes these two seemingly opposing ePortfolio approaches and suggests a method for putting the two in balance in order to achieve the best outcomes from both approaches.

EPORTFOLIO: PRODUCT VS. PROCESS

With electronic portfolios gaining more and more national and international attention in the field of higher education, many valuable questions concerning challenges and implications of ePortfolio adoption need to be addressed. Amongst these questions lie issues of standardization, ownership, and perhaps at the heart of the debate: the tension between process- and product-orientated portfolios. Shavelson, Klein, and Benjamin (2009) have argued that ePortfolios lack standardization, scalability, and objectivity. Batson, a stout proponent of ePortfolios, has also acknowledged that one factor preventing ePortfolio adoption is the "lack of standards for the data being maintained in the ePortfolio repository" (Batson, 2009a). Additionally, Batson has argued that for students "portfolio-for-the-matrix has left them estranged from their own work and the student-centered technology that was supposed to be has lagged behind accreditation management technology ... If there is only one ePortfolio platform on campus, it is bound to become an institutional ePortfolio" (Batson, 2009b). Some of these issues stem from the tension between process- and product-oriented portfolios and the pedagogical values and concepts different people attach to these various types of portfolios.

Some view product-based portfolios as being purely assessment-driven, which can in turn inhibit reflective, authentic facilitation of learning. Others view process-based portfolios as being too loose, too flexible and hence preventing scaffolded, guided facilitation of learning. Opponents of ePortfolios claim that this can create a hodgepodge of standards, which lack coherency. Since types of electronic portfolios are as diverse as the people who create them, the suggestion that there is a bifurcation between portfolios that are adopted for the collection of assessment data, product portfolios, and those that are instituted for the facilitation of learning, process portfolios, should not come as a surprise. Additionally, these two types of portfolios can simultaneously be thought of as wholly different, serving different purposes and different audiences, and as being one and the same. For instance, each of us comes to the concept of portfolios with our own ideas as to what they are and what audiences and objectives they serve. Some view ePortfolios as nuanced educational tools, used for encouraging student growth and self-assessment, for assessing learning across groups of students, and for developing a culture of assessment between faculty, students, and administrators; however, all too often people develop one set opinion on what an ePortfolio is and how it can best be used to meet their needs. Because of this somewhat homogenizing approach, we often fail to see the value of utilizing electronic portfolios for different purposes. This perspective applies to the dichotomization sometimes existing between product and process portfolios. While these types of portfolios have been referred to under various terms—such as showcase and workspace (Barrett, 2009) and process and showcase (Abrami & Barrett, 2005), for example—from here on we will refer to them as product and process portfolios. When a curriculum or program only approaches portfolios from a product perspective, it runs the risk of turning a valuable learning tool into an electronic storage closet. At the same time, product-oriented portfolios can add a layer of qualitative richness to the types of information gleaned from student activity and applied to improvements in teaching and student learning. Therefore, it can be helpful to discuss the relevant merits in the academy and other workplaces of both process- and product-oriented ePortfolios.

This section will provide overviews of product- and process-oriented ePortfolios. Additionally, it answers a question posed by Helen Barrett: "How do we match the needs of the institution for valid and reliable data for accreditation and accountability while still meeting the needs of learners for formative assessment to enhance and support the learning process?" (2004). At Virginia Tech we are able to engage in this process successfully, using a single ePortfolio platform system. Our system is one that embraces eFolio thinking as a way to synthesize process- and product-based portfolios. Whether a portfolio initiative places overarching value on product or process, as long as the project is imbued with "eFolio thinking," the process is likely to be successful and result in valuable learning.

Meyer and Tusin (1999) describe process portfolios as those that emphasize the learning of new skills, understanding, and progress. Students using portfolios for this purpose are more interested in improvement and learning from mistakes. Conversely, product portfolios have more emphasis on how outcomes reflect ability. Students using portfolios for this purpose are more interested in comparing themselves to and scoring better than others (Meyer & Tusin, 1999, p. 131). Helen Barrett (2009) describes process ePortfolios as being workspace portfolios, oriented to learning and reflection. With process portfolios, feedback is formative, assessment *for* learning. Product ePortfolios are described as being showcase portfolios, oriented to presentation and accountability. With product portfolio, feedback is summative, assessment *on* learning. Both types of portfolio have positive attributes they can bring to the classroom; both pose challenges as well.

While product-oriented portfolios hold value for the classroom, there is concern that when overemphasized, they can detract from the learning process. Johnson and Rose (1997) remind us, "When we only focus on portfolios as a product, we've missed their potential power, which comes from the process of creating them" (p. 8). In addition, Yagelski (1997) speaks of the integration of a reflective portfolio into a pre-service English course at Purdue University:

> Unwittingly, in trying to make the portfolio a comprehensive
> portrait of the students' work in high school classrooms over
> the semester, we had squelched the opportunity for careful
> reflection and ended up with what amounted to a collec-
> tion of documents; moreover, what reflection did occur was
> largely ... students ... evaluating their work for the portfolio
> *after* the fact and not in an ongoing fashion. (p. 230)

Because course teachers initially asked for a collection of a series of documents, of which most were specified course assignments, they were unable to achieve their desired goal of critical reflection. These arguments are not without merit. Certain challenges exist within product-oriented portfolios. Because of their product-based nature, these portfolios may allow more room for materials to be submitted at the last minute, and if this happens, students may not have as much critical reflection on how their materials meet their different learning outcomes. Wagner and Lamoureux (2006) note when implementing their outcome-based assessment ePortfolios, that "while students are currently encouraged to begin uploading to their ePortfolios early ... many seem to 'wait until the end'" (p. 545). An additional complication to assessment-driven, product-based portfolios is the fact that many students feel little ownership over their portfolios. This is a challenge Wagner and Lamoureux (2006) faced when a focus group student stated "We know it will help the program, but what's in it for us?" (p. 548). There is potential, with these types of portfolios, to place so much emphasis on the outcomes that students lose the importance of progressive reflection and engagement with their own learning processes.

On the contrary, product-oriented, assessment-based, and showcase portfolios can hold great pedagogical potential for courses, programs, and students alike. For students, showcase portfolios, which are also product-oriented, can facilitate ownership and engagement with programmatic outcomes and professional communities of practice. For example, when students are selecting their best pieces of work to showcase in a professional portfolio, with a prospective employer in mind as an audience, the student can feel more ownership over the materials and a stronger sense of involvement and value from the creation process. As they prepare these portfolios, students have the opportunity to see the connections between all they have learned in their courses and program and their intended professional communities. Additionally, in these types of portfolios, students also often have more opportunities to customize their portfolios and make them more personal, something that often contributes to ePortfolio motivation. As one student noted, "I also wondered if there was a way to make it more customized. I think that students are more attracted to things that they can make personal, as in color, font, background, etc" (Hakel, Gromko, & Blackburn, 2006, p. 395).

Beyond their ability to guide a student's professional development, product-focused ePortfolios are able to collect effective data that can give long-term, comparative information leading to curricular improvement. This can be done in ways that are more authentic and student-centered than traditional test-based assessment formats. In addition to some of the challenges of their outcomes-based assessment ePortfolio, Wagner and Lamoureux (2006) also note that faculty felt they were becoming more intentional in their assessment, and students saw the ways in which the assessment of ePortfolios contributed to the improvement of the program: "I see program changes as a reward. I'm only a sophomore and will reap the benefits from the revisions in the program" (p. 548).

Similarly, while product-focused portfolios have much to contribute to the pedagogical environment, the very process of creating these products that make up the portfolios, especially portfolios that emphasize learning-focused outcomes, can contribute to students making deeper connections between their programs of study and their professional communities of practice within various workplaces. Process-focused portfolios tend to be the ones most associated with reflection, self-assessment, and growth of learning. As Yancey (2001) states, portfolios make learning visible:

> Portfolios bring together visibility, process, and reflection as students chart and interpret their own learning. Students are responsible ... for explaining what they did and did not learn, for assessing their own strengths and weaknesses as learners, for evaluating their products and performances, for showing how that learning connects with other kinds of learning (in the classroom and without), and for using the review of the past to think about paths for future learning. (p. 19)

While process portfolios do not necessarily represent the type of presentation a student would want to introduce to a prospective employer, they do represent the types of learning and vehicles for authentic feedback that students would want to show their instructors, exam committees, and programmatic administrators. Additionally, there may be some documents within these portfolios that students might want to display within a showcase, and the progressive reflections embedded throughout such portfolios better help students to not only know which materials they might want to display, but also how they want to portray themselves to their intended audiences.

A useful way to think of these two ePortfolio paradigms is from a perspective that blends the two approaches. Meyer and Tusin (1999) say as much when they note that, "Within the average cases, we found preservice teachers' knowledge about and experience with portfolios to be complex mixtures of process and product" (p. 135). After studying the relationship between preservice and inservice teachers' pedagogical values, along with their knowledge of and experience with portfolios, Meyer and Tusin (1999) concluded that using portfolios in methods courses seemed to elicit more use of portfolios for professional development purposes, as opposed to the desired outcome of using portfolios for learning processes. They suggest that "Faculty must ask all preservice teachers to reflect upon all the different forms and purposes of portfolios, and to synthesize what is similar and different among their methods portfolios, students' portfolios, and professional portfolios" (p. 137). See also Carl Young's (2009) more recent work. This advice is applicable to all who embark on an ePortfolio initiative: it is important to strike a balance between product and process portfolios in order to maximize their learning and professional potentials. David W. Denton conducted an Eportfolio study along these lines measuring writing reflection improvement after an intervention with preservice teachers (2012). See also C. E. Shepherd and M. Hannafin's (2011) work on the effects of ePortfolio development on preservice teachers' inquiry and growth in the *Journal of Technology and Teaching Education.*

In her "Balancing the two faces of ePortfolio," Helen Barrett (2009) systematically and thoroughly displays the differences and relationships between process and product ePortfolios, and suggests that balancing the two types of portfolios enhances learner engagement with the portfolio process. The challenge, of course, is finding a way to balance all that ePortfolios have to offer: immersion in learning processes, formative and summative assessment, curricular and programmatic development and improvement, and professional development. Each program must determine for itself its own needs and goals, priorities, resources, and timelines.

At Virginia Tech, the ePortfolio Initiatives office is working with faculty to slowly evolve a process in which ePortfolios can facilitate product-oriented collection of data *and* process-oriented critical reflections on growth over time. Through our use of the Open Source Portfolio tools in our instance of the Sakai collaborative learning environment, we have devised a way for faculty and program administrators to collect student documents for summative assessment of learning and of the overall program. In addition, we can embed reflection prompts and students are able to reflect on their progress in their courses and programs throughout their duration. Finally, through the flexible nature of our tool set, students are able to create ePortfolios for assessment that balance process- and product-oriented approaches. Additionally, students can also easily reuse specific documents to create professional ePortfolios that they then use to gain competitive jobs and internships. Though we are just at the beginning of these efforts, we have already seen exemplary levels of student engagement with this blended approach. Faculty are able to collect the data they need for assessment and accreditation purposes, and students are able to see the ways in which their learning and development as professionals have grown throughout their academic career. Students have additional ownership over their work and related reflections, as they are able to customize these pieces to further their professional development. In fact, many students are recognizing that even if prospective employers do not actually see their electronic portfolios, the very act of creating their portfolios helps prepare them for the rigorous process of acceptance and eventual membership in their professional communities. When

227

students see the connections between their learning processes and their outcomes, we have truly achieved a synthesis of process and product.

FOLIO V. EFOLIO THINKING: EXTENDING THE PORTFOLIO DISCUSSION

Much of this discussion, which emphasizes the blending of process and product, is encapsulated within the framework of "eFolio thinking." This is a notion that we extended from Chen and Mazow's (2002) "folio thinking." Their term focuses on the cognitive predilection of any type of learning-focused portfolio to "encourage students to integrate discrete learning experiences; enhance students' self-understanding; promote students' taking responsibility for their own learning; [and] support students in developing an intellectual identity" (Chen & Mazow, 2002, p. 2). Those goals are solid foundations upon which to build an ePortfolio program. On the surface, these principles seem fairly process-oriented. The focus is on students' processes of learning and growth, responsibility and understanding. However, in order to sustain these processes, student activities, complete with artifacts created along the way, will provide the touchstones needed to assess the growth and learning touted in each portfolio. Well-designed portfolio programs of any nature would do well to ground themselves in folio thinking.

1. To extend that, we offer four additional enhancements based on the electronic nature of ePortfolios:
2. ePortfolios can offer an easier management of the collection, selection, and reflection process for students;
3. ePortfolios can offer a greater variety of communication potentials—easier sharing with a greater variety of individuals in order to provide a greater breadth and depth of feedback;
4. ePortfolios can offer a method of gaining more meaningful data analysis for the student, instructor, and administrator; and
5. ePortfolios can offer a greater potential for long-term transportability, and more importantly, long-term growth and development.

Without reviewing the obvious details of the differences between paper- and electronic-based portfolios, the four propositions comprising "eFolio Thinking," highlight several significant differences.

First, online management of portfolios, including those centralized in learning management systems, encourage students to take a long-term focus on the collection, selection, and reflection on the contents of their portfolio. Centralized storage encourages students to reuse materials and to do so more easily, extending initial reflections with deeper understandings at a later time. The integration of common blog-type elements, replete with full search engines greatly expands the "cataloging" capabilities of portfolio authors.

Second, as an extension of that concept, electronic environments offer portfolio creators a greater ability to share their work with audiences. Traditional audiences, such as instructors or academic committees, can be reached more easily, often with just an email containing a link. And that same email can simultaneously reach professionals working in the field, management considering applicant pools, family members, and interested other parties, all with the same amount of effort. With the integration of social networking tools, electronic portfolios can turn from pure product-oriented containers to discussion spaces surrounding touchstones of an individual or group's work, such as in the case of Margo Tamez' electronic portfolio created for her dissertation which quickly became a central point of focus in a national debate on immigration (Schaffhauser, 2009).

Third, electronic portfolios offer the ability for many different audiences to have access to an array of data for analysis of student learning. As we have known for years, ePortfolios offer individual students a way to track their development over time (Cambridge, 2001; Doig, Illsley, McLuckie, & Parsons, 2006; Hutchings, 1990; Michelson & Mandell, 2004; Steffani, Mason, & Pegler, 2007; Zubizaretta, 2004). In addition, ePortfolios that are designed well offer course instructors, program advisors, and academic assessment teams an enormous amount of direct evidence of student learning (Schneider, 2009), especially if the students' reflective voices are given a role in that assessment (Batson, 2009b). By carefully aligning the reflective learning process with the collection of artifacts that demonstrate that learning, students can measure their own progress against departmental or institutional requirements. At the same time, course instructors are gathering representative work from early, middle, and late in the term by which, with rubrics or other measuring scales, they should be able to detect the amount of growth that a student has undertaken in the course. Accumulating over several terms, departments can then assess the work that is being done in key courses by sampling from an array of students' portfolios demonstrating work and reflections on that work in those courses. This can be the grounding for continuous programmatic development. That sort of effort is one that the program or institution can use to demonstrate to accrediting bodies the on-going effort at programmatic improvement as well as achievements already made. Pure product-focused portfolios would not achieve these multi-layered goals. Institutions may collect key assessment data, but if they are only looking at lists of student-generated artifacts, they lose a significant voice in the assessment process: the student's own acknowledgement of learning. Similarly, pure process-focused portfolios, those based only on reflection and not as interested in core, guided products for programmatic portfolios, can inhibit the student's ability to measure his/her own success at achieving departmental goals. The sheer collection of exemplars by promoting successful portfolios can enhance each student's ability to meet departmental learning requirements and to grow beyond them.

That last aspect, the ability to break out of guided learning and to take on values of lifelong learning is the fourth aspect of eFolio thinking. This aspect links back to the first, in that ePortfolios encourage the author to take a long-term view of their development, but it extends the first in the affordance of transportability and the facilitation of lifelong development (Barrett & Garrett, 2009; Cambridge, 2009). Cambridge (2009), in his analysis of the potential of electronic portfolios to offer lifelong and integrative learning, focuses on two types of "selves" that can be created more easily with electronic portfolios: the "networked" and the "symphonic" self. In each case, the portfolio author has the opportunity to use the materials and reflections created over years to build a growing picture of him/herself as a learner, as one engaged in growth. While not fully technologically resolved, many elements of a portfolio are transportable if created with "eFolio thinking," that is, if the artifacts and reflections of a portfolio are created using technologies that show promise for long term read-

Student Portfolio Domains	Professionalism and Ethics	Multidisciplinary Teamwork	Multifaceted Communication	Disciplinary Knowledge	Systematic Analysis	Experiential Learning
Journal/Reflection						
HNFE 1004						
HNFE 2004						
HNFE 3025						
HNFE 3034						
HNFE 3114						
HNFE 3224						
HNFE 3234						
HNFE 4004						
HNFE 4125						
HNFE 4126						
HNFE 4624						
HNFE 4644						
Other Coursework						

Figure 1. Dietetics' Program Assessment Matrix.

ability, such as the Portable Document Format, then there is a good chance that the electronic portfolio can follow the student throughout life, gathering significance and meaning as the author grows. With even a simple Internet search, one can find dozens of examples of portfolios begun as early as kindergarten. With a proper approach, these kindergarten authors can continue to set goals and to mature as learners throughout their lives. (See also Lunsford, 2006 on writing technologies and the fifth canon.)

The four elements of eFolio Thinking focus on the electronic portfolio's ability to connect, reflect, and synthesize students' learning so that different audiences can benefit from the work contained therein. By designing ePortfolio programs with the principles of Folio and eFolio Thinking at the center, we can all improve our learning, both as students and as instructors.

TOWARD A BALANCE: TWO EXAMPLES AND A CONCLUSION

In order to wrap up this chapter, two examples will be offered from work done at Virginia Tech, in two very different departments. Through these examples, we hope to show how eFolio Thinking can be put into the design of a successful, and sustainable, portfolio program which meets needs of academic

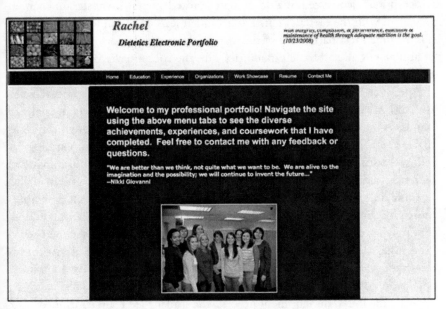

Figure 2. Sample Dietetics Student Presentation Portfolio.

and workplace environments. Both departments are radically different in their needs and outlook, yet both departments were able to design a successful eP-ortfolio program.

The first example is from the Didactic Program in Dietetics, based in the Department of Human Nutrition, Food, and Exercise (see Figures 1 and 2). This program has approximately 80 majors, accredited by the Commission on Accreditation for Dietetics Education. In that capacity, they have had a long-standing paper portfolio process in their department. This portfolio was a "product-focused" portfolio, asking each graduating senior to submit a collec-tion of 10 key assignments from their course of study, ranging from materials created in their sophomore year to assignments created in their senior year. These binders were collected, year after year. In January 2008, the program co-ordinator, Dr. Susan Clark, contacted the authors of this chapter, who all work for Learning Technologies, more specifically, for the ePortfolio Intiatives office. Dr. Clark was interested in the ePortfolio approach, initially to facilitate the easier collection and dissemination of the ten required artifacts. After recreating their paper-based, product-focused portfolio program in an electronic format, Dr. Clark recognized that there was a greater potential to the portfolio program if we adopted more of a process-focused stance and incorporated some more reflection and student-centered learning in the ePortfolios.

To accomplish this, we formed a student-led "Student Management team," which initially consisted of a dozen hand-picked students, chosen for their en-gagement with the dietetics curriculum and at least an initial interest in portfo-lios. For the most part, none of the team had a particular technological interest or ability, but all had basic capabilities with the computer. This team, again *led by the students*, helped to reshape the assessment-focus of the ePortfolio from the product-focused "10 artifacts in a binder" portfolio, to a process where the students can pick and choose which work of theirs best meets the national standards indicated by the professional accrediting agencies. Though the 10 ar-tifacts are still collected, in order to provide some consistency among the port-folios, the students also outlined several options from the curriculum that each dietetics student should consider for inclusion as evidence for one of the six learning domains that they identified. The students also focused on designing a more satisfying and useful web-interface that the individual students could use for applying to internships, which most dietetics students do after their senior years. These internships are highly competitive, and the students all felt that an electronic, easy-to-access portfolio would give them a competitive edge in the application process.

After the initial development process, the student-led team continued to ex-pand the culture of eFolio Thinking within their student body. They published papers and attended conferences to make presentations to other dietetics faculty about the significance of their work (Clark & Bailey, 2008; Clark et al., 2008, 2009a, 2009b). They also began a "Peer Mentoring" program that provides new dietetics portfolio students to gain advice and technological support from the students that have been engaged in eFolio thinking already. In this, they have created a student-centered, sustainable model for ePortfolio adoption in their program. In addition, their ePortfolios have shifted from one of pure product-gathering to one that incorporates reflections on key aspects of the dietetics professions and allows student choice of artifact to guide the collection and "evidence" of assessment that the program is using to gain accreditation.

The second program that we wish to discuss took a similar approach, in that it included student voices in the creation and adoption of the ePortfolios early on in their process. In this case, however, the Department of English at Virginia Tech does not have a professional accrediting agency to which they have to report. They had to begin by defining learning outcomes for their three primary options to the major: Creative Writing, Professional Writing, and Literature, Language, and Culture, in the process of outlining reasonable student learning outcomes, mostly to stay ahead of the curve of assessment that was gaining hold on campus. They wanted to be a department that took seriously the charges of a culture of assessment, namely that of a mode of continuous curricular improvement. To this end, they also began with a product-focused portfolio, centered mostly on programmatic assessment (see Figures 3 and 4).

LLC with Core	30-45 Credit Hours	46-60 Credit Hours	61-75 Credit Hours	76-90 Credit Hours	91-105 Credit Hours	106-120 Credit Hours
Core: Value of English Studies						
Core: Self analysis and evaluation						
Core: Critical Reading and Literary Analysis						
Core: Effective Research						
Core: Oral and Visual Presentations						
Core: Multicultural Context						
LLC: Analysis of Literature and Culture						
LLC: Knowledge and Understanding of Contexts						
LLC: Research and Engagement of Critical Discourses						

Legend

	Ready		Completed
	Pending		Locked

Figure 3. English Department Assessment Matrix.

However, early feedback from students indicated that they had no interest in or understanding of the dimensions of programmatic assessment, and their reflections made this clear. At this point, the English Department engaged a "Student ePortfolio Leadership team," whose task it was to consider what it would take for English majors to build more successful ePortfolios. For the various creative outputs of the students, a student-focused process ePortfolio was developed. Though anchored by key assignments throughout the English major's three years (beginning in the sophomore year with a course entitled "Introduction to English Studies," and which has now been renamed the "English Studies ePortfolio), the focus of this portfolio was on the learning processes that were central to the English degree. See Schnurr (2013) for more examples of

Figure 4. Sample English Major's ePortfolio.

leadership discourse and interaction cases through media (pp. 150-174). They created spaces for students to reflect on why they picked a particular option out of the three, on what they planned to do with the degree after graduation, on how they use the skills of an English major outside of the classroom (perhaps in a service learning or internship experience), and on how they see the synthesis of the English skills culminating in a picture of themselves as an English major (this last is accomplished through a synthesis reflection in the student's senior seminar). The students also are able to provide examples of artifacts that meet the six learning outcomes for graduation. The department uses these submissions for their annual "assessment day" activities, where they get a chance to look across the curriculum to see how their students are self-identifying the learning outcomes that they are achieving. This gives the department a chance to review curricular design, and to plan for a continual mode of improvement of their curriculum. However, this is no longer the only activity of the ePortfolio. Students are engaged in conversations about the curriculum and their individual plans with advisors, course instructors, and peer mentors. They are engaged in long- and short-term planning, and focused on the learning they are doing in the department. All of those are facilitated by new technology-enhanced assignments, such as a digital narrative, that take the students to new understandings of the contemporary English major. Similar to the dietetics group, this program shifted their focus from one of pure product-based assessment to include more eFolio thinking on synthesis, reflection, and connection between the curriculum and their lived experience.

Both of these examples show that ePortfolio projects need to balance priorities of learning and assessment, in-the-moment experience with archival records, needs of students with those of faculty and administrators. Following the principles of Folio and eFolio Thinking, this can be done through careful design and curriculum matches. Ultimately, this gives us all a win-win situation: students learn more, and we learn more about what and how students are learning. In addition to this sort of internal transfer of knowledge, such thinking is important for students matriculating to workplaces.

Programs such as these show that, through eFolio thinking, the notions of communication, dialogue, and synthesis are central to creating sustainable portfolio programs. At Virginia Tech, we have found that successful ePortfolio programs, in other words, those that embrace both process and product, reflect eFolio thinking. Through open dialogue with all participating parties, teaching faculty, assessment committees, advisors, administrators, and yes, even students are brought into dialogue through the ePortfolio development. Concerns revolve around capturing useful assessment data yet giving the students voice and room for authentic learning. However, if the dialogue is truly open and admitting, especially from the perspectives of the students who will be creating the ePortfolios, these concerns can be brought into balance. Additionally, the notion of synthesis between experience and learning or between artifact and reflection, which is central to ePortfolios and eFolio thinking, also reflects the synthesis employed by bringing together both process and product sides of ePortfolios. Because ePortfolios exist electronically, they provide for more synthesis, for example, synthesis of other types of assessment data and authentic learning activities, or synthesis of learning outcomes and professional ePortfolio presentations. eFolio thinking encourages students to engage in a process to create a product that will aid their learning and professional development, and when done well, aid all of us in assessing the individual's learning in more meaningful, useful ways.

REFERENCES

Abrami, P. C., & Barrett, H. (2005). Directions for research and development on electronic portfolio. *Canadian Journal of Learning and Technology*. Retrieved from http://www.cjlt.ca/index.php/cjlt/rt/printerFriendly/92/86

Barrett, H. (2000). Create your own electronic portfolio. *Learning & Leading with Technology, 27*(7), 14-21.

Barrett, H. (2009). Balancing the two faces of ePortfolios. Retrieved from http://electronicportfolios.org/balance

Barrett, H. C., & Garrett, N. (2009). Online personal learning environments: Structuring electronic portfolios for lifelong and life-wide learning. *On the Horizon, 17*(2), 142-152.

Barrett, H. & Wilkerson, J. (2004). Conflicting paradigms in electronic portfolio approaches: Choosing an electronic portfolio strategy that matches your conceptual framework. Retrieved from http://electronicportfolios.com/systems/paradigms.html

Batson, T. (2009a). Where is the student voice in assessment? *Campus Technology*. Retrieved from http://campustechnology.com/articles/2009/11/04/where-is-the-student-voice-in-assessment.aspx?sc_lang=en

Batson, T. (2009b, July 1). Why do we assess? *Campus Technology*. Retrieved from http://campustechnology.com/articles/2009/07/01/why-we-assess.aspx

Batson, T. (2011). Situated learning: A theoretical frame to guide transformational change using electronic portfolio technology. *International Journal of ePortfolio, 1*(1), 107-114.

Cambridge, B., Kahn, S., Tompkins, D. P., & Yancey, K. B. (Eds.). (2001). *Electronic portfolios 2.0: Emergent research on implementation and impact.* Sterling, VA: Stylus.

Cambridge, D. (2009). Layering networked and symphonics: A critical role for e-Portfolios in employability through integrative learning. *Campus-Wide Information Systems, 25*(4), 244-262.

Chen, H. L., & Mazow, C. (2002). Electronic learning portfolios and student affairs. *Net Results.* Retrieved from http://www.naspa.org/netresults/article.cfm?ID=825

Clark, S. F., & Bailey, J. (2008). Developing an e-portfolio system through student-faculty collaboration. *Dietetics Educators of Practitioners, (Fall)*, 15.

Clark, S. F., Bailey, J., Holmes, A., Johnson, L., Hendricks, M., Willis, G., ... Zaldivar, M. (2008). Student collaboration integrating the electronic portfolio with Sakai online learning technology to assess student learning outcomes for the Didactic Program in Dietetics. *Journal of the American Dietetic Association, 108*, A66.

Clark, S. F., Holmes, A., Hendricks, M., Willis, G, Miller, R., Griffin, E., ... Zaldivar, M. (2009a). Dietetic students collaborate to design an assessment based electronic portfolio. *Journal of the American Dietetics Association, 109*, A17.

Clark, S. F., Holmes, A., Hendricks, M., Willis, G, Miller, R., Griffin, E., ... Zaldivar, M. (2009b). Students collaborate with faculty to design an electronic portfolio system to measure student learning outcomes and professional development. *North American College and Teachers of Agriculture, 53.* Retrieved from http://www.nactateachers.org/attachments/article/1854/NACTA%20Journal%20vol%2053%20supplement%201.pdf

Denton, D. D. (2012). Improving the quality of evidence-based writing entries in electronic portfolios. *International Journal of ePortfolio, 2*(2), 187-197.

Devanney, G., & Walsh, P. (2002). Collect, select and reflect: Using the electronic portfolio in teacher preparation. In C. Crawford et al. (Eds.), *Proceedings of Society for Information Technology and Teacher Education International Conference 2002* (p. 593). Chesapeake, VA: Association for the Advancement of Computing in Education.

Doig, B., Illsley, B., McLuckie, J., & Parsons, R. (2006). Using ePortfolios to enhance reflective learning and development. In A. Jafari, & C. Kaufman (Eds.), *Handbook of research on ePortfolios* (pp. 158-167). Hershey, PA: Idea Group Reference.

Greenberg, G. (2004). The digital convergence: Extending the portfolio model. *EDUCAUSE Review, 39*(4), 28-37.

Hakel, M. D., Gromko, M. H., & Blackburn, J. L. (2006). Implementing electronic portfolios at Bowling Green State University. In A. Jafari, & C.

Kaufman (Eds.), *Handbook of research on ePortfolios* (pp. 388-397). Hershey, PA: Idea Group Reference.

Hutchings, P. (1990). Learning over time: Portfolio assessment. *AAHE Bulletin, 42*(8), 6-8.

Lorenzo, G., & Ittelson, J. (2005). An overview of institutional e-portfolios. *EDUCAUSE Learning Initiative,* 2005. ELI Paper 1. Retrieved from http://www.educause.edu/ir/library/pdf/ELI3001.pdf

Lunsford, A. (2006). Writing, technologies, and the fifth canon. *Computers and Composition, 23*(2), 169-177.

Meyer, D., & Tusin, L. (1999). Preservice teachers' perceptions of portfolios: Process versus product. *Journal of Teacher Education, 50*(2), 131-139.

Michelson, E., & Mandell, A. (Eds.). (2004). *Portfolio development and the assessment of prior learning.* Sterling, VA: Stylus.

Schaffhauser, D. (2009, November 1). Here, there, and everywhere. *Campus Technology.* Retrieved from http://campustechnology.com/Articles/2009/11/01/ePortfolios.aspx

Schnurr, S. (2013). *Exploring professional communication: Language in action.* London: Routledge.

Shavelson, R. J., Klein, S., & Benjamin, R. (2009). The limitations of portfolios. *Inside Higher Ed.* Retrieved from http://www.insidehighered.com/views/2009/10/16/shavelson#Comments

Shepherd, C. E., & Hannafin, M. (2011). Supporting preservice teacher inquiry with electronic portfolios. *Journal of Technology and Teacher Education, 19*(2), 189-207.

Stefani, L., Mason, R., & Pegler, C. (Eds.), (2007). *The educational potential of e-Portfolios: Supporting personal development and reflective learning* (Connecting With E-Learning). New York: Routledge.

Wagner, M., & Lamoureux, E. (2006). Implementing an outcome-based assessment ePortfolio. In A. Jafari, & C. Kaufman (Eds.), *Handbook of research on ePortfolios* (pp. 539-550). Hershey, PA: Idea Group Reference.

Weimer, M. (2002). *Learner-centered teaching: Five key changes to practice.* San Francisco: Jossey-Bass.

Yagelski, R. P. (1997). Portfolios as a way to encourage reflective practice among preservice English teachers. In K. B. Yancey, & I. Weiser (Eds.), *Situating portfolios: Four perspectives* (pp. 225-244). Logan, UT: Utah State University Press.

Yancey, K. B. (2001). Introduction: Digitized student portfolios. In B. Cambridge (Ed.), *Electronic portfolios: Emerging practices in student, faculty, and institutional learning* (pp. 15-30). Washington, DC: American Association for Higher Education.

Young, C. The MAEd English education electronic portfolio experience: What preservice English teachers have to teach us about EPs and reflection. In D. Cambridge, B. Cambridge, & K. B. Yancey (Eds.), *Electronic portfolios 2.0: Emergent research on implementation and impact* (pp. 181-192). Sterling, VA: Stylus.

Zubizarreta, J. (2004). *The learning portfolio: Reflective practice for improving student learning.* San Francisco: Jossey-Bass.